IN THE PSYCHIATRIST'S CHAIR

IN
THE PSYCHIATRIST'S
CHAIR

Anthony Clare

PROFESSOR HUGH DUDLEY

NELL DUNN

JUDGE CHRISTMAS HUMPHREYS

DAVID IRVING

GLENDA JACKSON

NEMONE LETHBRIDGE

PETER MARSH

SPIKE MILLIGAN

ARNOLD WESKER

CHATTO & WINDUS

**THE HOGARTH PRESS
LONDON**

Published in 1984 by
Chatto & Windus · The Hogarth Press
40 William IV Street
London WC2N 4DF

British Library Cataloguing in Publication Data
Clare, Anthony W.
In the psychiatrist's chair.
1. Psychiatry
I. Title
616.89   RC454

ISBN 0 7011 2793 7 Hardback — ₤
ISBN 0 7011 2837 2 Paperback

Phototypeset by Wyvern Typesetting Ltd, Bristol
Printed in Great Britain by
Redwood Burn Ltd.,
Trowbridge, Wiltshire

Contents

TO JANE

Acknowledgements

The interviews on which this book is based were broadcast on BBC Radio 4 in the autumn of 1982, and were edited and produced by Michael Ember. His consummate expertise, steady support and unshakeable belief in the value of the enterprise were at all times crucial. I am indebted too to Jenny Rivarola who obtained much valuable background information and who always provided useful insights. The support of Monica Sims and Alan Rogers in backing the series from the outset is appreciated. Grateful acknowledgement is made for permission to quote from the following: *Artaud* by Martin Esslin, reprinted by permission of Fontana Ltd; *Conflicts: Studies in Contemporary History* by Sir Lewis Namier, reprinted by permission of Macmillan Ltd; *Introductory Lectures on Psychoanalysis* by Sigmund Freud, reprinted by permission of George Allen & Unwin Ltd; *On Becoming a Person* by Carl Rogers, Houghton Mifflin and Company; *Swann's Way* by Marcel Proust translated by C. K. Scott Moncrieff and reprinted by permission of Chatto & Windus and The Hogarth Press; *Clinging to the Wreckage* by John Mortimer, reprinted by permission of Weidenfeld & Nicolson Ltd; and *The Presentation of Self in Everyday Life* by Erving Goffman, reprinted by permission of Penguin Books Ltd. The nine participants who agreed to be interviewed and to the interviews being published are saluted for their trust, as is Carmen Calill, who from the moment the idea of the book was put to her supported the project with her characteristic verve and energy. I am grateful to Jeremy Lewis of Chatto & Windus for his patience and persistence in seeing that the book finally materialised.

Finally, I must thank my family — my wife, Jane, to whom this book is dedicated, and my children, Rachel, Simon, Eleanor, Peter, Sophie and Justine, who in their various ways make ventures such as this worth the effort.

Introduction

The idea for the radio series in which these interviews occurred was a joint one. It arose out of discussions between myself and my producer, Michael Ember, held from time to time and over a number of years. I had met Michael during the early 1970s when, on the basis of some articles and book reviews I had written for the *Spectator* and *New Society*, he invited me to participate in 'Stop the Week'. At that time and for some years afterwards, my radio appearances were largely a hobby. They were, for the most part, unrelated to my professional work as a practising psychiatrist. Occasionally, I did undertake some work which brought hobby and professional work together. One example was a series entitled 'Let's Talk About Me' devoted to an exploration of the burgeoning boom in self-exploration and experiential psychotherapy in California, which was a joint enterprise with BBC producer, Sally Thompson. Another was when I helped with the production of a three-part series on family relationships entitled 'Thicker than Water'. In general, however, radio (and such TV as I did) remained a hobby.

From time to time, however, Michael Ember and I met people, on and off the airwaves, who appeared as curious as we are about what drives, sustains and motivates people through their lives, how they survive setbacks, and if and how they cope when disaster does occur – in short, what makes them tick. When, with the blessing of Monica Sims, then Controller of Programmes, Radio 4, and Alan Rogers, the Director of Current Affairs and Magazine Features, the opportunity arose to put a series together, we chose individuals from various walks of life and, to our immense satisfaction, the overwhelming majority welcomed the invitation and agreed to participate. Our main problem concerned a title for the series. 'What Makes you Tick?' captured the essence of the enterprise, but seemed flip and superficial. When 'In the Psychiatrist's Chair' was first mooted I felt uneasy, since I felt that while the great majority of listeners would recognise that the interviews were not psychiatric interviews as such, but interviews with a psychological emphasis conducted by someone who was a psychiatrist, such a distinction would not be readily apparent to everyone. There would be those who would think that this was psychiatry by radio with those interviewed cast in the role of 'patients', subjected to a relentless clinical analysis by a 'shrink', and the whole enterprise approximating in some way to 'therapy'. However, no other title remotely suited and, for all its possible disadvantages, 'In the Psychiatrist's Chair' did possess the merit of honesty; it made plain that there would be a psychiatric flavour, and that the interviewer was indeed a psychiatrist.

Another problem about attempting a psychologically-oriented interview is that for many such an approach is for ever associated with John Freeman and 'Face to Face', the series of television interviews screened at the end of the 1950s. One interview in particular is recalled – the one in which the bluff, irascible and seemingly unapproachable Gilbert Harding broke down and wept while recalling the death of his beloved mother. In the years that have passed since that event, the interview has acquired almost mythical status. Freeman actually carried out a series of remarkable interviews but few people appear to remember more than a handful, of which Harding's and, perhaps, those with Evelyn Waugh, Tony Hancock and Carl Jung, are the most frequently recalled.

The Harding interview deeply divided audiences at the time. Some people regarded the whole episode as a deplorable lapse of taste and an appalling violation of a man's private feelings. It seemed to epitomise the voyeurism and emotional exploitation which, such critics insisted, were the inevitable consequences of this kind of no-holds-barred interrogation. John Freeman's rightly praised interviewing technique may well have accentuated the impression of inquisitorial dissection. Throughout the series he consciously adopted the style of the detached, aloof, impassive and disinterested psychoanalyst. His approach mirrored the stereotype of the psychiatrist at that time as a sort of psychological surgeon, skilfully, unhurriedly and unemotionally stripping away defences and exposing repressed and buried traumas hidden in the patient's unconscious. As Harding wept, the virtually unseen Freeman (the camera lingered occasionally over Freeman's shoulder) appeared to remain utterly unmoved, his calm, steady, high and slightly reedy voice mercilessly picking and probing.

There were others for whom this approach vindicated the whole notion of in-depth interviewing. The image of the interviewer as detective, armed with a model of mental functioning and personal development which, however speculative, had the merit of raising hopes of catharsis and release, of sudden insight and dramatic confession right in front of the camera, was irresistible. The problem was that it set back the case for the in-depth, psychologically-oriented interview by several decades. Such an interview has become synonymous with soul-baring, emotional exhibitionism and the demonstration of psychiatric pathology. The fact that today the interviewer does not have to be as remote as Freeman or the subject as distraught as Harding got lost amidst the welter of argument and counter-argument, in which the one shared assumption appeared to be that this kind of interview involves the liberation of unacceptable, disturbing, even objectionable material.

It is arguable whether such a view of the interview and the interviewer is applicable today. The public in general is more sophisticated and more knowledgeable. The popularisation of psychology has meant that many people are reasonably familiar with such notions as the contradictoriness and ambivalence of human relationships and the interaction between intense emotion, symptoms and behaviour. Whatever is true about the nature of the unconscious itself, it might be said that since the time of Freud it has been shrinking. Less is buried there, for the very good reason that people are nowadays not surprised, let alone shocked, by notions of latent homosexuality, murderous fantasies involving parental figures, or infantile sexual feelings. Nowadays the issue for the interviewer is not so much uncovering what we have repressed and forgotten as attempting with us to make sense of and face that which we already know. It is doubtful, too, whether many viewers now would be surprised to see an apparently brusque and unfeeling man weeping over his mother's death. I suspect that the interest would lie more in identifying the impulses behind Harding's apparent need to keep people at a distance and his dislike for intimate personal contact.

In the series of nine interviews reprinted here, my purpose has been to cast some light on the mainsprings of the individual's life and values. What is it that propels such people forward, that enables them to survive or sees them through crises and disasters, that feeds the notion of excellence or difference which so many driving, ambitious and achieving individuals appear to possess? Several participants reveal the extent to which in the past they teetered on and, in some instances, fell over the divide between survivor and casualty – and illuminate that other thin line which divides those who have never sought professional assistance from those who have. One assumption, at the heart of these reflections, is the fairly reasonable one that the fulfilment of certain ambitions demands the sacrifice of others. This is what I mean by 'price'. All of us to some extent pay it: the dedicated surgeon, the assiduous playwright, the single-minded actress, the committed Buddhist, the driving businessman – all forgo certain aspects of living to pursue their chosen paths, and some exact a price from those around them in this pursuit.

No interview, however long, can reveal the whole picture or tell the whole truth. The biographical conversation cannot discover all that lies within a single lifetime. The factual history has no end. It is grounded in dispositions which we can never comprehend and seems equally determined by the vagaries of chance, situations in constant transformation, opportunities and all sorts of external events. Given the constraints of such an interview, and the fact that it is a one-off, in which only a fragment of an individual's life can be examined in any detail, we must accept a final product that is inconclusive. These individuals are only glimpsed within these interviews, but what cannot be known or is not directly addressed may perhaps be felt through the telling.

This is one facet of these interviews, one of the many which distinguish it from a clinical interview. The psychiatrist, like the family doctor, builds up a picture of his patient through a series of consultations over a period of time. I only met my subjects at the time of the one interview which each of them gave. They were not patients, they did not bring problems, and the process involved was not therapy. Fortunately, few listeners ever for a moment imagined that the title of the series meant that this was psychiatry by radio. Whereas the transmitted interviews lasted between forty and forty-five minutes, the studio interview usually took nearly twice as long. Editing the interviews to fit the scheduled slot was Michael Ember's task and he carried it out admirably. Editing runs the risk of superficiality, even distortion, but the final products provided the answer to such doubts, and the listeners' written responses strongly supported our feeling that the subjects emerged in a more rounded, more complete, more truthful way.

The interviews reprinted here (and for the most part they include material which had to be edited from the transmitted versions because of the constraints of time) are the only answer to the other popular charge levelled against this form of interviewing, namely voyeurism. People do of course get a vicarious pleasure from listening to the defects and the problems of others and the popularity of phone-ins and agony column programmes testifies to this impulse. But there are other less ignoble responses and the programmes when they were transmitted certainly provoked many. Some listeners took heart and reassurance from the fact that none of us is free from flaw or complex, from disappointment or dilemma. They drew encouragement from hearing how some people have rejected utterly their original backgrounds and have created totally new identities, how others have clung with an abiding intensity to all that has gone to make them what they are. They have heard how some have negotiated certain crises in their lives, crises which have been disastrous and catalytic. Some of the subjects feel confident that they know themselves and life's answers. Others readily admit to being baffled. None of the participants seriously challenges the maxim that in the lost boyhood of Judas, Christ was betrayed, but each in his or her own way illustrates how complicated, unpredictable and even mercurial the effects of childhood and our earliest and most formative experiences can be.

'But how can you be sure that the person is telling the truth?' has been one of the commonest doubts expressed to me about the whole enterprise. I have been tempted to reply with Pilate's famous doubting query, 'What is truth?' One avenue to the truth is perceived form and movement reflecting psychological events and mood. The understanding of expression was dubbed by Karl Jaspers 'this vision of the soul of things'. Of course the radio listener was not well placed to assess the subject's appearance, manner and expression, but I was. Empirical confirmation is obtained by establishing a demonstrable relationship between the expression as understood – say a smile – and the rest of human reality accessible to us in speech, general behaviour and so forth. Throughout the series I pressed individuals from time to time concerning their impressions, explanations, justifications – perhaps sometimes to excess. But the issue of whether what was revealed is the 'truth' seems to me a side issue. More importantly, is what is discussed of a piece, does it fit what else is known of the individual and of similar individuals? Can the listener (reader) empathise, doubt, mull over the material, secure at least in the view that what is being said is possibly true? In this kind of discussion it is not so much a question of 'facts' to be unearthed as of a picture to be painted and considered.

Graham Greene has written that analysis and auto-analysis 'reinforce the Christian concept of guilt'. He was drawing attention to the way in which psychoanalytical exploration invariably dwells on the negative side of an individual's life and personality. That view certainly underpinned some attitudes towards the series when it was first mooted. It was seen by some critics as an exercise in disparagement and voyeurism. The implication was a simple one: if it is to be a successful in-depth approach then it must reveal the less attractive, hidden, submerged aspects of our character; so why do it?

My own view is that the preoccupation of psychiatry with the negative and the flawed has been somewhat over-emphasised. Psychiatry is indeed concerned with such matters, but it is also concerned with personal strength, individual survival, positive impulses, drives and values. What keeps a man from breaking is as crucial a question as why he does break. What enables us to survive is as relevant as what pushes us over the brink. In so far as any light has been cast on such issues in the case of the nine individuals who are the subjects of this book then the exercise, for all its shortcomings and limitations, may have been a success. Only the reader can judge.

GLENDA JACKSON

We see the theatre as a truly magical enterprise. We address ourselves not to the eyes, not to the direct emotion of the mind; what we are trying to create is a certain psychological emotion in which the most secret recesses will be brought into the open.
ANTONIN ARTAUD

During the past twenty years or so the idea of drama as therapy for various psychological symptoms and difficulties has aroused a considerable amount of interest. 'Psychodrama' involves staged scenes in which patients act out parts but without scripts. Their own past is available to them in a form which allows them to perform a recapitulation of it. Other patients play significant individuals in the central figure's life and indeed the various participants can switch roles so that a patient can play not merely himself but his father, mother, brother or whatever. At the heart of the therapy is the belief that through the restaging of crucial events and experiences in the lives of distressed individuals, a 'working through' is achieved and some final resolution of hitherto truncated or blocked complexes can be achieved. In addition, however, there is the notion that emotions aroused, channelled and expressed through the psychodramatic situation are so affected as to alter the individual in his or her everyday life.

Indeed, the classic account of the origins of psychodrama implies just such an effect. Shortly after World War I, the highly theatrical central European psychiatrist, Jacob Moreno, began experimenting with drama as therapy. Initially, what he termed the 'Theatre of Spontaneity' was intended as entertainment pure and simple, and professional actors, taking their cues from the audience and current events, would improvise the plot, the action and the dialogue. One of the first actors hired was a footloose bank clerk destined for a Hollywood reputation named Peter Lorre. The origin of psychodrama as therapy is traditionally related to two individuals involved in this theatrical innovation, named George and Barbara. Barbara was a young actress who tended to portray gentle, frail and wistful women on-stage. She was married to George, a playwright and close friend of the young Moreno. George revealed to Moreno that Barbara, off-stage and in more domestic surroundings, was a temperamental and irascible shrew whose viciousness and hostility were playing havoc with their marriage. Moreno suggested that Barbara broaden her on-stage range, and he persuaded her to play somewhat more unsympathetic roles: disagreeable and violent women, petty criminals and prostitutes. This she proceeded to do with such verve and energy that her fellow performers became disturbed and felt she should cease lest in some way she suffer psychological harm. In fact, the change of roles had quite the opposite effect. The more she played such parts on the stage, the more she became reasonable, sweet-tempered and relaxed off-stage. After a few months, the marriage recovered.

From this spontaneous and inauspicious beginning psychodrama took off. It does of course differ from orthodox theatrical experience in that it dispenses with lines, preordained characters, and structured plots, and its therapeutic effects are attributed to the abreactive effects and opportunities afforded patients as they portray their dramatic life crises through public, highly dramatic performances. But it is interesting to note that the story of George and Barbara involved the *orthodox* theatrical process as exercising some potent cathartic power over the actress, and asserts that what happens to the performer on-stage can have powerful consequences for the individual's emotional life away from the theatre.

For some time I had wanted to put some of these points to an actor or actress. Of course it is quite possible that my curiosity concerning the impact of the acting process on the actor's psychological functioning and personal relations derives from a profound misunderstanding of drama itself – some critics have suggested as much. However, for a variety of reasons I felt that Glenda Jackson would be an actress well qualified to cast any light on such issues and, in addition, would be interested and able to reflect on the impulses and influences at work in the operation of one actress's craft. Many of her most memorable performances have been of women whom, charitably, one might describe as emotionally over-heated. There is her portrayal of Tchaikovsky's highly neurotic wife in Ken Russell's *The Music Lovers* (the poor woman ends up in a Russian mental hospital) and of the flamboyant Gudrun in *Sons and Lovers*, again directed by Russell. There is her remarkable portrayal of an asylum inmate in

Marat-Sade and an appropriately histrionic appearance as Sarah Bernhardt in *The Incredible Sarah*. There have, of course, been many other performances which have not demanded such white-hot emotionalism, but these have stuck in my mind precisely because they so strikingly contrast with the off-stage impression of Glenda Jackson as a cool, intensely private, even detached, person. She is not greatly given to turning her own life into drama. Interviewers have obtained her opinions on acting, theatre-going, membership of the Labour Party and the limitations of the Labour Party. But apart from learning that her marriage of some seventeen years to a producer broke up in 1975, that she lives with her thirteen-year-old son in South London and that she believes that the life of an actress is selfish because it tends to exclude other people, not a great deal has emerged about what exactly makes this exceptionally gifted actress tick emotionally and psychologically.

True, there are the readily available autobiographical details. Glenda May Jackson was born on 9 May 1936 in Birkenhead, Cheshire. Her father, a bricklayer, and her mother, a part-time cleaner, named her after an actress of the time, Glenda Farrell. The eldest of four girls, she won a place at West Kirby Grammar School but, not the easiest of pupils to teach, she left with only three O-levels. She spent a period behind the counter at Boots before she arrived at the Royal Academy of Dramatic Art by way of some YMCA amateur dramatics and elocution lessons. Since that time, she has become an internationally renowned actress on stage, on film and on television, has been awarded a CBE, has won two Oscars and a clutch of Emmys, and has been honoured by a D.Litt from Liverpool University.

What is particularly interesting to me as a psychiatrist is the extent to which Glenda Jackson can sustain the regular demands made by her craft on her emotional boiler-room while maintaining an off-stage and personal life. The more highly-charged the performer, the more pertinent the question becomes concerning the ease or the difficulty with which the on-stage fantasy can be distinguished from the off-stage reality. It may seem an obvious and crystal-clear distinction, and no doubt in the great majority of cases it is. But others have remarked upon the blurring of the boundary. For example, Goldsmith said of David Garrick: 'On the stage he was natural, simple, affecting; 'twas only that when he was off he was acting.' More recently, Joan

Plowright remarked of her husband, Laurence Olivier, that he does not know when he is acting and when he is not.

In her published comments on acting, Glenda Jackson has always contrived to make it sound very hard work. I have been intrigued by this. Many psychiatric patients are patients precisely because they experience anxiety bordering on and teetering over into terror if called upon to engage in the most basic, the most innocuous of public 'performances', such as eating in a public restaurant, shopping, or engaging in small-talk at an office party. The actress makes a career out of the portrayal on stage of such individual, highly personal actions. How does Glenda Jackson cope with the risk-taking, the stage-fright, the terror of failure? Are such anxieties exorcised by the actress simply engaging in the feared activity over and over again and acquiring ease and confidence with each successfully negotiated performance, a process in which behaviourists place such great faith and which is termed positive reinforcement? Or does an actress such as Jackson retain an acute sense of pre-performance panic? And if so, how does she negotiate it?

Like many people who deliberately push themselves to take risks, Glenda Jackson confesses to a multitude of anxieties, but is quite reluctant to contemplate ever having such anxieties treated. For her they are the source of the mysterious force, the 'energy' of which she repeatedly speaks. In this view she is closer to Rainer Maria Rilke, the poet, who was afraid of psychotherapy because he believed it might clear everything up to the detriment of that part of his mind which he believed held the key to and nourished his creativity. While I am sympathetic to such views, I tend to feel that they attribute an excessive potency to the therapeutic process. The anxieties of which Jackson speaks are elemental and are not easily removed without the active and willing participation of the individual concerned. In addition, Jackson's anxieties, for all their intensity and power, are still within her control; they may continually threaten to overwhelm her but for the most part she has successfully combated the threat and in her ability to overcome such basic fears lies, as she vividly describes it, much of the satisfaction in her own work.

One theme, common to a number of other interviews in the series, concerns the role of chance in the subjects' lives. (What Jackson terms 'accident'.) In one sense it might seem that the process which the individual describes as his or her life story, and in which someone such as myself seeks for connections, influences, choices, is largely a matter of chance occurrences and coincidences, and largely out of our control. Indeed, there are those who see in the North American vogue for psychoanalysis the same desperate search for the reassurance of control which drove our ancestors into the arms of astrologists. In Glenda Jackson's life story, as she relates it, there is a marked emphasis on the chance factor. Had she been born conventionally pretty she might well have settled down, married and had a family without ever embarking seriously on her own career. Like many teenage girls before and since, she suffered on account of what she perceived to be a physical unattractiveness. To cope with it she emphasised another aspect of her personality altogether, namely her talent to amuse, to lark about, to be the one making the ghostly rappings on the school-room door. It is a strange process this, whereby one reacts against some apparently remorseless force, and in reaction carves a particular and highly personal niche. Glenda Jackson sees the emergence of herself as a world-class actress as largely a matter of chance. The Second World War, which whisked the young Nell Dunn away from her beloved nanny, was from the perspective of a three-year-old a chance event with enormous consequences for the girl's subsequent character and confidence. The possession of any talent may itself indeed be a matter more often than not of pure chance and yet its impact can be, and usually is, as portentous as any exerted as a consequence of careful planning and prudent reasoning. Yet Judge Christmas Humphreys, from a Buddhist perspective, would have no truck with chance, and that doughty determinist, Sigmund Freud, albeit from a radically different philosophical vantage-point, would doubtless have approved the judge's vehement insistence that there is no such thing as fate but that in every action, choice and option there is a plan, an order, a purpose which can be deciphered. Again, there is Peter Marsh insisting that one is what one is because of programming, some maverick gene — again a chance event — and that the search to understand or explain entrepreneurial individuals — of which he sees himself to be one — is doomed to failure.

Chance or no, much in our lives is affected by what we decide we can influence and can do. Glenda Jackson expresses admiration for those who open themselves to whatever life throws at them, who desire to experience rather than retreat into safety and security.

Without the lows there cannot be peaks – this is the message this actress emphatically repeats throughout her interview, a theme which is echoed in the very last interview with Spike Milligan. From the vantage point of the clinic, such courage can be understood as the expression of someone who, in the last analysis, believes herself to be a survivor. There are others who are nothing like as confident that they can negotiate the lows and gaze longingly but unavailingly at the peaks scaled so confidently by the Jacksons of this world. Whether what is at issue here is some kind of faith, a leap in the dark akin to that taken every time the actress steps out in front of the footlights, I do not know. But the emphasis placed by Glenda Jackson on her work as the support to see her through difficult times suggests that for her at any rate it is work which holds the key to her survival. The wish to work, the director Peter Brook once observed, is the actor's strength, and it is the possibility that work will run out which is the performer's greatest worry. It is an understandable worry, though no less a worry for that. In Glenda Jackson's case one hopes it is an unnecessary and an unfulfilled worry: but one senses in her determination and her belief in work for work's sake that without the stage she would very quickly seek and probably find an alternative outlet for that energy of which she speaks and which she exudes off-stage as well as on.

ANTHONY CLARE: How do you feel, Glenda, about talking about yourself and revealing the private person as distinct from the public persona?

GLENDA JACKSON: I think I'm enough of an egomaniac to enjoy the idea of talking about myself. How much it will reveal I really don't know, because I don't think I've ever had a conversation like this before.

CLARE: Do you often reflect on what has brought you where you are?

JACKSON: Well, if I ever do reflect, it seems to have been a process of accident, and I don't know whether I actually accord any validity to the theory that there are no such things as accidents. I joined the amateur dramatic society because I was bored with my life in Boots Cash Chemists, and I felt there was more that I could do and that there was more to be done. If a friend had introduced me to a particularly active political party, or some other activity that engaged my interest as completely as amateur acting did at that time, and had said to me, 'You should do this professionally', I might have done something quite other. So it seems to me quite accidental that my interest was aroused by acting.

CLARE: Let's look at where you *do* come from. Was your family back in Birkenhead particularly emotionally charged, a 'high voltage' family?

JACKSON: It didn't seem to me at the time, though the strongest blood lines are Welsh and Irish, which I suppose combined to produce some sort of Celtic doom and gloom occasionally – and there's always the reverse of that. But no, I would have thought it was an incredibly placid, very supportive family. We all lived very near to each other. My grandparents were very near, my father's sister lived just round the corner and was virtually another mother to us. It was a very female family because we were four girls, and of course the war took the men away . . . we were a family that was run by its women.

CLARE: Does that mean your mother was a powerful person?

JACKSON: Oh yes, yes.

CLARE: In what sense?

JACKSON: In simply being able to do everything. I'm not saying that she did it without moaning or groaning. She still moans and groans. I think I've inherited that from her – I'm a great moaner and groaner. But it's a way of . . . holding up the energy that makes it possible to actually get over a particular problem, whatever it is.

CLARE: Sometimes in that kind of environment one can develop a distaste for other people's moaning and groaning. You can do it yourself, but it's not something that you tolerate very well in others.

JACKSON: I think that's probably true. In our particular family we were never encouraged to cry particularly openly. We were expected to get on and do things.

CLARE: Would you say that's contributed to any aspect of yourself now?

JACKSON: In a profession that can be extremely airy-fairy and inordinately self-indulgent, it has kept me almost abnormally rooted on the ground, and that has been of enormous benefit – that capacity to see work for work's sake and not the peripheral glitter which can sometimes confuse people. People sometimes think that the glitter is all, and not see that it is mere top dressing.

CLARE: But there was not theatrical influence in your early life?

JACKSON: None at all. No.

CLARE: Why were you called after an actress?

JACKSON: (*laughs*) It was either Glenda Farrell, or Shirley after Shirley Temple. I think it was simply that they were my parents' particular favourites. One of their entertainments was going to the cinema, and they obviously figured prominently in their thinking.

CLARE: What sort of person were you in early adolescence?

JACKSON: I was the plain friend, I think. I was extremely fat, very acne-ridden. Rather – well, I suppose shy is the only word I can think of. I wasn't particularly outgoing, so I developed an attitude – whether this is with the benefit of hindsight, I don't know, but it might have been deliberate at the time – of preferring not to be in social situations, in finding greater pleasure in a book, or a solitary walk, or going to the pictures, or something like that. I didn't have a particularly wide circle of friends.

CLARE: How much of a burden, psychologically, was this plainness, because it recurs in some of your wry comments on film stars?

JACKSON: I think it's something I'll always carry because when I was growing up girls were expected to conform to a particular kind of image. And I didn't fit into that. I think part of the defence mechanism was to eschew it, to pretend I felt there were more important things in life than the way you looked. Indeed I think if I had been pretty in the accepted sense of the word then, I probably wouldn't have had a career. I probably would simply have married and settled down, which was the pattern for that society and certainly for the family from which I came. Women had to work because they needed money. They didn't have a career; their career was children and home.

CLARE: You're saying that had you not been a plain adolescent, you mightn't be an actress now?

JACKSON: This is very true, yes.

CLARE: But it's a common theme that runs through adolescence. Some, particularly girls, suffer terribly about being physically unattractive, being thin or lanky, being socially unacceptable – some suffer to the extent that they end up as patients of people like me. So I'm interested to know how those who survive such anxieties, and indeed conquer them, manage or compensate? One way is to retreat into an academic interest. But you didn't do that. You weren't academically terribly successful.

JACKSON: No, not at all.

CLARE: So what did you do?

JACKSON: I think I was the joker. No, perhaps joker isn't the right word. I was the one who would, for instance, climb on to a roof that we had been forbidden to climb on at school, who was locked in a cupboard during an English lesson and made ghostly rappings on the door. I think there were about five of us who went around in a tiny gang at that time.

CLARE: You were a tomboy?

JACKSON: Not really, because I'm too lazy to be particularly physically active. I didn't shine on the sports field or anything of that nature. I think I was slightly anti-establishment, but not in the revolutionary or radical way that people attack the establishment now.

CLARE: You weren't politically very interested?

JACKSON: Not at all. I had no awareness of political parties while I was at school.

CLARE: What about religion?

JACKSON: Religion I brushed against slightly. My family were Presbyterian, and we lived very near a Presbyterian church.

CLARE: How was that? You mention a Welsh and an Irish background?

JACKSON: Yes, well I think it was an amalgam of Welsh chapel and possibly Irish Protestantism that came out as Presbyterian. Or it could simply have been that the Presbyterian church was the nearest to where we lived, and that's where we were sent to Sunday School. I don't know.

CLARE: What about your three sisters? You were the eldest?

JACKSON: There is four years to the sister after me; there is about a four year gap between us all.

CLARE: And what was your adolescence in relation to them like?

JACKSON: Well, to my sister closest to me, it was animosity naked in tooth and claw. We loathed each other, I mean really brutally loathed each other. I regarded her as a burden because I had to take her with me wherever I went. And that relationship stayed pretty much like that until I left home to go to drama school. And I think it was probably distance then that lent enchantment, and we managed to establish a much more equable relationship. But I think the affections actually skip, in that I'm closer to my second sister and she is closer to my younger sister – that seems to be how it's balanced itself out.

CLARE: As sisters, are you very alike?

JACKSON: Physically we're alike, and I think there are characteristics which we share, but we seem to lead very different lives.

CLARE: Are they surprised that you ended up as an actress?

JACKSON: If they were surprised they would never show it – that's part of the way we behave. I think they're surprised by the enormous success that eventually came because they'd seen me for many years going home with holes in my shoes, and no acting work. But they've never let it overwhelm them.

CLARE: When you left school with three O-levels I think they were in literature, language and geography . . .

JACKSON: That's right, yes.

CLARE: But you didn't do anything with them?

JACKSON: No, no.

CLARE: Not immediately at any rate?

JACKSON: I didn't do anything with them ever. I went to the Labour Exchange and trotted off to the jobs they sent me to. Eventually I got a job in Boots Cash Chemists, and there I was.

CLARE: How long did you do that for?

JACKSON: Two years.

CLARE: Why did you do it?

JACKSON: I had to work – we needed the money. I think there was a certain snobbery in that it was a step up from Woolworth's! And I didn't have any qualifications for anything other than, I suppose, work in a shop.

CLARE: At that stage, there was no idea of acting?

JACKSON: None whatever. I'd done none of it at school at all. I'd been to the theatre with the school, and we'd gone to the panto every year, but they were my only theatrical visits.

CLARE: You were gripped more by the cinema?

JACKSON: Oh yes, hugely. I'd go every night if I could get the money and permission.

CLARE: Were there any stars you identified with?

JACKSON: The ones I can most closely remember were people like Joan Crawford and Bette Davies, that Forties ilk of leading female actresses.

CLARE: Do you know why?

JACKSON: I think probably it was that they seemed very capable of conducting their own lives regardless of the dramas that they had to deal with, and in the face of quite often large emotional vulnerabilities. They weren't merely tough, which implied that they could never be hurt. They could be hurt, but could still come up smiling.

CLARE: That is an aspect of a person's personal life you would admire?

JACKSON: Oh very much so, yes.

CLARE: Because?

JACKSON: I think there's something essentially courageous in opening yourself up to whatever life throws at you and experiencing it and keeping open to what comes up next, as opposed to becoming frightened and enclosed and wanting to shove all that away, and not wanting to be hurt any more. I don't think you can have the peaks without the lows, and if you cut off the lows then you're going to cut off the peaks as well.

CLARE: You talk a lot about the energy you store up before performances.

JACKSON: Oh yes, yes.

CLARE: Certainly many of your early roles were of highly charged, almost abreacting women, which leads even the amateur psychologist to wonder – not just in relation to you, but to any actor or actress – the extent to which it provides them psychologically with a way of dealing with what they in their personal life have to control and master and discipline. It allows them, in a sense, personally to abreact.

JACKSON: That's quite interesting, because when I've been going through personal emotional crises, the thing that's worried me – quite apart from the actual emotional crisis – is, is it going to limit my ability to work? It seems that what I would call my private life could restrict my ability to work properly, not the other way round.

CLARE: Well, let me press you. One or two things you've said elsewhere suggest that it could work the other way round.

JACKSON: You mean the work could affect the private life?

CLARE: . . . in terms of this thing called energy. When you were talking about acting elsewhere you said that it is selfish in that you have to conserve yourself emotionally, you haven't got time for the emotional distractions of every day because, in a sense, they sap and tap these precious reserves. It certainly conjures up a life of some emotional isolation for those who venture into the public arena.

JACKSON: I think you have to go back a bit further as far as I'm concerned. I'm very work-oriented. I come from a family in which the work ethic is very basic and is valued. And along with the value of work is the idea that you get nothing without earning it. As I have always had this strong work ethic, my work has always been central to me. I have always expected other people to have this same attitude to work, and because I have that attitude to other people's work, I expect other people to have that attitude to mine, and that sometimes doesn't occur. That can create frictions which still puzzle me. I'm still amazed that people can be jealous of or distressed by work being given importance in this way. After all, acting is a very here-today-gone-tomorrow kind of profession. In a curious way this underlines for me the importance of concentrating on it when it's *there*. But that can affect others personally. They can feel jealous of work, or cheated by the time that one gives to work, or they attempt to reduce my attitude to work – and that does surprise me.

CLARE: But isn't there also the vague feeling that such single-mindedness, such – and I use the word carefully – self-centred single-mindedness, is achieved at a very high price, often paid by others? It's a question that inevitably takes us to a personal experience in your life – the breakdown of your marriage.

JACKSON: Yes. I think it's very difficult for me to define precisely why that broke. I don't mean why the actual break came, but what had led up to whatever it was that made it possible to break. I always accepted the validity of the other's work and therefore in a way it seemed like a kind of betrayal to me if there was any friction about my work. Do you see what I mean? It still comes as a shock when people say, 'Oh, you're putting that which is only a performance – it's only a play, it's only a film – before me. That's where you're living your real life, you're not living your real life here with me.' But they *are* separate. Whether all those accusations about work would still have been levelled at me if I'd done something which is regarded as rather more beneficial to the human race, I don't know – I think my attitude to work would stay the same.

CLARE: You mean if you were a busy surgeon coming in late at night . . .

JACKSON: Yes – or a busy traffic warden. My attitude to work would always be the same regardless of what that work was.

CLARE: But you feel a spouse, for example, would be more self-effacing in the face of work as a life-saving surgeon than as an actress?

JACKSON: I don't know whether that would be the case, because I've never done anything else in which one could see whether it's the job that creates the threat, or the attitude to work.

CLARE: To go back to the autobiography: you married before you were on the stage.

JACKSON: Oh no, I was on the stage 'cos we actually met in rep.

CLARE: Your ex-husband was involved in the theatre?

JACKSON: Yes, oh yes.

CLARE: And in fact, it was a long marriage.

JACKSON: Yes, very.

CLARE: But you're saying that the tensions between . . .

JACKSON: As I say, I don't know what really created the tensions that made it possible for it to break, even though my actions in the end broke it.

CLARE: In what sense?

JACKSON: In that I was the one that left and found somebody else. But what had made that situation possible? I think it's a bit too easy to say that I'd become successful, although the last five years of that marriage were when I had become overtly successful, by which I mean people could put a face to my name and I'd earned a lot of money, and you know, I was doing a lot of films.

CLARE: You mentioned someone else. Was that a relationship that lasted?

JACKSON: No. It lasted off and on for about five years, I think, but no longer than that.

CLARE: In view of what we've been discussing, is the tension between Glenda Jackson the actress involved with her work and Glenda Jackson the person involved in relationships with other people, something you muse on much?

JACKSON: Not really, no. I think what causes, or what rather caused, problems was less Glenda Jackson the actress than Glenda Jackson the name, and I think that caused grave frictions. That's one of the reasons why the second relationship fell to pieces.

CLARE: How do you mean?

JACKSON: I suppose the public figure aspect of it. I know it is there and I try very hard not to use it. I try very hard not to capitalise on the peripheral bonuses that being a well-known figure, and a comparatively popular well-known figure, can give you. You are asked for your autograph or people say, 'You come to the head of the queue' and things like that. If I'd been an actress whom nobody recognised or knew, I don't think those problems would have been there at all.

CLARE: Is it very difficult for somebody who has achieved fame and public recognition in the sort of profession you're in to sustain a personal relationship offstage which is personal, intimate, private, self-fulfilling?

JACKSON: It's possible, but it probably does create difficulties. I don't want to sound like a tired old feminist here, but I think it's the balance between who is the more successful that can create those kinds of difficulties.

CLARE: What about the other aspect of the relationship between acting and one's personal emotional life which intrigues someone like myself with no knowledge of acting – the extent to which you know when you've stopped acting? I was struck by this problem when I read about an account of you rehearsing, I think it was in *Sarah Bernhardt*. There's a break-up or a marital row or some relationship row, and you didn't care much for the way the director did it; it was clearly too low-voltage for you, and you and the other actor rehearsed it, and it ended up a very fiery exchange indeed. I wondered what experiences you drew on, or where the energy you drew on comes from? That leads me on to ask what happens when you're in exactly that sort of situation in your own life?

JACKSON: Oh it's much easier in the films than it is in real life, because you know exactly what everybody's going to say, and you know where the flying dishes are going to land!

CLARE: You don't in real life?

JACKSON: No, I think that's one of the great dangers of real life, you never know what anybody's actually going to say. Where the energy comes from I don't know. That's part of the mysterious process. And do you take it home with you? When you're doing a film you may, because you've never completely played the character, because it's a process that takes several weeks to complete. There's always part of you that's worrying about the problems that are coming. But you're very, very tired at the end of a film day because you start at six and you finish at six and there are always hours of travelling. With a play there's nothing left to take home. There's nothing of the performance to take home because you've burned it all out on the stage.

CLARE: That brings me back to a point raised earlier – this question of whether you burn out and have to recharge; that your life makes such demands on your emotional fuel, that this places *particular* difficulties in personal relationships?

JACKSON: Well, I've been in emotional crises in my life when I've also been playing highly-charged emotional people, and the emotional energy that I've used on the stage has in no way reduced the emotional crisis when I got home. It doesn't seem to work like that.

CLARE: Do you find that at times people will say, 'You're acting'? Is there any tendency for them to see the public in the private?

JACKSON: I don't think it's true, because acting is something that you have to be able to repeat again and again and again. It's just one of the easy cracks that people throw at you because they expect it to be painful.

CLARE: You've said acting is something you serve, it doesn't serve you. You've never been stage-struck, you didn't have a theatrical indoctrination in your early childhood. You've never thought it glamorous. You've never thought it great fun. You don't see it as something to do on a rainy day. You don't see it as a game. It sounds very like work. What you're saying is, 'I do it for the same reason that you do psychiatry.' Is that why you do it?

JACKSON: Yes, I think so. A lot of my negative statements are simply because acting isn't regarded as a serious, hard-working profession in this country. It's still regarded as something that under-developed, child-like adults play at. At its best, and it's at its best I suppose when it's engaged in the best possible material, such as a great play, it seems to me it is great. One of the reasons why a play is great is because it is actually showing us ourselves – it's showing us people not as they like to pretend they live, or even as they would like to live, but as they really live. Obviously the first name that comes to mind is Shakespeare. And that's part of what acting in a way does for me. It puts me, however haltingly, lamely, partially, in touch with a mind like Shakespeare's, and with his view of people – which is another way of seeing oneself, because you can recognise yourself in great plays. They constantly ask the same questions: Who are we? Why are we? What are we? And that's why I think acting is serious, why I think it's an occupation for serious adults and not simply play-acting children. Obviously, the opportunities to work with that quality of mind and talent are very rare, so you have to be able to accept the dross with the gold. You can't really cheat on that, you can't say, 'Oh well, I'll only half act this, because it's not Shakespeare, it's not up to the standard that I would like it to be.' You have to work completely on whatever you're doing, even though it may not rise to your own particular standards of excellence. So it's always difficult. For someone like me, who has to be made to work because I'm essentially lazy, that's one of the reasons I do it. It's constantly interesting.

CLARE: Do you ever feel on a treadmill?

JACKSON: No, I've never felt on a treadmill. I've sometimes felt, and I think I feel now, that I'm in a tunnel with no light at the end of it. The actual opportunities are not there, because I'm a woman of a particular age, and there's nothing really around which is going to stretch a little bit more of me.

CLARE: Does that worry you?

JACKSON: Yes, it does because there is no point in acting unless you're doing it for the best that you can possibly be. If demands aren't being made on you, then there is no point in doing it, it's a totally silly way to spend one's life. That does worry me, yes. I can see this year, but I can't see beyond that – and then I think one has to make the decision. Does one wait? Which I don't think I will. And then the next big decision is, what else do I do with the energies that I've got left?

CLARE: How worried do you get?

JACKSON: I worry to the point of actually growing an ulcer, to the point where it physically expresses itself and I physically shake – go into a kind of rigor, which has happened to me occasionally throughout my life. The other symptom is that I can become terribly passive. I just cut out and wait. My worrying doesn't produce in me the energy to make the step forward – it has to abate and *then* I can make some kind of step.

CLARE: Have you ever worried that you were going to break down?

JACKSON: I did think that I had actually broken down, during the two-year period when I didn't work at all in the theatre, and I was doing, oh, odd jobs all round the place. I did really think I was in the middle of a minor nervous breakdown.

CLARE: What age were you then?

JACKSON: I must have been about twenty-two – twenty-three I think, and I was married. My husband was away. He was working in Bristol, at the Old Vic, and I was up in London, and it was very bad. I went down to Bristol to be with him, but couldn't get a job in the theatre, so I got a job as a waitress in a hotel in Bristol, and that, I think is what saved me. If I was ever in that situation again, that would be my particular salvation – hard physical work.

CLARE: Were you so low as to feel that life really had lost its purpose?

JACKSON: My prevailing sense was the most overwhelming panic and terror that life itself was going to end. It was at the time of the Cuban missile crisis, and I was absolutely convinced that every aeroplane that went over was carrying the first bomb that was going to be dropped. It actually took a concrete external fear form for me.

CLARE: Did you tell people that?

JACKSON: I don't think I did, no. I had one very bad night when I had this terrible shaking, and I went to see the doctor the next day, and I was given some form of tranquilliser. The effect was so horrendous, I threw the bottle into the dustbin and would never take anything like that again.

CLARE: Did you dream then?

JACKSON: If I did I can't remember what the dreams were. I can remember waking up in a cold sweat, but that happens to me still. I sometimes wake up with my teeth firmly clenched, covered in cold sweat – I've been in some nightmare.

CLARE: But you can't recall it?

JACKSON: Not directly. The most recurring nightmare is always of being chased – I take to the sky to avoid my pursuers, but they tend to be able to walk in the air too, so on it goes.

CLARE: I get the feeling that you drive yourself.

JACKSON: The reasons always seem to me valid at the time, I don't think I go looking to be driven particularly.

CLARE: But you make it sound an effort.

JACKSON: Yes, oh yes.

CLARE: Each time?

JACKSON: Yes. Certainly – work is an effort, because it's so easy to do it so badly. I suppose the fear of doing it badly is what drives me in that sense.

CLARE: What's so terrible about doing it badly?

JACKSON: When you ask it baldly like that, the possibility of failure isn't so terrible; and certainly in the profession I pursue failure is a very subjective definition. But the feeling when you're doing it badly is horrific, partly because you've always had a glimpse of how it could be, so there's that personal dissatisfaction; and you're doing it in public, and there's that innate sense of nakedness which is disturbing.

CLARE: But presumably it has happened?

JACKSON: Oh yes, good heavens yes.

CLARE: But doesn't that condition you against the next time?

JACKSON: No, it doesn't, actually. There's no law of diminishing returns in the possibility of failure. Obviously you learn more from your failures than you do from your successes. But there's no way – I certainly haven't found it yet – of sedating that area of panic.

CLARE: Your dedication to work and your professionalism: are they things you would pass on to your son?

JACKSON: I would hope that he would have something he wanted to do in the way that I had something *I* wanted to do. I'd hate to think that he'd be entering his adolescence and the adult world with no ambition, with no desire to do anything or be something. But if he did, I'd feel it had probably been my fault that he had no particular desires or aims. If he *did* have desires and aims I hope he'd acknowledge that you have to be your own strongest critic, that is *your* standards that you have to meet, and that they should probably be higher than most other people's.

CLARE: Are there aspects of being Glenda Jackson that you wish you had been spared?

JACKSON: I would like him not to be as easily frightened as I am. I would like him to be not fear*less* in the sense of physically fearless, although I would quite like him to be that, but I would like him to be imaginatively fearless, because I'm not. Imagination fills me with fear a great deal of the time, and I think that's the thing I'm afraid of most, fear.

CLARE: You've only mentioned failure as the thing you fear. What other fears have you?

JACKSON: I'm plagued by all kinds of fears. I'm afraid of flying, I'm afraid of choking to death. I'm afraid of dozens and dozens of things. But the thing I'm most afraid of is fear, disabling, limiting me in some way.

CLARE: What do you do when you're in a state of fear?

JACKSON: Nothing, actually – nothing practical. When you're afraid on the stage you just wait – you're not afraid on the stage, you're afraid before you go on, and all you do is wait and the curtain goes up and you don't have time for that kind of indulgence. I have imaginatively frightened myself when I thought I was being physically threatened. I sat up and switched the light on in a bedroom in New

York, and I believed that someone had broken in. I could actually hear them rifling through the drawers, and opening packages and things like that. And I thought, 'Well just lie still and pretend to be asleep and they'll go away.' I couldn't do that – I had to sit up and switch the light on and confront them. Of course there was no one there, it was noise coming from a well downstairs.

CLARE: Would you fly, for example?

JACKSON: Oh I do fly. I sit there gripping the arms until my knuckles go white and with every bump on the plane I'm convinced that something dreadful has happened. I had an actual experience of that: I was flying back from America and the oxygen masks dropped in front of our faces, and I remember – I take a certain pride in it now, but it hasn't ameliorated the fear – I turned to the person I was travelling with and we both laughed. And I thought, Well that's a good way of facing it. In fact, of course, it was an accident: as the captain said, he'd pressed one button and things happened – which didn't make the remaining seven hours any easier.

CLARE: Would this come as a surprise to anybody who knows you reasonably well? How private are you about such aspects of yourself? Do many people know you?

JACKSON: Many people *don't* know me although many people think they *do*, which makes it quite difficult to have a conversation like this. Because you and I are virtually total strangers it's much easier to have this conversation. But if I meet people for the first time socially, it's very difficult for them to cut through what they *think* they know about me, and for me to cut through what I can see coming off them.

CLARE: In my professional life I meet women, about the same age as you, not actresses, whose social life is very circumscribed and the opportunities for them to talk, to let things out, are very restricted. They would be very surprised to hear that for a world-renowned actress it can be rather similar.

JACKSON: Oh absolutely similar – and I can understand that they would be surprised. But I used to take my son to school and I often felt totally outside that group of mums standing at the gates, because there they were chattering away to each other. They tried to make me a part of their group and all we were talking about is how they're doing, and the prices of things in the shops and totally banal things. But that sense of belonging to a community, a group . . . of course I couldn't sustain it because I'd go away for three months and wouldn't take him because I was working. And there's that sense that, to go back to what we were saying earlier, I'm somehow different, as a breed, as an individual human being. And that's very hard sometimes to break through.

CLARE: One of the differences about your career is that it's a very remarkable form of risk-taking – to go on stage in a live performance, night after night, to portray yourself on celluloid in an often very uninhibited way, as you've had to do, to perform on television. An actor or actress performing is itself a source of drama – just to see if it can come off to the watcher, to the viewer. That certainly creates in me a feeling that actors, actresses, particularly successful ones, are remarkably strong, tough; indeed the image no doubt of you would be of a tough, strong, hard-working actress.

JACKSON: I think resilient is a better word than tough because it can be a killing profession, and I mean that quite literally. It can be punitive in the toll it can take on those who wish to follow it. Tough, which implies unfeeling and unbreakable, isn't true. Resilient certainly. You have to be able to bounce back, and that, touch wood, I've always managed to do, up to now. But you have to have that. Otherwise it would be absolutely impossible.

CLARE: In the light of all this, if you had a daughter, would you have put her on the stage?

JACKSON: No. And I'm praying to God my son doesn't want to go on. It's hard enough to do for yourself, but to actually watch that external part of you go through it must be far worse.

CLARE: Would you prefer not to have done it?

JACKSON: Oh no, no. Because I've been one of the very lucky ones, and I've been given opportunities and been able to fulfil them. But I know many, many people who started the same time as I did who were not given those opportunities. It can be crucifying, because there are so many pursuing so little, and there are so many myths and fantasies about it and about the kind of person who actually wants to go into it. It's very, very difficult, certainly when you're beginning, even to be treated as a human being. You're just an object, a shape, a size, a weight, a colour . . . and that can go on for a very long time, and can be hugely damaging, I think.

CLARE: Was that one of the reasons you are tempted to ascribe a lot of what's happened to you as accidental? It's an easier way of explaining why *you* emerged.

JACKSON: I was very lucky, I was given an opportunity to work at a particular time and many, many people are not.

CLARE: Who would have been?

JACKSON: We'll never know, will we? That's one of the curious things about this business. There'll always be a case to disprove what I'm saying, somebody who, at the age of fifty, suddenly becomes a major acting talent. It may only happen once in twenty years, but there it is, that exception proving that particular rule.

CLARE: One last question. In North America particularly, also in Europe and, to some extent, here, many actors, actresses, people in the media often have a professional analyst, consultant, adviser. I'm not for a minute suggesting this is an admirable practice. But I am struck none the less that they do, and they treat them in various ways as gurus, or as ears, or just as people with whom they can let off steam. You haven't, as I have understood you to say – indeed there's no immediate person in your life who would play that role. Is that because it's something you've never thought of, or because it's something with which you would prefer never to be involved?

JACKSON: It's something I've never thought of and I would never involve myself in unless I regarded it as being based on very strong medical grounds. It would strike me as cheating in a professional context because, as you were saying earlier, the point about acting is it is a high-risk profession and you can't really take the risks if you've cushioned yourself against the possibility of failure.

DAVID IRVING

One would expect people to remember the past and imagine the future. But in fact, when discoursing or writing about history, they imagine it in terms of their own experience and when trying to gauge the future they cite supposed analogies from the past; till by a double process of repetition, they imagine the past and remember the future.
SIR LEWIS NAMIER, *Conflicts: Studies in Contemporary History*

David Irving was chosen as a subject for interview firstly because he is an historian. If we are to begin to understand another person we need to know his history. Every good case history grows into a biography. Psychological illness and health are rooted in a person's life as a whole, and cannot easily be isolated from it if they are to be understood. Irving is a biographer who has made the life of one awesome figure of the twentieth century, Adolf Hitler, his particular interest, one might even say obsession. Hitler has fascinated Irving. His own claim to fame and, indeed, notoriety rests on one book, *Hitler's War*, with its flat assertion that the Führer knew nothing about the extermination of the Jews and would not have sanctioned it if he had. His first book, *The Destruction of Dresden*, published when Irving was only twenty-three was nearly as controversial, while *The Destruction of Convoy PQ17* led to a lengthy libel action and damages in excess of £40,000 awarded against Irving. Accusations of anti-semitism were fuelled by Irving's celebrated challenge to professional historians that he would pay £1000 to anyone who could produce evidence proving Hitler's knowledge of the Jewish extermination, and by an apparent preoccupation with the number of Jews in the Hungarian communist party at the time of the uprising in 1956. This emerged in his book *Uprising: One Nation's Nightmare: Hungary 1956*, which was published in 1981 and savaged by critics (a 'bucketful of slime', was how Neal Ascherson dismissed it). In common with virtually every book written by David Irving however, it contained material gleaned from documents, memoranda and other records previously unknown or unavailable to professional historians.

For David Irving is not a professional historian. Indeed, he never obtained a university degree, a fact that he clearly regards as significant in some way, for it features in much that he and others have written about him. The impression of Irving as a maverick iconoclast, playing practical jokes, as it were, on professional historians while outshining them in their own specialised areas of research was one I had formed from reading about the man. (In the interview he confirmed my impression, admitting to a penchant for playing tricks.) In the circumstances, my desire to explore the relationship between the psychological make-up of an individual historian and his craft seemed likely to bear fruit in an interview with this unusual man.

He was born in Essex on 24 March 1938. His parents separated when he was quite young and he was brought up, along with his two brothers and his sister, by his mother. It was a particularly military family, in that his father had been a Royal Naval Commander and both his brothers had served in the Royal Air Force. Irving attended a direct grant minor public school and then went to Imperial College in an experimental scheme designed to turn arts students into scientists and engineers. It turned him into neither, however, and he left before completing the course, after failing a vital subject. He then spent a year as a steel worker in Germany's Ruhr before returning to England to take up a place at University College, London. However, he left after two years without completing his degree, having begun his ultimately successful career as a writer.

At the time I invited David Irving to take part in an interview he was separating from his Spanish-born wife. Nevertheless, he promptly accepted, expressing an interest in psychiatry which he attributed to the fact, unknown to me, that one of his four daughters had undergone a schizophrenic-type breakdown, from which she had recovered. In material published about him, I detected a somewhat intriguing attitude towards women. For instance, the *Evening News* on 14 April 1978 reported Irving as declaring that he had 'deported' his wife and daughters to Spain because 'the climate of education in London has become so ugly and the atmosphere of pornography so disgusting in the West End'. Deportation had been Irving's word and I found it somewhat forceful, authoritarian even, in the context of a family decision over a suitable place to live.

As it turned out, the interview itself provoked a considerable amount of comment from listeners, many of whom were clearly surprised by Irving's cool, detached discussion of feelings, and his straightforward belief that his life's work as an historian had been somewhat retarded by his decision to marry and have a family. Some listeners were chilled by the dispassionate nature of his relationship with his mother, his wife, and perhaps most unexpectedly of all, his twin brother, with whom he readily admitted having little in common. To some extent, Irving's unemotional comments reflect his desire to be rational and his admitted fear of feelings and passion. To this extent, he is more like the public stereotype of the academic don than he might care to accept, with his emphasis on the importance of facts as against conjecture and the need for control in one's personal relationships and in one's life generally. 'I occasionally catch myself succumbing to feelings,' he admits at one point, while later he expresses admiration for Hitler's computer brain, into which relevant data would be fed at night 'and in the morning he'd wake up and the decision would come plopping out'. To a psychiatrist, such admiration of cold rationality unencumbered by emotions often suggests disturbance and pain in earlier life. The fact that the one experience which provoked intense feelings in Irving was the death of his father is additional, though still circumstantial, evidence in support of the argument that the loss of his father from the Irving household when David Irving was quite young was that traumatic event.

Early on, from Irving's account, he strongly identified with his absent father. Others in the family expressed anger at being left to carry on without support but David, for reasons that are merely hinted at in the interview, repressed or actually felt no personal bitterness. Indeed, he describes how the more reprehensible and disreputable were the views expressed by his family of his father, the more the man went up in his personal esteem. While, in itself, such a process of identification does not explain why some individuals become outsiders, deriving much satisfaction from shaking conventional views, assumptions and codes of behaviour, it can hardly be said to retard such a development. From early on, David Irving appeared to derive much quiet satisfaction from being an outsider. Troublesome at school, the recipient of an intriguing (and ambiguous?) piece of advice from his public school headmaster, a loner in adolescence, a steel worker in a foreign country, and a solitary historian, part of no academic group or university clique, he remains a lonely figure. Yet unlike several of the other participants in the series, such as Nell Dunn, Spike Milligan and Glenda Jackson, he does not regret or complain of it but appears to welcome a certain solitariness, and even encourages and provokes it.

During the interview, Irving talks proudly of how, when writing *Hitler's War*, he imagined himself in the Führer's shoes when Hitler was supervising the German war effort. In the circumstances, Lewis Namier's observation, quoted at the beginning of this essay, to the effect that people who write about history imagine it in terms of their own experience, seemed to me at any rate peculiarly apposite. I was interested in the extent to which Irving identified with Hitler. Irving seemed surprised by my interest and, as a consequence, on one or two occasions the interview was diverted into discussions of Irving's views of the Holocaust, anti-semitism and the racial theories of the Third Reich, although these never were intended to be the main subjects for discussion.

Finally, there is the issue of Irving's family history of mental illness. Irving himself wished to discuss it, but it raised sensitive questions. On the one hand, I was criticised by the secretary of the Watford Group of the National Schizophrenia Fellowship because I had not persuaded Irving to refer to his daughter's illness by name, especially as his daughter had recovered. It was felt that a splendid opportunity to bring schizophrenia out in the open and discuss it properly had been missed, perhaps because of an over-sensitive preoccupation with the issue of stigma. On the other hand, there was criticism of the mentioning of his daughter's ill health, although at no stage was anyone named. In the end, I felt the issue was important enough, and David Irving's attitude to it of sufficient interest and relevance, for the illness to be mentioned but without providing too much detail of its exact nature.

Since being interviewed, David Irving has produced another book, this one devoted to the private diaries of Dr Theo Morrell, Hitler's private physician. In the course of it Irving muses on the fascination with which we regard those who wield power and influence. In their own way, those who write about such powerful individuals are every bit as fascinating.

ANTHONY CLARE: How does a historian like yourself, professionally involved in unearthing facts and details about the past lives of others, feel about taking a look at the acts and the feelings, the emotions, the impulses, in your own past that have gone to make you what you are today?

DAVID IRVING: I'm fascinated by it. I've never done it before. I'm curious to see what's going to come out. In fact I was rather perplexed when I got the invitation from you. My first instinct was that you were going to ask me about Hitler's make-up and psychological structure, and when I read the letter again and saw you were interested in myself I was rather baffled.

CLARE: Does anything about such a process worry you?

IRVING: Undoubtedly I'm concerned about what's going to come out. A lot of my friends have said I'm a fool to come here and sit in front of you and lay myself bare.

CLARE: Did you ask any of them why you should feel reluctant to come?

IRVING: Because I'm a public figure, to a certain extent. I live by my credibility. People who buy my books assume that they're going to read something that other authors have had reasons not to publish, either because they're academics or because they're professional official historians; and my own credibility is entirely based on the prestige that I've won over twenty years of writing. I'm also moving into a different field now, in politics, in which my credibility is also important; and I suppose my well-advised and well-intentioned friends thought I was walking on to very thin ice indeed in coming here and answering your questions.

CLARE: If there was an identifiable influence in your life, what would it be?

IRVING: Many people have influenced my life over the last forty-three years. I suppose the very first influence in my life was my headmaster, of course, at public school. He's still alive, a man to whom I look back with great affection, a man with whom I still regularly correspond. I blame it all on Brentwood School, in fact, because the education there was so liberal and it encouraged the boys – it was a boys' school at that time – to develop their own interests with such enthusiasm that I don't think that I would be what I am had I not had the start that that school gave me.

CLARE: What sort of man was he?

IRVING: He was – still is – an upright and handsome man with a humorous face, well-spoken, well-intentioned. I remember my closing interview with him when we filed out of the school, having got our necessary A-Levels and O-Levels. I went to shake hands with him and say goodbye, and he said, 'I give you one piece of advice, Irving, and that is you must never leave a place in such a way that you can't return to it at any time in good faith and meet a welcome there. So no matter how often you feel the temptation to stalk out and slam the door behind you, don't do it.' It was a piece of advice I've been very grateful for over the last thirty years.

CLARE: That linked with some aspect of your personality that he had observed?

IRVING: Well, I'd been one of the most troublesome children. I was the only one who was repeatedly caned.

CLARE: Why?

IRVING: Oh, for various transgressions. It's difficult to recall precisely what I was caned for. They weren't beastly crimes like shop-lifting or drug pushing or anything like that. But I remember the very last episode I was caned for was an April Fool's Day prank when another boy and I unveiled a red flag over the school's main gate in such a way that they had to have the local fire brigade called in to bring it down. And, I suppose, in a way I've been unveiling red flags over main gates ever since.

CLARE: Indeed, there's something of the prankster about your personality.

IRVING: When I write a book I always try to ensure that on every page I write there's one piece of pure joy to those who will recognise it – either a private joke or an in-joke or something which makes somebody sit back and chuckle.

CLARE: Always chuckle?

IRVING: Well, the chuckle has a positive, a plus sign, in front of it. There's also a negative chuckle sometimes – a gasp of dismay – when something comes up that they didn't know about.

CLARE: We'll return to the prankster Irving in a moment. The teacher you described was a major male influence in your life. One is struck by the fact that your father left your mother when you were quite young. How young were you?

IRVING: I can only vaguely recall it, of course, because one gradually became aware of the fact that one was growing up in a family where there were no men. My only memory of my father at that time was of his making one very unhappy visit back to our country house and having a terrible argument with my mother in the garden and dashing a can of pea seeds out of her hand – she was planting in the garden. It was during the war, and those peas were scattered all over the garden and we had peas growing for years afterwards. And I never saw him again until the year before he died. I remember he did come back, in fact, for about three days when I was about fourteen or fifteen, and an attempt was made to reconcile them. He was living in Wales, we were living in Essex. I don't know who tried to effect the reconciliation but I was very proud, and I remember going to school that day and casually dropping in conversation the fact that I was going to be with my father that evening. But it was a very short-lived reconciliation.

CLARE: And your feelings?

IRVING: When I think about the deaths of my parents? Of course, my mother's death made me very, very unhappy but I can now overcome that: but I can never ever describe my father's death without tears in my eyes.

CLARE: Do you know why?

IRVING: I felt very sad for him. He had no family for the last twenty or thirty years of his life – he lived with a housekeeper in Wales, and we did what we could for her afterwards.

CLARE: Did you ever feel angry about him?

IRVING: Never.

CLARE: Never?

IRVING: Attempts were made to make me feel angry about him. Occasionally things would be said like, 'You're growing up just like your father.' When he died I sent telegrams to all the family and told them the funeral would be at a certain time and place, and his own brother didn't arrive, I remember. I was rather puzzled by that. Four or five weeks later his brother wrote me a long letter about twelve pages long telling me what a rascal my father had been, in great detail – various escapades he'd been involved in, mostly womanising – and after that my father went up enormously in my esteem. He'd obviously turned into a very human character.

CLARE: I'm puzzled you didn't feel much anger because your mother had to struggle, didn't she, to bring up you, your twin brother, and your sister?

IRVING: It must have been an enormous struggle and I think one of the most unkind aspects of human life is that just as I, the youngest child of four, was beginning to make good, just as my books were being published, she died. I remember that all I could say the night I got the news of her death was, 'How unkind, how unfair.' Just when you're in the position to give her what she had missed all her life, she dies.

CLARE: What sort of woman was she?

IRVING: She was a children's illustrator, very straightforward, patient, constantly sighing. I suppose life must have been very hard for her. We lived out in the country. She had to keep the four of us just from her income as an illustrator for the nursery world. Occasionally she broadcast on 'Woman's Hour' and earned a few pounds like that but it can't have been very easy at all, and after she's gone, of course, you regret it bitterly. The evening before she died, I had an argument with her about something petty. She'd come up to see our youngest child who'd just been born and I was reading out a passage of one of my books to her and she only wanted to play with the child and I remember saying to her, 'You just don't change. You can't be interested in anything I do at all.' And she said, 'But I'm just playing with Josephine.' And then the next day you get the news that she's died and afterwards you kick yourself for the rest of your life.

CLARE: Was she not greatly interested in what you did?

IRVING: Not greatly interested, but when *The Destruction of Dresden* was published she was very worried about it. She said, 'What kind of son have I nourished here, who publishes books like this?' In fact, the book caused the family quite serious problems. At the time, my eldest brother was an officer in the Royal Air Force, and my twin brother was also in the Air Force. Both of them were summoned to the Air Ministry and called to account for themselves. It was quite an awkward period for the family.

CLARE: Had you actually ever discussed Dresden with your brothers?

IRVING: No, not with either of them. You see, our family was very far-flung. They were serving in the Air Force at the time of my parents' death — one in Cyprus, the other in Singapore.

CLARE: But one of them is your twin!

IRVING: My twin brother, yes.

CLARE: You must have grown up with him quite closely?

IRVING: No, because from very early on it became obvious that we were anything but identical twins. He's short and plumpish and bald and wears check suits and smokes a pipe and he's a civil servant and talks in a whisper. He lives in Paddington, about three miles away from me. Occasionally we meet – about once every three years – and we get on well together as long as it's not more often than that.

CLARE: What sort of adolescent were you?

IRVING: I was completely uninterested in girls, for example, until about twenty-one, and this gave me a lot of time to study. I used to learn everything I possibly could.

CLARE: Were you noticeably different from your friends when you say you weren't interested in girls until twenty-one?

IRVING: I think that certainly by the time I got to university I was different because I remember the university milieu of rugby teams and the beer-swilling engineers at Imperial College, crowding the union bar – I wasn't part of that at all. I didn't touch alcohol until I was thirty. I used to have a glass of sherry perhaps, but certainly no kind of wine drinking or beer drinking till I was thirty – and I stopped it when I was forty.

CLARE: And your first sexual experience?

IRVING: That would have been . . . I would say it was when I was twenty-three, when I was a steel worker in Germany. A very unsatisfactory affair. I was sufficiently intelligent to realise that you are not going to get any lasting sexual pleasure from a chance encounter anyway, and that really I was just fulfilling a duty, I suppose, which was expected of me by this particular woman.

CLARE: Have you changed much? I sense that you're a person not greatly taken with women.

IRVING: I greatly enjoy the company of intelligent, bright and, above all, beautiful women. If a woman isn't conventionally beautiful then it's unlikely that I'm going to find out if she's got brains or not because I'm not going to ask.

CLARE: And if she hadn't, would it worry you too much?

IRVING: Then I wouldn't go out of my way to share her company and I would divest myself of her company as soon as possible.

CLARE: So the looks wouldn't be enough?

IRVING: Looks wouldn't be enough, but on the other hand if they hadn't got the looks, I wouldn't find out about the brains. I'm sure I do tend to put women down.

CLARE: In what way?

IRVING: Looking around as a historian and reflecting to yourself what women have done, the answer is not very much. They've achieved very little compared to men over the millions of years that *homo sapiens* has been on the earth's surface. They haven't produced a Mrs van Beethoven or a Mrs van Gogh, or a Mrs Le Corbusier or any great creative talent that one can think of.

CLARE: George Eliot?

IRVING: They write largely for themselves. When I last put this theory to him about women not having produced anything, my publisher said, 'Well, David, you've got to realise that it was a woman who invented Tippex Fluid' (the correcting fluid). And I said, 'Well, it was women who invented the typing mistake too.' This may be flippant but it's a disappointing view of women, because there's not very much that they can offer by way of disproof. They haven't produced very much and they can't say they haven't had the chance or the talent because they have had the chance to sit in their corners and write Ninth Symphonies and they haven't been doing it.

CLARE: So what would be your explanation for why they've singularly failed?

IRVING: I suppose it's something biological. I can't say. I've not really investigated it in any great detail but I would imagine that they're just built in a different way. I may be enraging thousands of female listeners who are all fuming and saying, 'But at this very moment I'm writing a novel or inventing something very important.' But the fact is they haven't done it and I can only assume it's because they haven't got the . . . the physical capacity for producing something creative.

CLARE: You have four teenage daughters – what do you think they'd make of such a statement?

IRVING: I see my four teenage daughters during most of the evening. In fact, I hear what they're up to most of the evening because it's blared at me from a loudspeaker down the length of the corridor in my apartment, and I don't think that they're going to be writing any Ninth Symphonies either. I've tried pointing them in the right direction. I've suggested them various educational careers they might follow. But they're just not interested in that. It may be that they're conditioned by the environment from the very first moment they're given dolls to play with and prams to push. They're not given work benches and electronic kits and things.

CLARE: Do you think this view of women has affected your personal and sexual relationships – for example with your wife?

IRVING: This is quite possible, yes.

CLARE: In what way?

IRVING: I think if I was a woman I would be deeply indignant about sex because I think that, for a woman, the sex act must be regarded as an act of male aggression in some way and it must be humiliating and undignified and in some way perverse, and the idea, to me, that women can enjoy this act is rather ludicrous. They do appear to enjoy it, and I'm very grateful that they do, but it all seems rather odd to me.

CLARE: How do I know that you're not having me on?

IRVING: Difficult, because I have no visible signs of mendacity. I don't go red. In fact, if I do go red, it's usually when I know that I've been accused of something which I know that I'm completely innocent of, and in my fierce efforts to prove my innocence I am liable to go red and blush in all the ways that ordinary people blush when they're lying.

CLARE: I'm not suggesting you are. But some listeners might say that if I didn't ask that question, I'd be yet another psychiatrist gullibly believing what I'm told. It's unusual for a man these days to tell me that he regards the sex act, from the point of view of a woman, as an act of aggression. Some women tell me that.

IRVING: Well, I discussed this with my American publisher. He was there with one of his secretaries and she said, 'I don't think the sex act's aggressive at all.' So I said, 'Well maybe I've been doing it wrong all these years.' The sex act – it isn't the final five or ten or fifteen minutes, it's the days or months that precede it which are far more important to me.

CLARE: Is that because for you the sex act is a relatively infrequent activity, because you've other things to do?

IRVING: I'm a very busy person and in fact I regularly work about sixteen hours a day. I suppose that over the last two weeks I've not had more than five hours or six hours sleep every night. I go to bed as late as I can or I write as late as I can. I get up at six. Then I go for a half hour's run round Mayfair at seven o'clock in the morning. This kind of thing does tend to preclude any other kind of activity.

CLARE: Do you prefer male company?

IRVING: No, no. I like stimulating men to talk with. I've got two or three very good men friends, men that I like talking with, men that I can have a good belly laugh with, men that I can talk to privately in a way that I wouldn't like newspaper men to hear me talking.

CLARE: Did you ever fear that you were a homosexual?

IRVING: I think all men are terrified of any kind of homosexual proclivities. I think all men, too, probably go through a homosexual phase. At public school, particularly at a boys' public school, that's where a lot of it happens. I'm sure that boys go through a phase where they're far more interested in other little boys than they are in their bigger sisters. I remember there were a couple of boys at school I was very interested in. You go out on the football field and there's a certain amount of comparison that goes on – but it's a very passing phase, and it's so unimportant that probably for the next twenty years, you never think about it. You don't have any kind of relations with these boys, but there's a certain amount of prurient interest in other boys that you never quite get over – you go to the changing rooms and you go to the showers and there's the same kind of shifty looking around that you see when you go to a beach in the South of France where all the girls are walking around topless. Frankly the men are not so interested, but you see the girls there lying on the beach, ostensibly reading books, but all looking around at the other girls.

CLARE: How do you feel about homosexuality itself?

IRVING: I think homosexuality's a great tragedy. I think it deprives men of normal heterosexual relationships and in that sense is a tragedy. I think it's a tragedy too because it exposes men who suffer from that to all sorts of society pressures – but more than that I wouldn't like to say.

CLARE: You went to Germany after you'd dropped out of Imperial College. Why did you go to Germany?

IRVING: I'd dropped out of Imperial College because of examination failure. I tried in the last year to hold down a job at the same time as I was doing the course, and it just wasn't possible. We hadn't got the money for the scholarship. And the danger then came up that I would be called up for National Service, and I regarded two years' National Service as a waste of two years of my life.

CLARE: What year was that?

IRVING: That would have been in 1959, and National Service was just winding up. I had been deferred all the time I was at university and that deferment was now going to drop and I was going to be called up at any moment. Rather than that I volunteered for the Air Force for three years as a short-service officer. They would have sent me to Cambridge for three years to study Russian. You didn't have to wear boots, you didn't have to wear uniform, you would be at Cambridge for three years learning Russian – a useful kind of acquisition I thought. I passed the Russian language tests and I got 98.97 in the aptitude tests, and the man said it was the highest they'd ever had. And then I failed the medical. This was very annoying because it rather drew a line through the plan I'd made for myself for the next three years, and I thought, 'Well, you can't just go straight out into the outside world and on to building sites. You've got to do something adventurous, manly, build yourself up a bit, and earn money.' The steel worker image fitted there, and it would give me the chance to learn a foreign language properly, to learn German, which I'd done at school as an A-level subject.

CLARE: Were you ever regarded as a German in Germany?

IRVING: No, but I'm regarded as a German in England. People come up to me frequently and say, 'You're really German aren't you?' And I say, 'No, why?' And they say, 'Well there's something about your voice or the way you construct your sentences.' I don't believe this is true but it happens too often to be pure coincidence.

CLARE: Your Spanish wife's parents thought you were a German. Why?

IRVING: Probably because at the time I got to know her I was working in the steel works and all the letters came from Germany with German stamps on them, so it was a natural kind of mistake that people can make. I know they were very disappointed to find out I was English.

CLARE: How did you feel about being mistaken as a German?

IRVING: I don't mind it one way or the other because I don't tend to classify people in ethnic or racial or national characters and say, 'German bad, English good.' I think this is a very elementary error that people of a lower order would fall into.

CLARE: Did you have views about the Jewish problem when you went to Germany?

IRVING: No. When I'd been at Imperial College, in 1956, we had the Hungarian uprising and the Anglo-Israeli invasion of Suez, and I remember joining in all the Israeli demonstrations and being very fiercely pro-Israeli and anti-Arab. I wouldn't be now, having investigated the record and seen the extent of collusion that went on and considered the rights and wrongs of the situation more. But it's interesting to note that at that time I was completely blind to any problem in that respect.

CLARE: And since then?

IRVING: Again, it's very difficult to remain on a completely narrow path. I would say that the Jews in this country create big problems for themselves by identifying a person they dislike for one reason or another as an anti-semite, because this instantly provokes in that person a reaction. And I'm fighting down that reaction all day long. In my book on the Hungarian uprising I go into great detail investigating the fact that the Hungarian people perceived their government as being largely Jewish. The Communist regime in Hungary was largely Jewish. This is an objective fact and it caused a lot of unhappiness, which eventually led to the uprising. When this book was published, a book to which I devoted a lot of very serious research and which I thought was a very fine piece of work – and I don't often say that about my books – I had a lot of slime poured on me by the national press in this country who accused the book of being anti-semitic. This is a very unpleasant position to be in, because you find yourself defending a position that you haven't really stated in the first place.

CLARE: Now, one might say, that one controversy is forgivable, even accidental, two an unfortunate coincidence – but three and maybe four! We're not talking just about *Uprising*, your Hungarian book. There's *PQ17: The Destruction of a Convoy*. There's *Dresden* itself. There's *Hitler's War*. There's the fact, which I think you've indicated to me, that you rather like to put in the odd little grenade. You didn't say precisely that, but it amounted to it – if you came across something which wasn't necessarily terribly relevant but you knew would needle people, you'd stick it in. I'm struck by that because one of the critics, I think it was Neal Ascherson, commented that at times in your Hungarian book you unnecessarily inserted the adjective 'Jewish', or some description such as 'velvety eyes', or some nagging and rather emotive stereotype phrase.

IRVING: I think this reflects on them rather than on me. I had to put in the adjective 'Jewish' in various places in that book just the same as I put in the adjectives 'Catholic', 'Protestant' and 'Calvinist', but the only people who objected to this description are people like Neal Ascherson and Arthur Koestler and other critics to whom it has become a buzz word. I'm very sorry that society is in such a state of acute destabilisation on the Jewish issue that it is impossible to describe somebody as being Jewish even if he is Jewish without arousing his sense of outrage. In this book it was important because the Jewish issue had played an important part. All other historians and writers have ducked the issue, and they went through religiously rubbing that word out. Everybody else was described as Catholic or Protestant or Calvinist, but these people were not so described and I had to take a deliberate policy decision to state the facts, and I must admit I did it in a very cowardly way. Every time it was stated that anti-semitism played an important part in the uprising, I tried to make sure I was quoting the words of some psychiatrist, preferably a Jewish psychiatrist, because I knew that it was an explosive issue, and that it wasn't going to do the prospects of the book – particularly in the United States – any good.

CLARE: Do you have any sympathy for the position of the Jew, given the fact that the application of the adjective 'Jewish' isn't quite the same in the 1980s as the application of the adjective 'Catholic'?

IRVING: They have got themselves into a very exposed position, and it's very difficult to see how they can turn the clock back so that they are no longer the centre of interest that they have made themselves. The only way I could have avoided it would have been to write a book about something completely different. An analogous situation arose over the book about the destruction of convoy PQ17. When Captain Jack Broome first started litigating against us, the book was in the hands of another publisher. The publisher's advice to me was to say, 'David, I've had a brilliant idea. Can you not possibly write the book with no reference to Captain Broome at all? Just go through the manuscript and cut out every reference to him.' And I said, 'But he was the commander of the escort! It was to him that all the Admiralty signals went.' To me the idea of ducking an issue like that was so outrageous that we just went straight ahead, with catastrophic financial results for myself and Cassells, the eventual publisher of the book.

CLARE: Returning to the more private person, you married a Spanish woman. I gather you split up last year. Can you tell me why?

IRVING: I suppose it's the so-called legal profession who have done the damage there.

CLARE: Not you?

IRVING: Not me at all. I'm absolutely blameless. Who could be more innocent than I? A great tragedy of this country is that we have the laxest divorce laws in the world, I think. To get a divorce, virtually all you have to be able to do is to claim that your marriage has broken down. The mere fact of applying for divorce is proof that the marriage has broken.

CLARE: Your wife applied for the divorce?

IRVING: The initial steps were taken by Mrs Irving who, after twenty years of marriage, began to feel vaguely uncomfortable, that she could have done better somewhere else, and that her life was entirely wasted. I suppose all sorts of illogical feminine emotions began milling through her. I defended the family as long as I could against the legal profession for the next three years, although I could have made it very easy quite simply by capitulating. Finally, in May last year, I had to divorce Mrs Irving because the legal profession was taking such a toll of my time and the family's capital that I had to go ahead and switch the whole thing off.

CLARE: Your marriage went through some rather unusual periods. About three years ago your wife and four children were sent off to Spain. You were reported as saying in a newspaper interview that the climate of education in London had become so ugly and the atmosphere of pornography so disgusting in the West End that you'd sent them there for their protection.

IRVING: This is true. Ten years or fifteen years ago, we took the decision to move to Mayfair. The lease on our property expired, and we had a choice between living in Mayfair in the heart of London next to the American Embassy or a country house somewhere in Surrey. I thought to myself, if you move to Surrey you are really going into retirement effectively. Move to London, move to a flat in Mayfair, then you're still on the way up, your ambitions are all going to come to fruition and you can go ahead. What I didn't realise, of course, is that bringing up young children in London, in central London, is a major problem. Everything is on their doorstep, including some of the ugliest things – and you can't watch over four children twenty-four hours of the day.

CLARE: But many people do manage to bring children up reasonably successfully in the centre of London.

IRVING: Yes, I'm sure. I'm sure there were all sorts of reasons why this was a problem. The children grew up realising that they were in quite a well-known family. They grew up in conditions of great affluence. They had things which I never had as a child, and this must have rubbed off on them in a disadvantageous way.

CLARE: Did they suffer by being your daughters?

IRVING: No. No. The history teacher at the school said, 'We don't think very much of your father's writing,' so I said, 'Well, you ask your school history teacher what he knows about the Battle of Waterloo. You'll find he won't teach you very much.'

CLARE: What did your daughters think of being transferred to Spain?

IRVING: They objected. Traumatic, I'm convinced of that in retrospect. They were convinced it was a joke. The actual journey out to London Airport took place on April 1st three years ago – they thought it was an April Fool's joke and that at the last minute Daddy would confess it had all been an April Fool's joke, and that we were going to turn round and drive back that afternoon. Finding themselves being put on the plane with their mother was no joke at all.

CLARE: But the eldest at this stage was fifteen!

IRVING: The eldest was fifteen and they lost their friends in London temporarily – which I wasn't sad about, because the two elder children had made friends I wasn't happy about.

CLARE: But your relationship with your fifteen-year-old was such that you could put her on a plane to Spain?

IRVING: With her mother, yes. They were looking forward to it too, because they always liked Spain. I took steps to ensure that they came back to London quite frequently – every three or four months they would spend a week in London – so I did realise that it would cause problems.

CLARE: Do you regret it?

IRVING: Yes.

CLARE: Why?

IRVING: Because of the effect it had on the elder two children. Things happened when the children were no longer under my supervision that wouldn't have happened had I been keeping an eye on them.

CLARE: Has that been traumatic to your relationship with them?

IRVING: I'm sure: but I've kept as stable as I can under the circumstances, and I've put up with their reproaches, and I know that my reasons were watertight at the time. In fact, together with Mrs Irving, we drew up a memorandum on the precise reasons why we were doing it so later on there could be no dispute why we'd taken the decision to move the family out.

CLARE: Do you think that makes any difference?

IRVING: I think so, yes. Because later on – I know this only too well as a historian – memories do cloud. One is liable then to be at the short end of the stick and to be accused of having done things for all sorts of different reasons. And we were both very clear in our minds on that April 1st why we were taking that step.

CLARE: But there's a difference between the cognitive process and the emotional process: you can have all the reasons in the world for sending your daughters off to Madrid but it doesn't get over the emotional trauma of their not wanting to go and your wanting them to.

IRVING: It wasn't a question of my wanting them to go. It was a question of getting them safe. We had got them out of their school. They were suffering damage. They were in danger of suffering even worse damage if they stayed on. It was a very sad state of affairs – a lot of parents of children at that school faced the same problem.

CLARE: I sense that you lay a great deal of emphasis on the value and the virtue of logic whereas feelings, for you, are often irritating – they're subjective.

IRVING: Well, they are, I think you're dead right. I do try and work out logical reasons for doing things, cost-effective reasons for doing things.

CLARE: Do people ever say that you've no feelings?

IRVING: Oh yes. I'm frequently accused of being callous and brutal.

CLARE: And are you?

IRVING: I don't think so. I think that running a family is rather like running an army and somebody has to be there to say, 'Right, I've taken this decision and I think it's the right decision.' It may turn out to be wrong but . . .

CLARE: But it's not like running an army.

IRVING: I think so.

CLARE: But you're not related to the commandant-general.

IRVING: A general would regard his troops in rather the same kind of paternal way that a father would regard his sons.

CLARE: You mean that the accusations that are made about you as a historian are made about you as a father – that you're brutal and insensitive?

IRVING: I don't think anyone's accused me of being a brute as a historian. I think, rather differently, that they regard me as being brutally clinical and brutally objective as a historian.

CLARE: That is better put. Let me rephrase the question. Brutally clinical, brutally insensitive as a father and a historian?

IRVING: You've got to realise that a mother and four daughters form a small mafia, and they tend to club together when it comes to screwing anything out of their father. I'm sure that lots of fathers are going to be nodding their heads sagely and saying, 'Too true'.

CLARE: I've no doubt, and now you're playing to them!

IRVING: Dead right.

CLARE: But the fact of the matter is that when somebody has made an accusation against you, you marshal facts to meet this objection; but the common denominator is that you are described in a uniform way by different groups of people who know different aspects of you. Does that ever make you think that they might actually be right?

IRVING: No, I think you're using language in a clever way. We both agreed that I'm a brutally objective writer and a brutally clinical writer, but I think that this is not the sense of the word 'brutal' that we would use to a father who brutally beats his children. It is just a clever play with words, really.

CLARE: Words, as you well know, can be very dangerous. You can play with them, indeed. For example – to come back to your historical arguments – I sometimes think that it is almost an Irving 'prank' against organised professional historians to say that if they can produce a written piece of evidence showing that Hitler actually ordered the extermination of the Jews, you'll give them a thousand pounds. I've often felt this was something of a practical joke. After all, Hitler did a variety of things without writing orders. And he had a way of using words to describe the Jews – tuberculous bacilli, for example – which makes one feel that their being exterminated in vast numbers wouldn't exactly have caused him a loss of sleep?

IRVING: I agree entirely. I don't think I've ever said anything different from that, but I agree that it does cause me an immense amount of malicious pleasure to see the discomfiture of the established academic historians – and you can make what you want about my interpolating the word academic – writhing under their own inability to prove someone's responsibility for the biggest crime in history.

CLARE: But it's also caused a great deal of agony – hence the accusation of insensitivity.

IRVING: Whom has it caused agony to?

CLARE: It's caused agony to many Jews and, indeed, people who feel for them because of the strong implication . . .

IRVING: (*interrupting*) Did they want to be killed by Hitler? Why should . . .

CLARE: (*interrupting*) They believe they were killed by Hitler and what he represented. The man epitomised and personified the German nation at its most powerful and, in some ways, its most insensitive. To suddenly chop the top of it off and say that 'it didn't know about one of its major achievements' is to suggest in some way that Hitler is being let off the hook.

IRVING: Well, I'm not letting him off the hook entirely, as you know, because anyone who has read my book *Hitler's War* knows that I specified in great detail all his other crimes.

CLARE: For the small malicious glee of discomfiting the professional historians, you're prepared to risk the insensitivity of it all and the pain it causes to many ordinary Jews?

IRVING: I think that ordinary Jews are enraged, if at all, because I have detracted from the romance of the notion of the Holocaust – that six million people were killed by one man, rather than by a hundred rather grubby and ordinary criminals; but I can't help it, because that's my sincere view. I don't think there's any evidence that it happened any differently. I haven't got any axe to grind. I'll be quite happy to accept if I'm wrong.

CLARE: Do you have passionate feelings about anything?

IRVING: I've a passionate feeling for sticking my neck on a chopping block, if I think I've got something right – and I don't really care if I'm going to lose tens of thousands of dollars if I print something that's unpopular. I could be a very rich writer indeed now and I'm not, I'm a very poor writer, but I could be very rich just by having written orthodox history.

CLARE: Your feelings don't worry you? You never feel sometimes that your feelings are out of control?

IRVING: I occasionally catch myself succumbing to feelings.

CLARE: What sort of feelings?

IRVING: Of great remorse or, I suppose, self-pity. I was very, very sorry when my father died, and I can never describe his death without breaking down. It's a matter of great regret to me, but otherwise I can keep a pretty mask-like countenance. And people do begrudge me that.

CLARE: Do you ever worry about being mentally ill?

IRVING: I think a lot of people who are intelligent or work with their brains are deeply worried about the prospect of either falling mentally ill or being mentally ill.

CLARE: Have you ever felt that you were breaking down?

IRVING: I've sometimes had to work so hard, particularly over the last two or three years, when I've been working desperately hard to get a book finished, because publishers are about to foreclose on me and on top of that something else happens and on top of that something else happens. I remember a very close friend in London said to me last year, 'David, I've got to hand it to you. This last year, you've seen your marriage break up, you've seen one of your children fall seriously ill, you've published two books, you've formed a political group. You've done all that and you're not collapsing.' But sometimes I felt on the point of that.

CLARE: But in fact you're quite proud that you haven't.

IRVING: As soon as I thought I was about to, I decided the best way to avoid it was to improve my physical well-being, so I started taking very serious physical training steps.

CLARE: You don't derive support from personal relations to see you through the dark nights?

IRVING: It's very difficult to establish personal relations with somebody of my age. It would be a great miracle to find somebody with whom I could relate.

CLARE: I was thinking of one's family.

IRVING: Well, they have been taken away from me. The daughters will automatically be allocated to my wife.

CLARE: While you were going through this strain and stress, they were all around – still are, as I understand.

IRVING: They still are, yes. I'm defending that position as long as I can, but there's not very much I can do about it.

CLARE: Why are you defending it? They don't seem to give you a great deal in terms of emotional support or strength.

IRVING: I think that teenage children need to have both parents as long as they possibly can.

CLARE: You mean they need you?

IRVING: I could have copped out three years ago and saved our family £50,000 in legal fees. I decided to take the stonier and harder and more expensive course, and just fought on.

CLARE: I understand that you feel that they need you: do you need them?

IRVING: I think all parents need their children in a certain way. Parents get a lot of selfish pleasure out of watching children grow up. It's a very hit-and-miss affair, bringing children up.

CLARE: When you were writing *Hitler's War* and *A Pathway to War* and so on, did you ever identify with Hitler?

IRVING: I think you have to. You have to identify with your subject. Not just with Hitler but with whatever subject I am writing about. I'm identifying solidly with Winston Churchill now, which is quite a quantum leap. In the case of *Hitler's War*, my readers will remember that it's actually written from behind his desk. You hope you're getting everything as Hitler himself saw it. An ambassador doesn't go to see Hitler, he comes in to see Hitler and the book closes the moment Hitler raises the pistol to his right temple and shoots himself. It's quite an interesting way to write a book – and the interesting thing is having climbed into that skin, to be able to climb out of it once you've finished.

CLARE: What other things about Hitler do you identify with?

IRVING: His ability to exclude extraneous detail when making decisions. He regarded his brain as some modern computer into which he would feed all the relevant data, and then he would sleep on it and in the morning he'd wake up and the decision would come plopping out. I like to regard myself as having that kind of attitude to decision-making.

CLARE: You must have formed some view about his mental . . .

IRVING: Capacities?

CLARE: Not so much his capacities as his status. You know and I know that so much has been written about Hitler and his mental condition.

IRVING: Here again, it's purely subjective, isn't it? We were told throughout the war years one thing, but I've gone to great trouble in recent years, simply from writing my own biography, to find out what his own doctors thought about him – doctors who were men of regular professional upbringing, including army doctors who are about as square as you can get. And the opinion of every one of these doctors except one was that Hitler was sane until the end. That one was Hans Karl von Hasselbach, and he said that he thought Hitler was beginning to get delusions of grandeur towards the end, but then Hasselbach didn't treat him for the last six months of his life so he's not really qualified to judge.

CLARE: You've had some personal experience of mental illness with your daughter.

IRVING: Until we had this illness in our family, I was very, very sceptical. I'd read a court report and I'd see a psychiatrist being called in to give evidence, and I'd become very impatient. Having written a very detailed diary of how it affected our family was the only way I could get her off my shoulder and keep my brain clear to write. I wrote down, every day, every single detail of this tragedy, and all the remarks and statements. I read court reports of certain cases and I can see identical symptoms and identical illnesses in my view, and I become very impatient with the judge who won't listen to the medical evidence.

CLARE: I prefer not to talk about the illness of your daughter in any detail because . . .

IRVING: Yes, it's a very common illness indeed, in fact. And I think one reason why I can talk about it is that we have been told that she is as cured as can be expected. She has made a miraculous recovery and she is coming off medication.

CLARE: Do you feel in any way responsible?

IRVING: No. I would have felt responsible, I suppose, if I hadn't gone into it in more detail and if I hadn't learned a great deal more about this illness since it happened.

CLARE: Why would you have felt responsible?

IRVING: Because I would have believed that any kind of mental illness was brought on by the environment. For example, a brutal father might cause a mentally ill child. But, in fact, this is the kind of illness that is latent in a lot of people. Millions of people, four million people in the United States, have this illness – it's latent in them, and it needs just something to trigger it off.

CLARE: Which can, of course, be a brutal father.

IRVING: It can be, but in this case it was almost certainly something that the child had been taking – slimming tablets.

CLARE: What would you like to do – be it through politics, writing, whatever? What is it that you want to say?

IRVING: I've always wanted to influence people and destinies. For the last twenty years as a writer I've been influencing people's opinion, and now I want to start influencing their destinies.

CLARE: Why?

IRVING: Well, I suppose everybody has some kind of talent, maybe only a small talent, maybe a large talent. I was telling my oldest child, the one who was ill, 'This illness has an advantageous side, and that is that a very large number of geniuses – Van Gogh, Michelangelo – all had that illness and we just have to find out what is your particular talent that you're going to be great at.' I suppose the talent I have is enormous ambition and energy and personal drive and a pretty clear sense in myself that I'm right.

CLARE: About what?

IRVING: About ways of doing things, about the way things have to be done. Existing, established parties in this country are incapable of doing things in ways that are right; they are just going to continue doing things in ways that they have been done in the past.

CLARE: You once described yourself, I understand, as a mild fascist.

IRVING: Yes, I'm not sure which is more objectionable, being described as mild or being described as a fascist, but both are wrong.

CLARE: Did you so describe yourself?

IRVING: No, it was a *Daily Mail* journalist.

CLARE: How would you describe yourself, in relation to your ambition?

IRVING: I don't think there's any one political adjective that would describe the way I feel. I suppose I'm a very patriotic, dedicated, clear-thinking person. I've tried very hard to keep myself ready for this moment in as much as I've never smoked, never drunk – and I'm very anxious not to gradually deteriorate in the way that people otherwise might between the ages of forty and fifty.

CLARE: You make it sound as though there's a moment of destiny approaching.

IRVING: Oh yes.

CLARE: Has your experience as a historian not made you suspicious of people who have a sense of personal destiny and a feeling that other people's lives should be placed in their hands?

IRVING: Somebody has to do it. Somebody has to take the decisions, and I think the important thing is that that person should be a person whom the rest of the people can trust. And I think that if I've been doing anything for the last twenty or thirty years it's been trying to establish that people can't frighten me into adopting views that aren't right.

CLARE: Supposing your sense of destiny is correct and the British people turn to you, what would you want to do for them?

IRVING: I'm not saying that they're going to turn to me. I'm sure that somewhere in England there is somebody else like me to whom they may turn. Maybe me, maybe somebody else, maybe somebody who hasn't even applied his mind to it. I have forty years, I think, in which to do it. Time isn't running out very fast for me.

CLARE: You probably won't answer this question but I'll ask it none the less, given that you're embarking on a public career. Do you ever doubt whether you are the person for this kind of enterprise, because of psychological aspects of yourself, or because your life up to now has illustrated not just your strengths but some of your weaknesses?

IRVING: I think we learn from our weaknesses – the important factor is not to pretend that one is perfect, but on the other hand never to lose one's self-esteem and one's self-confidence and the belief in one's own future.

CLARE: Even if there have been times when that belief has contributed to somebody else's suffering?

IRVING: I don't think it ever has.

CLARE: A man can assert himself fully and confidently, and not ever at the expense of his fellows?

IRVING: Certainly not in my personal knowledge.

CLARE: So, looking back, there is nothing for which you feel ashamed?

IRVING: I think it was a mistake to get married.

CLARE: Because?

IRVING: Getting married takes twenty years out of your life. Getting married, raising a family and dedicating yourself and your resources to raising a family is like blood-letting. It should be one thing or the other. It may have been my one cardinal mistake.

CLARE: Because it's harmed you?

IRVING: Yes. I have always had these ambitions, and I think that getting married was an unnecessary deviation.

CLARE: Otherwise it's been a successful life?

IRVING: I don't regard any aspect of it as a failure. In fact I regard the illness of my child as having been a test granted to me by God which most parents are not granted.

ARNOLD WESKER

There is, in fact, a path from fantasy back again to reality and that is – art. The artist has an introverted disposition and has not far to go to become neurotic. He is one who is urged on by instinctive needs which are too clamorous; he longs to attain honour, power, riches, fame, and the love of women; but he lacks the means of achieving these gratifications. So, like any other with an unsatisfied longing, he turns away from reality and transfers all his interest, and all his libido too, on to the creation of his wishes in life.

SIGMUND FREUD, *Introductory Lectures on Psychoanalysis*

This famous passage, from one of Freud's introductory lectures on psychoanalysis, has not without reason infuriated artists and helped to create one view of psychiatry (with which psychoanalysis is invariably confused) as a field in which highly simplistic and reductive explanations of complex human activities hold sway. If the Freudian conception of creativity is correct, then, as Anthony Storr has remarked, it would surely be better to have none of it, for reality is generally preferable to fantasy, and it is a dismal state indeed to find oneself lacking 'the means of achieving' any of the gratifications listed by Freud.

While W. H. Auden agreed that Freud's view of creativity was 'misleading', he none the less argued that it was valuable in that it drew attention to two facts. First, no artist, however 'pure', is disinterested, but rather expects certain rewards from artistic creativity. Second, the artist starts from the same point as the neurotic and the day-dreamer, namely from emotional frustration in early childhood. In the same essay, Auden reminded his readers that the popular notion of the artist as in some way socially maladapted has been a long-standing one and not entirely without justification. This particular school of criticism points invariably to the fact that Beethoven was deaf, Milton blind, Pope deformed, Proust asthmatic and Van Gogh psychotic.

What drives the artist to create, what psychological processes are at work? It was inevitable that when my producer and I were drawing up a list of subjects to interview we should wish to include a writer.

There seemed to be advantages, too, in selecting a writer whose work appeared to draw in a fairly open manner upon the experiences of early childhood and adolescence. Of Arnold Wesker, the critic John Russell Taylor has written, 'More than any other dramatist – more even than with John Osborne – it is virtually impossible to consider the plays apart from the playwright; to separate judgement of the plays as works of art from judgement of the political opinions which are sometimes given effective dramatic expression in his works.'

It might be added that it is difficult too to separate the plays from the psychological tensions and conflicts within their creator – but that was, in itself, a hypothesis to be tested during the course of the interview. What I knew of Wesker suggested that he would be prepared and able to reflect on these and similar issues. He was born in Stepney in the East End of London on 24 May 1932. His mother was a Hungarian Jewess, while his father was Russian. Both were tailor machinists. He was educated at Upton House School until he was sixteen, and his first jobs after school were as a furniture maker's apprentice and a plumber's mate. He spent his two years' National Service in the RAF and then, after many jobs including kitchen porter, ended up as a pastry cook. It was while he was a porter in 1956 that he met and married Doreen Bicker; the Weskers have two grown-up sons and a daughter. Wesker married on a £300 Arts Council bursary, awarded to him for his play *Chicken Soup with Barley*. It was the first of a celebrated trilogy, completed by *Roots* and *I'm Talking about Jerusalem*, and since then Wesker has written a stream of plays including *The Kitchen, Chips with Everything, Their Very Own and Golden City, The Wedding* and *The Merchant*, in addition to numerous short stories, television plays, reviews and articles.

What makes Wesker a particularly interesting subject is that he has declared that one motive for writing plays is that he might be able to provide people with an insight into their lives which they might not have had before. That aspiration raises the question of whether his plays, heavily impregnated as they appear to be with the scents, flavours and feelings of his own childhood and family, provide him with equivalent insights, and whether the process of transmuting his own experience into art exorcises spectral traumas, enriches satisfying memories, and dissipates blocked emotional tensions.

The central figure in his trilogy of plays, Ronnie Kahn, bears more than a passing resemblance to the young Wesker. Ronnie's mother,

Sarah, is the dominant figure in the Kahn household, a battling political activist with visceral Marxist principles, a massive organiser of the lives of those within her immediate sphere of influence. Ronnie's father, in contrast, is weak, ineffectual and uncaring. In creating such family characters, how far was Wesker drawing on his own memories of the characters and the relationship of his parents? And how far, if at all, does Wesker share the preoccupations of the characters within the play – the need for a driving belief, the fearful inevitability of patterns of behaviour being handed remorselessly down from one generation within a family to the next, and the fear of failure (and actual failure) which permeates so many of his early plays?

The first play of the trilogy ends with Ronnie Kahn showing every sign of following his father into inconsequentiality, while his mother cries despairingly, 'If you don't care you'll die.' Wesker's own public life has largely been that of a man who at times seems to care too much, to take issue too often, to write just one letter of protest, clarification or reply too many. He certainly has been no stranger to controversy. In the 1960s he was an ardent campaigner against nuclear weapons and was briefly in prison with Bertrand Russell. In the mid-1970s, after a two-month stint with the *Sunday Times*, he wrote a play, *The Journalists*, which Royal Shakespeare actors refused to perform; the result was an acrimonious dispute which eventually ended in a settlement in Wesker's favour. Between 1961 and 1970, he was Artistic Director of Centre 42, a cultural movement for popularising the arts, mainly through trade union support and participation, and in furtherance of his stated intention to write plays not merely for those for whom plays are a legitimate form of expression but also for those who normally find the world of art and the artist strange, intimidating and even alien.

In addition to his identity as a playwright in the public eye, Wesker, from the psychological vantage point, is of interest because he is an outsider. A Jew of immigrant parents, a writer about the experiences of a working class of which he is questionably a member, a spokesman who idealises that class in terms of its energy, raw passion and spontaneous feelings and yet has himself left it behind, he is, in the sense that so many of my subjects were – Peter Marsh, Nell Dunn, Spike Milligan, David Irving – on the fringe. Those most preoccupied with their own identity, most intrigued by the myriad ethnic and racial factors, religious and political convictions, personal influences and chance happenings which go to mould an individual's sense of his own self are, more often than not, likely to muse on the extent to which they do and do not belong to class, creed, ethnic group and nation.

Arnold Wesker's interview followed hard on the heels of David Irving's, and the contrast is quite striking. Where the historian expresses an uncompromisingly low opinion of women and idealises an absent father, the playwright admires feminine strength and is suspicious of what he sees as a certain male arrogance and phoniness. Irving complains of Jewish self-preoccupation, while Wesker reflects on the fact that only abroad does he feel himself to be an Englishman; here he feels alien. For Irving, family life and the rearing of children, while important, are none the less processes which come between him and his life's work. For Wesker, they are his life's work.

The contrast provoked an immense response from listeners – and an involved one too, in that several correspondents commented on how aspects of Wesker and Irving reminded them of individuals within their own lives. Both interviews powerfully evoked family strength, pressure and influence, even if neither provided a clear, unambiguous insight into quite how, at the end of the day, such factors mould one man into a playwright and another into a historian. There may still be those who feel that one can watch Wesker's plays and read Irving's books without knowing anything about either of them and be none the worse for it. I know I can do neither without thinking of what each said to me in that anonymous little studio in the bowels of Broadcasting House.

Yet Arnold Wesker expressed reservations about being a subject at all, and quoted Samuel Johnson to me to the effect that 'questioning is not the mode of conversation among gentlemen. It is assuming a superiority, and it is particularly wrong to question a man concerning himself; there may be parts of his former life which he may not wish to be made known to other persons or even brought to his own recollections.' In the last analysis, Wesker agreed to participate and, to my mind, the result suggests that, in this respect at least, the good doctor was wrong.

ANTHONY CLARE: Arnold Wesker, you did agree to be interviewed in this series – so what was it that overcame your own and Dr Johnson's reservations?
ARNOLD WESKER: A mixture of reasons. I've come to recognise

over the years that being an artist is dealing in a market place, and it's essential to remain in the public attention. Secondly, I keep a diary, and every so often I write something in this diary to the effect that I don't really understand what's happening, and seem to understand less and less about myself. I just hope that the details I'm recording will mean something to someone, and it struck me that an encounter, an exchange with you, might reveal something to me. I must confess I've always been sceptical about psychiatry: it seemed to me that if you had a good, intelligent, perceptive friend, that would be adequate. I have studiously avoided going to a psychiatrist, although lots of people have said I ought to. I have often wondered whether going to a psychiatrist would, in addition to revealing things to me about myself, open up all sorts of other areas, into which I might dip as a writer.

CLARE: Were there other anxieties and reservations?

WESKER: Yes – that I would be lulled into a sense of false security, and reveal more than I would want.

CLARE: That is immediately very tempting in that it suggests that there are things you know of, which you would prefer not to talk about.

WESKER: Oh good God, yes. I think we ought to define the areas, or at least acknowledge that areas exist beyond which I don't think I would go, so that we know quite what this exchange is about.

CLARE: Would it be fair to ask if you can split your reservations into areas? Is there some aspect of yourself that you would prefer not to discuss?

WESKER: Under the general heading of the most private, yes.

CLARE: Given that you're aware of it, is it likely that you might discuss it in the course of this kind of interview?

WESKER: Yes, because there's another part of me which, unless I control it, has a desperate need to tell all.

CLARE: If you did tell all, what damage do you fear?

WESKER: One, that telling all would involve other people. And there is the other danger that in the great whoosh of telling all, one actually doesn't tell the truth: one reveals more what one suspects, fears, about oneself, without necessarily revealing the truth.

CLARE: But these were not sufficient to counter the major reason you gave for participating, namely keeping your name in the public eye.

WESKER: Ah, because there are all sorts of other areas I would hope were interesting enough to talk about. You must decide that.

CLARE: Fair enough. The very first area is your Jewish background.
WESKER: Yes. It needs to be described carefully. I think it's important to qualify a notion that perhaps I am partly responsible for, namely that of an East End writer. If you talk about having an East End background, it suggests poverty and unhappiness and deprivation and all that. Certainly there was poverty and certainly there was deprivation, but there wasn't unhappiness, not for me. My memories are of a battling family, but basically a happy one, in which there was a great deal of love. I am also slightly worried about the notion of a working-class writer. I don't know how helpful that is as a description, because being Jewish the whole atmosphere was one in which education and the arts were taken for granted, and we didn't participate in what are generally thought to be East End working-class activities. We didn't go to pubs or football matches, and it's necessary to be aware of that when thinking about my background as East End and working-class. It isn't quite the same as, perhaps, an Alan Sillitoe background.
CLARE: In view of this Jewish, East End, central European background, how do you see yourself? Would you describe yourself as an Englishman?
WESKER: Everywhere but in England! I feel very English abroad, but I don't feel English in England. I feel very alien. I was surprised to discover this. I'd never thought of myself as anything but an English writer until the responses to my work began to take on a special tone, and they bore no relationship to what I thought I was doing as a writer. I had to ask myself, 'Why is the work arousing hostility?' – and it was hostility, not simply criticism. I know that, however flawed any of my work might be, there's an enormous amount of thought and craft in it, so when the criticisms came I had to ask myself why, and I could only think that there must have been an alien voice, an alien tone to the work, which aroused the hostility of the critics. I suppose you could say, 'Wait a minute: so many of the critics are Jewish; how can that be?' And that opens up a whole other area of how anglicised certain Jews are, to the extent that they would prefer to forget that they are Jewish and are slightly embarrassed when confronted with the Jewish tone.
CLARE: Do you see this as a dichotomy – being Jewish or being English?
WESKER: Yes.

CLARE: You couldn't conceive yourself as being both?

WESKER: Well I am both, but it produces a conflict of emotions. There's a very strong part of me which loves England and loves the landscape and loves so many of its traditions, and I do really feel that England is a place where one breathes freely in a way one doesn't in all sorts of other places. But there is a marvellous phrase by George Eliot, 'The English are slow to move, like a stomach', and I find myself in conflict with this because I have a certain energy – I *had* a certain energy, I'm not sure whether this hasn't been stifled by the English slowness.

CLARE: Were your family very energetic, battling people?

WESKER: My mother was a marvellously energetic person. Her energy went into keeping the family together. But my father, no. My father was a very typical, recognisable Jewish character who preferred to read books and not work, and engage in conversation, and generally be nice to people and have people be nice to him.

CLARE: Was your mother politically idealistic?

WESKER: Yes, but she was an innocent. She was politically uneducated. She was a communist because communism for her was a symbol of equality and justice and she really didn't understand the implications of ideology leading to totalitarianism.

CLARE: But she influenced you?

WESKER: Yes she did, but the influences were the influences of values – human values, how you behave with people, being good, being courteous, being thoughtful, being loyal. This is very Jewish, and this very much influenced me, so that if I were to be described as a political animal, it would be simply as someone who cared about a society in which human beings realised their potential. It's the waste of life that distresses me. There was a time when, with her, I thought that capitalist society destroyed that marvellous human spark, that individual spark in human beings. That's why I was a socialist, because it seemed to me that socialism released the energy of the individual. But now we have enormous experience of socialism doing exactly the same, killing the individual spark, so that leaves me politically in a wilderness. My mother, on the other hand, died still imagining that communism was the answer.

CLARE: Did the differences between your parents lead to battle, argument, contention?

WESKER: Yes, they fought, they were a fighting couple. I was protected partly by an older sister, who is eight years older than I am.

CLARE: Were there just the two of you?

WESKER: Yes, just the two of us. She took the brunt of it – I think it distressed her more than it distressed me. I seemed to look for the positive in relationships and in people rather than the negative, so I enjoyed my parents for what they were, and for the love they gave me. Of course I was distressed by the quarrels between them, but on balance I was more influenced by their love and humour and the pleasures they took in us and the family.

CLARE: Do you identify yourself with one or other of them?

WESKER: I don't know what you mean by identify. I enjoy the best that I think I've inherited from them. I fear some of the other traits. I fear the weakness of my father's personality. I've just written something in which a character says that inside all of us there's someone waiting to give up, and I have this image of my father who gave up once he became ill. But I was supported very much by the memory of a mother who outlived him, who never gave up.

CLARE: There is no real evidence is there in your personality of someone who gives up?

WESKER: There are moments when I reach the edge and want to give up.

CLARE: A great cry in one of your plays is, 'If you don't care you die': is that why 'battle' is so important?

WESKER: That particular phrase was once uttered to me by my mother and it seemed to me resonant of all sorts of things. As a writer I would like to think that I operate on many levels, but – for a simplified answer – it seems as though nearly all my work is to do with people who attempt something in their lives and fail. The play is about the attempt and the failure and the abilities to survive that failure. I'm always impressed by the quality of survival in people, in my mother, in a lot of the friends who surrounded her. I wrote a play called *The Old Ones* which was very much about her people, her friends, and it was about that quality of defiantly going on.

CLARE: Did she want something particularly for you?

WESKER: Yes, she wanted me to have a safe, secure job, and not be a writer.

CLARE: What sort of job?

WESKER: Oh – electrician, anything that had a regular income. She herself was ambivalent. On the one hand she said that you must stand up and cry 'stinking fish', but being a Jew of that generation that remembered or lived very close to the pogroms of Europe, she also had that Jewish trait of saying, 'Ssh, Ssh, not too loud, they will hear.' She always used to say to me, 'You know, what you are doing, dear, standing up in public, giving interviews, making declarations like that — they'll get you in the end', and I must say that the spectre of their getting me in the end has grown with the years.

CLARE: She was alive when your early plays were put on?

WESKER: Yes, and there was a mixture of pleasure and bewilderment and fear: that it couldn't possibly be true and that — as indeed I feel, and I suspect most artists feel, and as I think John Osborne's play *Inadmissible Evidence* is about — sooner or later they're going to find out that there is absolutely no value or worth in one as an artist.

CLARE: I'll come back to that. Did your mother recognise herself in your early plays?

WESKER: Yes, of course she did and she was very distressed at the image, because she could only see me recording the quarrels and she didn't understand that was a necessary process before one could allow the character to emerge as a heroine. I saw her personally as a heroine, and that's how I allowed the character to become in *Chicken Soup With Barley*. I always knew that I wanted to write a heroic woman, and that's what I think I ended up with. But everything has to be earned. To this extent I am a puritan. I think everything has to be earned, friendships have to be earned, everything you produce in art has to be earned, your final moment has to be earned. I knew that if that woman was to be a heroine one had to show her with blemishes, and it was the blemishes that she saw. She didn't see the heroic person at the end.

CLARE: Did that leave scars in your relationship with her?

WESKER: I think it contributed — my mother always felt guilty for my father's illness, and if she didn't feel guilty for it she felt that we thought she was responsible for it, which of course was nonsense. There's a moment in the play when she snatches the cigarette out of his hand because he is not facing the reality that she is trying to confront him with and he has his stroke. And she saw that as me saying, 'You gave him a stroke.' Of course it was not. It was a dramatic moment, and the two came together.

CLARE: How do you know it wasn't you saying that she gave him a stroke?

WESKER: Because I don't believe it. You're a psychoanalyst and you'll say that none of us can be relied upon to know what we feel or felt; this may be true and there's no answer to that. I can only say that, whereas I do know a lot of things about myself that I don't love, that just isn't one of them. I understood both of them equally, and was as critical of each as I was loving of each.

CLARE: You say that it was a stormy relationship, that there were conflicts when you were a little boy. I wondered what that left in you? When I ask and get a picture, it is of a nice neat tidy package, where you loved her and you loved him.

WESKER: If you want to know what the scars are I can talk about the scars, but before I do, it must be observed that my sister took the greatest brunt. She was older and was vulnerable at the stormiest time. And I was cushioned from a lot of it. I do think you also have to take into account natures, and it seems that I have a resilient and generally – it sounds so soft and wet to say – joyful nature. Given the choice, my instinct is to laugh and celebrate rather than to be gloomy – which doesn't mean I am unaware of what is awful in man and the world. But there I am, I have that nature. I can remember when they quarrelled – I would attempt to reconcile them and say, 'Don't be silly', and send them up, as it were. That was my nature. But of course there were scars, and the one scar to which I can point is that, with the knowledge of my father as a weak personality and as someone who gave in, I find that I am absolutely determined never to give in on the one hand, and to be independent on the other. I think this spirit of independence contributes to the hostility I arouse, because I will not concede that anybody is doing me a favour, for example. If anybody suggests to me that my life wouldn't be the same without them, that's it. I can cope on my own. My wife might be distressed by this because she knows I am domestic. I can run a house. I can cook for myself, iron for myself, launder for myself, do anything she can do – and so this must irritate her in some way.

CLARE: Does it?

WESKER: Actually it doesn't, because finally she is doing it! She runs the house, she is a brick, the anchor not only of this entire household but of our circle of friends.

CLARE: I am struck through this that your mother, for all her blemishes, was a sterling and remarkable force that you identify with. When you talk of your father, while it's with sympathy and understanding, there's a feeling of 'that's not what I want to be. I must at all events avoid ever being that.'

WESKER: Absolutely. I bristle. I suppose in a way that's why I get irritated with the critics, because there's an air about them that but for their graciousness ... that I'm dependent on them.

CLARE: And that if you were just a little bit more agreeable you could come back to school?

WESKER: If I didn't answer back, if I didn't write those articles about critics, if I didn't even send them private notes. When *Caritas* was reviewed by the man on the *New Statesman*, he began his review by listing the letters I had sent him and the articles I had written. Obviously it impinges on their consciousness, and they say to themselves – they don't say it in such words, actually Harold Hobson did in a review, directly after I had criticised him – 'Writers should learn when to keep their mouths shut.' That's what I *should* do, and they don't quite understand – 'There's Wesker blowing his top again.' Well there you are – I do.

CLARE: Going back to your adolescence: how different were you from other boys in terms of, say, your interest in sport?

WESKER: Well, you've hit upon something. I never developed a passion for football. I think I made a token gesture. There was a time when a famous Russian team, the Moscow Dynamos, came and three-quarters of the school played truant to see them play Spurs. It was a foggy day anyway so we couldn't see much, but I never developed the habit of going to football matches. I was an energetic player of football, but I never really knew what to do with it when I got it. I developed no skills in cricket, I'm an average swimmer, and even in days of affluence I didn't develop the skill of skiing. So it was an interest in literature and cinema and poetry and this terrible habit of writing that set me aside.

CLARE: None of these are working-class passions.

WESKER: Not generally. There does exist, of course, a strong working-class tradition of literacy.

CLARE: How much did this feeling of difference affect you in later adolescence – say with girls? Were you self-conscious about these differences?

WESKER: I always enjoyed the company of girls much more than boys, and still do.

CLARE: Why?

WESKER: I don't know. One of the lectures I give is called 'The Women in my Work'. It seems as though seventy-five per cent of the leading characters in my plays and stories are women, and I've tried to account for this. Not seriously, just thinking about it off the top of my head. Maybe it's because I had a strong mother whom I adored. Maybe it's because in most artists there seems to be a greater amount of female genes than male, and that this enables the male artist to have greater sympathy with women. I don't know. I have this dark – not so dark – suspicion that women are superior to men in some strange indefinable way, and that men know this, and that this might account for male chauvinism. Or it may be that – and I won't go much further than this – a certain self-contempt or acute awareness of weaknesses in myself makes me think, 'How on earth can women possibly enjoy men – they are such absurd, arrogant, silly creatures?'

CLARE: Would you see yourself as arrogant?

WESKER: There are times when I catch myself, and I think, 'What on earth could a woman see in such a personality?'

CLARE: You empathise with women; were you successful as a young man with women?

WESKER: I seemed to be, but when it came to the crunch they all turned me down.

CLARE: Why?

WESKER: I think it was a mixture of things. I didn't seem to be going anywhere. I certainly didn't have academic skills which promised the life of a lawyer or an accountant or a doctor. I didn't have any craft skills – I wasn't going to be a tailor. I certainly didn't show any business acumen. Maybe there wasn't sufficient promise in my future. On the other hand I was too much of a handful for them in some ways – emotional, spiritual ways. Beyond that you'd have to ask them.

CLARE: You mentioned arrogance: but what else is there about men – and, indeed, yourself as a man – that makes you wonder about them and their attractiveness to anybody else?

WESKER: I watch men behave. Men embarrass me when they're with women. If you go into a restaurant and you see couples, men and women, and you look at a man and watch his face and his gestures, they just seem absurd and transparent without any . . . sense of poetry. The girls seem not to see through them, but I'm sure they do.

CLARE: If they did, what would they see? A sort of self-obsession?

WESKER: They see a man preening himself and trying to be what he isn't and to say the things he thinks will please them rather than the things he actually feels, talking about himself, having very little curiosity in them, having very little curiosity in the world, just offering the day's reading with great erudition.

CLARE: It seems phoney: is there a sort of phoniness about many men?

WESKER: I think there is. But when I say this to certain women they say, Oh no, they couldn't be without men.

CLARE: When you left school, what did you do?

WESKER: I decided that I had to earn a living and if I wasn't going to be an actor, I was going to be a writer, and I would write whatever I did. It was my responsibility to bring money into the house, so I followed in my brother-in-law's footsteps and became apprentice to a furniture-maker with whom I stayed for six months and then became redundant, because he was a man who worked on his own and big factories were easing him out. I felt I really wasn't made for the building trade: I ought to get near books, so I worked for Simmond's the booksellers in Fleet Street before going into the Air Force.

CLARE: This was the late Forties, early Fifties. It was an interesting time politically in this country. Were you very political at that stage?

WESKER: I was in a confused state, it was a few months into the Air Force. Until I joined the Air Force, I was a mixture of Zionist and Young Communist.

CLARE: Where did that come from?

WESKER: The communist from my parents both of whom were members of the CP and between the ages of fifteen and sixteen I was for six months a member of the Young Communist League. And that was all. I've never been a member of a political party since then. But I drifted into a Zionist organisation, and I did so mainly because there were rather attractive girls who were members of the group. Then I became very caught up in the whole idea of going to Israel, but I didn't. After about four years I drifted out of it. In the Air Force I met a young student at Oxford, because I was stationed near there, and through devious routes became introduced to a book of essays called *The God that Failed*, which was one of the major political landmarks for me. Whether it was a good collection or whether they were well-written essays or not, I don't know. All I know is that they shook my image of what was happening in the Soviet Union and what had happened to communism throughout the world. I suppose from that moment on I was what I thought of vaguely as a socialist, but I never joined the Labour Party.

CLARE: When you went into the Royal Air Force, was there anything in that extraordinary organisation which underlined the fact that you might be English?

WESKER: No, the Air Force continued to underline the fact that I was different.

CLARE: In what way?

WESKER: Because of the responses to me. This is how we measure ourselves, isn't it? We define ourselves by the way people respond to us.

CLARE: Is there a bit of you that wants to belong?

WESKER: Yes, I don't go out of my way to be an outsider. You must take my word for that. I don't calculate shocks, I don't calculate terrible attitudes. I think I am as honest and as immediate as I know how.

CLARE: What about the opposite, whereby you might lose some of your unique outsider quality?

WESKER: I wouldn't phrase it like that. I wouldn't say I want to belong. I would be much simpler and say that I want to be performed. I don't want to be applauded necessarily, I just want to be performed. Let posterity take care of the work. That means that one of the problems that, say, Peter Hall has with me is that I view the National Theatre as mine. I mean it belongs to me, it's the stage on which my plays sit easily and for which they're written. Whenever we exchange letters this is what I say, so this is what I mean. I want to be performed and recognised as belonging to English theatre. To that extent I want to belong.

CLARE: Your brother-in-law once said that each generation has a problem that it battles and tackles: war, depression, nuclear disarmament. You're a person who fuels on battles and that's been so over the years. What fuels you now?

WESKER: Very wise, my brother-in-law. I think he was saying that to each generation is given a particular task: the Spanish Civil War to one generation, the Second World War to another, CND to another, and so on. People have often asked me if I am involved with the resurgence of CND and the answer to that is no. Very simply, because I think one has a variation of what my brother-in-law said. One has only a certain amount of energy in one's life, or at least I've found I have. There was a period in my life when I could give energy to such things as CND and Centre 42, and then I devoted my energies to bringing up a family. At a certain moment I decided I really couldn't talk about how the world could improve itself if I didn't have the authority of having put together a good family.

CLARE: You were tamed by domesticity?

WESKER: You could call it 'tamed by domesticity', but that's diminishing it. I don't think it's tamed, and anyone who brings up a family knows that it's not a tamed animal that brings it up. It's so difficult to make a family work; I had at least to show that I could make that work. Otherwise talking about the way society should treat and handle people would have no credibility.

CLARE: You said somewhere that when you're in a solitary mood you look at yourself and see what you will not be – what you once wanted to be, may still want to be. What do you want to be that you won't be?

WESKER: A mixture of things. I would like to be silent like Pinter; I will never be. I would like to be economically independent, which means I would like to be a business man; I would like to know the value of the pound, not the value of a pound, but how to make one pound into five. It's a very special facility and I would like to be able to do that very coolly and efficiently and without greed, so that I could be entirely independent of management and artistic directors and critics, and mount my own plays and finance my own films.

CLARE: Why do you think you've been a writer? Is there anything in your life other than writing that commands even a tenth of the passion, the interest, the commitment, the involvement?

WESKER: Apart from my family?

CLARE: Apart from your family.

WESKER: No, not a tenth. There is something that intermittently commands a little bit of attention.

CLARE: What's that?

WESKER: Drawing. I've had moments when I've thought to myself if at the age of fifty I stop being a writer, and I begin to teach myself to draw – I've had twenty-five years at being a writer – and if it takes me ten years to learn how to draw and the nature of paint, I would have another fifteen years of being a painter. And then I would only be seventy-five. Picasso went on to eighty-five, ninety. Even if it took me fifteen years to learn, I would have ten years of work in me. But I don't suppose I ever will be.

NELL DUNN

No other person's ideas, and none of my own ideas, are as authoritative as my own experience. It is to experience that I must return again and again to discover a closer approximation to truth as it is in the process of becoming in me. Neither the Bible nor the prophets, neither Freud nor research, neither the revelations of God nor man, can take precedence over my own direct experience.

CARL ROGERS, *On Becoming a Person*

I wanted to interview Nell Dunn for two reasons. First, I read her book, *Living Like I Do*, not when it was published in 1977 but in 1980 when I was working, with Sally Thompson, on a book published the following year. Our book, entitled *Let's Talk About Me*, evaluated the self-exploratory psychotherapies which were mushrooming in California as the ultimate products of the Me Decade. Nell Dunn's book was a largely favourable account of a series of alternative life-styles including communes, assortative matings, *ménages à trois* and upwards and single-parent families. Although she recorded each arrangement very honestly and admitted at the end of the book that most had terminated short of finding Utopia, and although the picture that emerged of the various alternatives to the nuclear family was, in fact, a poor advertisement for the notion that here might lie better ways of organising family relationships, Nell Dunn appeared reluctant to discard her own hopes. I must have noted the fact because when, in 1981, I went with my wife to Nell Dunn's first and highly successful play, *Steaming*, I recalled the book and its implicit suggestion of an author in search of a personal identity. In *Steaming* a group of ill-matched women take their clothes off in a local Turkish Baths and, *en passant*, reveal their innermost feelings, fantasies, inadequacies and dreams. Once again emerged the themes of loneliness, dissatisfaction with current human relationships, and the difficulties men have in understanding women, and once again the author combined a sharp eye and ear for human difficulties and tensions with a warm heart, bordering on the sentimental, even naive, when it came to proposing remedies.

When I went to find out more about her I became even more intrigued. She was born in London on 4 June 1936. One grandfather was the Earl of Rosslyn, known popularly as 'the man who broke the bank at Monte Carlo'. A man of spectacular spontaneity, he once hired the Stoll Theatre for one night and booked Lily Langtry to play Ophelia to his Hamlet. Her other grandfather was Sir James Dunn, a Canadian philanthropist who left £25 million when he died. Nell Dunn was convent educated, but left school aged fourteen. At twenty-one she married the writer, Jeremy Sandford, and had three sons. The marriage, however, broke up after thirteen years and was dissolved finally after a further ten years' separation. It was during her marriage that she began her career as a writer. *Up the Junction*, her first book, sold half a million copies, won the John Llewelyn Rhys Memorial Prize and was filmed for both television and the cinema. Her first novel, *Poor Cow*, was also a bestseller and became a major film. Each of her books concerns relationships between women and how fulfilling such friendships can be; her own stated favourite, *Tear His Head off His Shoulders*, faces the difficulties which occur when a friendship between two women begins to suggest a sexual encounter.

Given such a background, there appeared to be little shortage of areas in Nell Dunn's life which merited discussion. On the surface, she appeared to have shrugged off the influence of her most formative childhood years and to have embraced a whole new baggage of ideas, attitudes, values and opinions concerning life and living. She had been born into wealth, had a convent education and lived within an upper-class milieu, yet she acquired a public persona through writing vigorously and, in general, favourably about working-class experience and unorthodox styles of life. In various interviews, she was quoted as insisting that she believed in the importance and the possibility of a genuine, lasting and satisfying heterosexual relationship; yet, to judge from her writings, her opinion of men is far from positive, most of her masculine creations being, on the whole, a miserable lot. Indeed, at times it is difficult not to feel that she believes that true sensuality is rarely encountered outside the working class.

How far, I wondered, were these themes in her work related to her own personal experiences as a child? How far did she draw on her own memories of her childhood? Was it fair or indeed wise to suspect, as I did, that someone like Nell Dunn is drawn to alternative and communal approaches to family life precisely because her own experience of family life has been largely unsatisfactory? Put like that it sounds demeaning and reductive, but looking at the cults, communes and groups in California made it difficult to avoid the conclusion that much of what motivated the search for alternatives, and provided a very strong motive for idealising what was found, was a dreadfully inadequate experience of life and love as a child.

As the interview unfolds, such issues quickly come to the foreground. Nell Dunn quickly entered into the reality of the interview as a discussion, a mutual process of reflection in which there are, of necessity, no right answers, merely possibilities which appear more likely than others. Her account of her wartime evacuation experience moved several listeners to write describing their own, others to inquire about research into the impact of the country's evacuation policy during the Second World War. Early on in the interview she provides a sharp and convincing example of what Abraham Maslow has called a 'peak' experience – a moment of intense happiness, which has been described as a sense of completeness, of absolute value and relevance, and a bubbling over of sheer delight. Its relation to the importance of her nanny is quickly noted.

More than thirty years ago, John Bowlby published his work on maternal deprivation and identified a number of short-term effects on the child and long-term effects on the development of the personality. Bowlby concluded that 'mother love in infancy and childhood is as important for mental health as are vitamins and proteins for physical health'. This view was immensely influential, provoking a review of deplorable patterns of institutional upbringing and leading to an improvement in the residential care of children. In the intervening years, however, there has been a reassessment of the emphasis on 'maternal' and greater attention has been paid to the complex notion of deprivation. The current view, most articulately presented by Michael Rutter, is that while it is clear that 'bad' care of children in early life can have 'bad' effects, the term 'maternal deprivation' is misleading in that in most cases the deleterious influences are not specifically tied to the mother and are not due to deprivation. In most cases, the evidence suggests, the damage comes not from 'deprivation' or 'loss', but from a lack or distortion of care.

Some idea of the complexity of this whole issue can be obtained from examining Nell Dunn's own story. At first glance, the issue seems uncomplicated. At a vulnerable period in her life she was taken from her family home and evacuated to America. It clearly was traumatic. The memory is vivid. She was taken to see a psychiatrist in New York. She returned when she was five and a half. A straightforward account of maternal deprivation exercising effects which are still visible forty years later. But other factors need to be taken account of before too hasty a conclusion is drawn. Had Nell Dunn returned to a harmonious and integrated household, perhaps her evacuation experience might have been diluted and eventually exorcised. Instead she returned to a home from which her father had already left. Single traumatic events, such as the evacuation, are popularly believed to underpin adult doubts, difficulties and disorders, but in general it is rare for a specific event to have long-term effects in the absence of additional, related and exacerbating situations and circumstances.

And so, not merely the evacuation, but the rupture from her beloved nanny, the quality of her parents' relationship before she left, the break in her home on her return, the subsequent isolation at boarding school, and her general lack of personal identity all need to be taken into account when Nell Dunn's vividly described personal development is pondered.

In her own way she represents the self-actualising individual described so approvingly by Carl Rogers, the influential American psychologist, and founder of the encounter group. In the encounter group the crucial activity is not treatment, interpretation, revelation or advice, but listening, listening 'acceptantly to myself', listening 'to the richness in each other'. In this way, Rogerian psychotherapy argues, can be developed 'a deep trust in the capacity of the individual to be himself, to accept himself, to express himself'. The paradox which runs through so many of the newer therapies is that we cannot change, we cannot move away from what we are until we thoroughly accept what we are. Nell Dunn, in her writings, has been strongly drawn to Rogerian ideas. She drew on her experiences as a member of a women's encounter group for much of the material in *Steaming*. The problem, and she acknowledges it implicitly in the interview, is that accepting oneself presupposes a notion of oneself. In her case, her concept of self is shadowy, even elusive. But she has not turned inwards in an engrossing exploration of her self as she would undoubtedly be advised to do by any of the many psychotherapy gurus in North America, but has sought to chart her own identity and define her own essence through her writing. For our sakes, as well as for her own, may she continue to do so for many years to come.

ANTHONY CLARE: How do you feel about talking in some detail about yourself?

NELL DUNN: Slightly mixed. I find it immensely interesting, but I am slightly nervous about doing it when it's being recorded, and also unsure about the whole thing of exposure. I feel a mixture of having a tremendous need to show off – which I feel is part of being a writer – and yet a strong need for privacy and almost secrecy. So I'm not quite sure why I do it, but I am interested in it.

CLARE: But don't many writers reveal a great deal about themselves anyway?

DUNN: I think so, but it's a little bit different because in a book or a play, you are wearing disguises, and you can take risks to explore the unknown bits of your thoughts or ideas. When we're talking like we are now, I have to take responsibility about saying, 'This is me', and I'm answering for myself; and I think that's more anxious-making, perhaps.

CLARE: Such anxieties you have – are they related to revealing things which you know and would prefer not to discuss, or to revealing things of which you know not, and are worried as to what they might be?

DUNN: I don't think either. A lot of the anxiety is to do with letting you down, and not saying anything at all interesting! Which perhaps relates directly to feeling I have to succeed in what I do and that . . . it's not enough just to be myself, and just to be present here telling you how things are for me.

CLARE: Where does that come from?

DUNN: It comes from an enormous need to vindicate myself. That sounds as if it's the wrong word – I'm not very good on words, although I'm a writer. But somehow to say, 'I am, notice me, care about me, comfort me.' It's a sort of constant waving of the hands, to say, 'Here I am.'

CLARE: Were you easily dismissed or missed or not noticed?

DUNN: I have a memory as a very young child – and it's a very important memory – that it was enough just to be me. And that was absolutely enough, and I was completely accepted. Quite an interesting thing happened about that. I have a very close friend – who in fact is the heroine of *Poor Cow* and in a way the heroine of *Steaming* — and she was at tea in my house with her mother, and I was sitting beside her on the sofa and her mother was sitting on a chair at an angle to the sofa — one of those old carpet chairs you used to have in cottages in the Thirties. I think I handed her a cup or took a cup and I sat there and I had this extraordinary heat enter my feet and go right up my body; it was a sense of pure happiness and pure warmth. So overcome was I that I became quite embarrassed and thought they must notice and think something peculiar had happened to me. In fact it passed after, I suppose, thirty or forty seconds, but I felt very amazed by it, and I explored a little bit where it could come from and pieced together little memories. I think it came from my nanny when I was very young. I used to go and stay with her and her mother when my parents went away for the weekend, in a cottage which had that kind of furniture. It was the same date and layout of a terrace house, which is the sort of house I've always tried to live in. I feel that I did know what it was like not to have to try to draw attention to myself, but that at some point I lost it; and it's as if I'm trying to get back to a sense of getting enough, and it's very difficult for me to get enough. One of the ways I try and get enough is by writing.

CLARE: Let's go back a little. You were born in London?

DUNN: Yes. Till the war, we lived in St Andrews' Place, in Regent's Park, and when I was three in 1939, I was evacuated to America. And that's about my first real memory.

CLARE: How long were you in America?

DUNN: For two and a half years.

CLARE: The first three years — had you a nanny then?

DUNN: Yes.

CLARE: What did your father do?

DUNN: I don't know. He went off to the war when I was evacuated and when he came back he worked for a time in the newspaper world, but as soon as he could, he retired to the country and just lived in a beautiful house and farm — that's what he liked best.

CLARE: And your mother?

DUNN: My mother I don't remember before the war, because I was evacuated without my mother or my father. During the war she was very keen on farming — that's what she loved doing. She loved the country — both my parents loved the country.

CLARE: Do you remember much else about those years?

DUNN: I remember being sent to see a psychiatrist in New York because I couldn't talk. I remember having to go into a room and being told to play and to break as many of the toys as I could, and becoming aware that he would see me through a glass panel, although I couldn't see him, and not wanting to break any of the toys but wanting not to be seen, and finding some way to stay in a corner. I think there were several sessions of this, during which other children were put in, and I really wanted to avoid playing with the other children. I found it very difficult to play, that I can remember.

CLARE: You sound a very lonely child.

DUNN: I had my sister, whom I was very attached to. She took care of me – she was two years older than me. But I think I was very shocked by the separation, and I don't feel that I was emotionally robust as a child – or indeed as an adult, for that matter.

CLARE: Do you think back much to those days?

DUNN: Sometimes I do.

CLARE: With what kind of feelings?

DUNN: Sad feelings, really. Not blame. I don't blame anyone. I think it was the war – parents who could afford to, sent their children to America. I know that. I recognise that.

CLARE: But that's a very rational judgement.

DUNN: Yes.

CLARE: Emotionally?

DUNN: Emotionally, a tremendous sense of loss and a sense of – what is it called when you've cut someone's legs off? – an amputation, in a sense.

CLARE: What do you think you lost?

DUNN: I think I lost a place where I was completely accepted and loved. And I lost some sense of the freedom of being allowed to be myself. It starts getting a bit solemn when I talk about it, and I don't want to make it sound too solemn – and it also gets a bit abstract.

CLARE: Did you lose something that you could accept and love?

DUNN: Yes definitely, although I hadn't thought of it that way – but yes.

CLARE: When you came back you were still quite young – five and a half, six. What did you do then?

DUNN: Well, then my father was still away and my parents' marriage was breaking up – although ten years later they remarried, they did actually divorce then.

CLARE: What was it breaking up over?

DUNN: They'd married young and my father was away for three years in the war, and my mother fell in love with someone else.

CLARE: Do you remember the someone else?

DUNN: I remember him because she married him.

CLARE: And did you live with them?

DUNN: I went to my boarding school, my convent, and during the holidays we lived half with my father and half with my mother.

CLARE: How much contact did you have with your father?

DUNN: A lot.

CLARE: What sort of man was he?

DUNN: Very private. Not good at being expansive, and not really good at having a good time, but at the same time he was very individual, with a lot of things that he cared about, like nature, things happening around him in nature, and poetry – he'd read us poems early in the morning. We'd get into bed with him, and he'd read to us.

CLARE: Did he find it difficult to express his feelings?

DUNN: Yes, I think he came from a culture and a background that didn't go in for a lot of expression of feelings.

CLARE: His background was affluent.

DUNN: Affluent, but unsettled.

CLARE: Why was that?

DUNN: His parents divorced as well, and they moved house a lot. I think his was an unsettled childhood.

CLARE: You had one sister. Any brothers?

DUNN: No.

CLARE: Did your sisters go to a convent as well?

DUNN: Yes, we went together.

CLARE: What was that like? What sort of convent was it?

DUNN: I loved it. It was a Roman Catholic convent with nuns.

CLARE: Were you Roman Catholics?

DUNN: Yes, we were brought up as Catholics – our grandmother was a Catholic. I was very happy there. I liked the order. In my life I don't like things being too adventurous. I like them being rather orderly and calm, and I rather like the same things happening every day.

CLARE: And that sums up the convent?

DUNN: Yes.

CLARE: Were there people there who were very influential? A particular teacher?

DUNN: Yes. There were two. One in the lower school when I was very young, who used to sing us lullabies at night. I had a sense of comfort from her, I remember, a sense of again being allowed to be. And then there was the English teacher when I was older, who encouraged me to read and write. I can remember when I was quite young – ten, eleven, twelve – having the experience once or twice of writing and really enjoying it and getting totally absorbed in it. In fact I had a lovely thing happen to me which I felt terribly moved by: I had a letter from someone I remember to have been my best friend when I was thirteen, who'd been to *Steaming* and who now lived in Buenos Aires, and was over here, and she reminded me that I had written a play when I was ten and that we'd all performed it.

CLARE: But you'd forgotten it?

DUNN: I'd sort of forgotten it, but I remembered it very clearly, and what I remembered was the feeling of utter delight and absorption and wholeness in the act of writing, which a lot of the time I don't get. I find it very hard work a lot of the time, but just occasionally I do get that feeling.

CLARE: Was there any writing in your family?

DUNN: No.

CLARE: What was living with your mother like?

DUNN: That was a more Bohemian world, with more people coming into it, much more coming and going. My mother likes people a lot and has a lot of friends.

CLARE: Is her background upper-class?

DUNN: Yes. She's a much lighter-hearted person. My father is dead and my mother is still alive. She has a gift for pleasure and enjoyment which I admire, which I feel my father hadn't really got, and that I haven't really got.

CLARE: Your mother married a second time. What did her second husband do?

DUNN: He was a painter.

CLARE: That was quite a change?

DUNN: Yes.

CLARE: Why did that marriage break up?

DUNN: He left my mother for someone else, after some time, twelve years or something, and then my mother went back to live with my father.

CLARE: Did that affect you?

DUNN: Yes it did. It's hard to say exactly how. I suppose I felt again shocked at the fragility of things.

CLARE: You mean of relationships?

DUNN: Fragility of relationships.

CLARE: You were very fond of your stepfather?

DUNN: Very fond of him. I mean I still am. I still know him.

CLARE: Were there other feelings apart from shock?

DUNN: I think puzzlement too.

CLARE: What age were you then?

DUNN: About twenty.

CLARE: You had left school at fourteen. Why?

DUNN: I was never really told why. My parents took me away. I think they thought it wasn't an interesting enough education, so I was sent to a convent in Rome and then a convent in Paris to learn languages. But in fact I was very bad at languages, and I read books a lot of the time. That was the source of any nourishment I had, because it was difficult for me to make friends when I couldn't speak the language.

CLARE: It must have been a very solitary existence.

DUNN: Very. I can remember in the Rome convent, there was one nun who was eighty who was English. She used to come and see me sometimes and bring me hot milk, and I used to really look forward to her visits which were perhaps once or twice a week; and she also arranged for me to have a bath – she said the English children usually have baths, and she arranged it. And I remember that was very important to me. But I don't remember being particularly unhappy. I think I had by then learnt to live quite a lot in books and my own thoughts.

CLARE: But other things would have suffered. What about your contacts with other adolescents, with boys?

DUNN: I had no contact really until I was seventeen, I suppose, when I came back to England.

CLARE: Would you have had a fairly orthodox Roman Catholic sexual education?

DUNN: Yes.

CLARE: Did that affect you?

DUNN: I'm not sure how much it affected me. I think it's such a mixed thing, the Catholic thing: it encourages and sets such a high standard of passionate love, and in another way it discourages any sort of sexual exploration of how you really are. When I was in Paris I used to see young men and obviously I could have talked to them, they occasionally tried to talk to me, but I didn't really want to. I didn't know how to go about it, so I avoided it.

CLARE: Until?

DUNN: Until I came back to London and started to go to the Courtauld Institute and study History of Art when I was seventeen. At that time it had very few students – there were about fifteen of us, in this lovely Adam house in Portman Square. I was aware then that I didn't know anybody, and that I didn't really know about people. I was living at the time in Eaton Square with my father, and I didn't really know that not everybody lived in Eaton Square or in a country house, which was the only other thing I knew about. I used to catch my bus in Sloane Square, but just occasionally I'd walk a little bit down the King's Road or something, and that felt really brave. I was extremely cautious, I think I'm very cautious by nature, and the only incautious thing I do at all is writing. In every other way I'm very cautious. Part of what I write about is people who aren't cautious, and I admire people that really live, who aren't cautious, who take risks in their lives.

CLARE: You tend to identify that with what's called the working class. Why is that?

DUNN: Possibly because I first met it very strongly when I was about twenty-one, and went to live in Battersea when it was a very working-class area.

CLARE: Why did you do that?

DUNN: Completely spontaneous. I was living in Cheyne Walk in Chelsea, and I had my first son, Roc, and I wheeled him in his pram over the bridge into Battersea. I used to do that quite often because I began to like going there. There was a group of women standing round some rags, and they started talking to me. I didn't know what to say, so I said, 'I'm looking for a house.' One of them said, 'Well, there's one in our road for sale', and took me there; and there was this really beautiful little Victorian cottage with sunflowers in the back garden and a vine, and I just wanted it. I felt this terrific want. It was for sale for fourteen hundred pounds and I had seven hundred pounds; I offered the man seven hundred pounds and he took it. And I wanted to move in straight away. I felt totally at sea in this great big house in Cheyne Walk with enormous panelled rooms; and then suddenly I was in this little cottage with two rooms downstairs and this little garden, and that's where I wanted to be. So I went to live there, and by living there I got to know everybody and I saw and heard a sort of everyday quality of life, where things are immediate. Amazing things I can remember seeing. There was a great row in the street; I looked out of the window, and this girl was fighting with her boyfriend. She picked up a piece of wood lying in the gutter, and hit him over the head, and he collapsed in the street and she walked away – I was so amazed by that. She just walked off round the corner, and then she peeped back, and he lay there, and then after a bit he got up and shouted at her and she came running back, laughing like anything. I felt tremendous envy for that amount of happening, that being allowed to happen. I found it both very exciting and funny. I'd lived in a much more remote world, and suddenly this seemed to be a world where you did things together, and things happened between you, and I think that was why I was attracted to the working class.

CLARE: Did you have any contact with your own class?

DUNN: I did have some friends. But not many. For reasons unknown to myself, I didn't feel happy in the upper-class world.

CLARE: Is this because you didn't know the rules? You didn't know how it worked?

DUNN: I think I was very bad at them – I felt it was too difficult for me, that the hoops were too high. I did know most of the rules, but I felt they were too difficult.

CLARE: You don't like formal parties?

DUNN: No, I don't and I didn't. I was married to a man who wasn't interested in formal life. He didn't have any expectations of my being that kind of wife. I also realised I really had no idea what marriage was about either. I don't think I had very much idea about what other people thought, felt, how they lived their lives. I really did have moments when I thought that the world of people was some kind of extraordinary theatre.

CLARE: You say you didn't quite know what marriage was about?

DUNN: I didn't really know what it meant to have a partnership. I remember years later someone talking about a partnership, and I thought, 'So that's what marriage is meant to be, it's meant to be a partnership. How funny, nobody ever told me that.'

CLARE: How did you come to get married?

DUNN: I think I was in love with the first person I went out with, and I married.

CLARE: The very first?

DUNN: The very first.

CLARE: Were you a virgin?

DUNN: Yes. I'd been out with – no, I hadn't been out with boys. I knew other young boys who had been around me. I think I was in love, and I thought, 'When you're in love you get married.' I was longing to have babies. My first son was born ten months after I was married.

CLARE: And your husband was Jeremy Sandford. He came from a background very similar to yours.

DUNN: Yes. His parents were quieter people. My parents were more wild and adventurous, where his parents lived rather quietly in the country.

CLARE: Jeremy Sandford was quoted as saying, 'I fell for a rich girl because money in girls is sexy and glamorous.' Were you sexy and glamorous?

DUNN: No! I think I was terribly serious and rather withdrawn. Jeremy was quite a lot older than me, and I think he did have fancy ideas which I didn't realise about me being glamorous and all those things. I was also not in the least interested in money, I wasn't interested in being rich. I don't know why – it just didn't seem to interest me very much.

CLARE: Because you'd no reason to think about it?

DUNN: I expect so.

CLARE: You also imbued working-class life with a certain disinhibition and spontaneity; but you also describe how you are actually not that sort of person.

DUNN: No. I don't feel a free person. The scene in the street in Battersea is for me a symbol of freedom, of being able to behave how you feel without too much thought for the consequences: I feel I don't do that. I spend most of my energy trying to make myself feel safe in one way or another, to draw things around me and make myself feel safe in that way.

CLARE: When you say 'safe', what do you fear?

DUNN: I fear pain that I can't deal with. I fear overwhelming feelings that I can't deal with, confrontations, expectations that I can't deal with. It's as if I sometimes feel people are actually too much for me, and what I long for is too much. Like last night, which in a sense was a lovely occasion for me – I was awarded a prize and a lot of people said such nice things about my play – and in fact I didn't sleep all night. I felt very overwhelmed and very anxious all night. I slept and woke and slept and woke.

CLARE: Why anxious?

DUNN: Because I can't keep everything safe and under control – a sense that I don't know what's going to happen and things are going to go wrong. I won't have the strength to put them right again.

CLARE: Did that ever happen?

DUNN: I think it happened when I first went to America when I was evacuated.

CLARE: It was that painful?

DUNN: It was very shocking to me. It's not a very good way of putting it perhaps.

CLARE: Did it happen again?

DUNN: I don't think it's ever happened quite so badly, but yes, I've felt a resonance of it in my life, and I've probably taken a certain amount of precautions against not letting it happen by not being so deeply involved with grown-up people whose power I'm in. I find it very difficult to love grown-ups as much as I love my children.

CLARE: You sound as though you strongly identify with children rather than grown-ups.

DUNN: Yes, I do. I can capture that sense of light-heartedness occasionally with my children. It interests me very much, that whole, light-hearted, frivolous – I'm never quite sure if frivolous is the right word – side of life that eludes me a lot of the time; and when it comes my way I'm so delighted by it. In writing I try to get some of that: I tried to with Josie in *Steaming*, when she talks about what she's going to wear – she's got this terribly serious council meeting to speak at, but really she's interested in the clothes she's going to wear. I love that in people. One of the things I love very much about women is that surface quality they have. The way they can imbue the surface of life with such a rich quality. A friend of mine, who's bringing clothes over from Sweden and selling them to her friends in people's houses, had an afternoon in my house lately. I really loved it – the whole thing of trying on clothes with some friends, and admiring each other. That feeling of light-heartedness went on right through the evening after it was all over. I felt incredibly all right, that's the best way of putting it. It seems peculiar that it should come from that; it often comes from a very surface thing.

CLARE: Whereas with men?

DUNN: I believe the most satisfying thing for anybody is a deep and honest relationship – for a heterosexual woman, obviously with a man. I'm trying to make that for myself, and sometimes it does feel within sight.

CLARE: A heterosexual relationship?

DUNN: I don't mean a heterosexual relationship, because homosexuals believe it would be a homosexual relationship. What I mean is a strong honest satisfying relationship – identifying that such a thing exists, and then making it for myself. It seems like two stages, and I've done the first bit. I do recognise that such a thing exists, and I can see fairly clearly what it means. And the second stage, of actually achieving it, I've begun to touch upon.

CLARE: In your present relationship?

DUNN: Yes.

CLARE: Which is of some years?

DUNN: Seven or eight years.

CLARE: What does your partner make of your distinction between seeing the possibility and then obtaining it?

DUNN: Immediately you say 'partner', I find even that a dangerous word for me.

CLARE: Why?

DUNN: Because he's going to somehow come over to my side of the fence and link arms with me and tell me what to do. That is just my reaction. I mustn't and can't speak for him, but I feel that we probably met and got together at about the same time in our development as people. So perhaps we're finding out together, and that's the good thing about the relationship. There isn't a master/pupil atmosphere about it. There's much more a feeling of two rather desperate people struggling to make something for themselves, and occasionally achieving something very nice for themselves.

CLARE: One of the things that strikes me about some of the things you've written, and indeed your play *Steaming*, is not that men come across as hostile or dangerous or macho or chauvinist, but that they almost get in the way. They get in the way of what is a better relationship: what is, in a sense, more spontaneous, more honest, less inhibited by all sorts of hang-ups, competition, sexual envy, jealousy – namely the relationship between women as portrayed in that play. In fact the only way men appear to be a threatening force is that they will close the place down. How much of that view is yours?

DUNN: The thing about the man threatening to close the place down was, in a sense, a joke against men – it was my way of having a go. It's been very hard for me to lose my fear of men. That's why I don't write about them very much – I'm frightened of them, and therefore I don't see them clearly. The fear is somehow based on a belief I absorbed some time in my growing up that men were more important than women, and that my validation as a woman came from being attractive and desirable to men. There is a fear that they have a power to strike me where it hurts, to take away my sense of being all right, my sense that I'm acceptable; I can't quite get rid of the feeling that they won't like me and they'll want me to go away and not be there because I haven't fitted in to those qualities that they want in women. I'm frightened, so I distance myself. I think that's getting better: curiously enough, it's getting better all the time. Perhaps that's one of the nice things about getting older.

CLARE: Would it be stretching things too much to say that that fear too has echoes of your 'going away'?

DUNN: Yes. Perhaps my earliest memory was being put on this great boat to America, and crying and crying as my mother and my nanny got further and further away in the distance and of the boat going out and this great big sailor picking me up and saying, 'If you don't stop crying I'll throw you overboard.' As I'm telling it to you now it's a remembered memory, I'm not telling it fresh. But I have remembered that very deeply, with so much fear and so much anger. For a long time I didn't cry, and I think that some of that fear and anger really solidified. It's very hard for me to get rid of it. I can rationally, but there is a bit of me that is still quite careful.

CLARE: And yet you try to get to grips with it through your writing. In *Steaming* you deal with the literal and the metaphorical meaning of nakedness, which I gather attracts you.

DUNN: I love Turkish baths and I love nakedness – I find women's bodies very beautiful and friendly and comforting. Is that 'metaphorically'?

CLARE: That's 'literally'!

DUNN: I think it has something to do with the idea of deep contact between people being ultimate bliss, being whatever is known as Heaven to me. Metaphorically, in *Steaming*, it's a plea for contact – that we're all in this together, let's share our experience, share our reality.

CLARE: But can you? I get the feeling that you're still looking out at the fight on the street, and that the working class for you is the Id. It's where it's all really hanging out. And you've come from a Super-ego, I suppose, the upper class. In a sense, if I may say so, you're quite middle-class, in that you fear and are attracted to the working class, but you live an impeccably middle-class life – career, striving for a relationship, the order, the discipline and the importance of your children.

DUNN: That's very true.

CLARE: And yet they get, indirectly or directly, the brunt of your assaults. It's not the upper class, it's the middle class that I sense that you feel most at odds with.

DUNN: I think that's another conflict. I feel a great respect for the middle class, yet there's a part of me that says that all this being sensible isn't enough. We've got to take risks, we've got to be wild, we've got to throw over the applecart and leap over the cliff.

CLARE: But you don't.

DUNN: No, I don't.

CLARE: Is this a subject that the people who know you discuss?

DUNN: Oh yes. I have one friend who says, 'It's all very well to write about the sort of lives you write about, but it's awful living them.' I feel very undefensive about being a voyeuristic writer. I think most writers are very voyeuristic, and it is a source of guilt in me, but it isn't something I want to hide. Does that answer the question at all?

CLARE: Yes. I can give you some sort of practical examples. I gather you were in, and may still be in, a sort of women's sensitivity group. Did you find it difficult in that setting to be open, to do some of the things you want to be able to do, that you admire being done?

DUNN: No. The only thing that I did find difficult was to express any disapproval, and I'm still frightened of that: I'm frightened of women's anger as well as men's anger, and I did find that difficult.

CLARE: You mentioned at times you like surface exchanges, the easy come-and-go between women. I was very struck by that.

DUNN: I notice odd things. I derive enormous pleasure from watching my next door neighbour, an old lady, hanging out her washing. The garden is very close to mine, and I open the window if I'm upstairs. I work at the back of the house and wave to her and we talk. I derive enormous sustenance from something as superficial and as everyday as that. People telling each other things that are difficult to tell, that are hidden and painful to them – which was something that was attempted in the women's group – is very important to me. Being an acceptable person, experiencing the enormous warmth from other people after having told about these things that I was ashamed of or disliked about myself – that kind of contact is very important to me. Most people know what marriage is. They know that marriage is a commitment to another person, and I didn't know that – I thought it was where you hid behind some sort of barrier and occasionally poked your head over the top to shout at the other person. My idea of survival was doing my very best to entertain the person I was with in order to keep them at a distance and make sure they liked me. It was a tremendous breakthrough for me to discover that there was something called 'my own experience' and my own thoughts and feelings, and that all I had to do was to share that, and that was all that was expected of me and was the most that I could give.

CLARE: When did this occur?

DUNN: Only in the last year, I think. Before that I was playing a much more hidden game, and I thought the way to survive was through my wits and manipulating the world as best I could – leaping from position to position.

CLARE: Why did you change? What changed you?

DUNN: Because I managed to actually clutch the experience of speaking and acting from myself. I don't always manage to hold on to that. I'm often frightened out of it.

CLARE: What are the factors that have contributed to this development of confidence? Your relationship?

DUNN: I think partly my relationship, partly my women's group, partly my children getting a little bit older and a bit easier, in a sense.

CLARE: You mentioned earlier a sensation of extraordinary peace you had with a friend. Have you ever had that feeling in a relationship with a man?

DUNN: Not so overwhelmingly. I have had it, I have touched on it, but not so overwhelmingly. Not quite so safe.

CLARE: Were you ever drawn to the notion of a relationship with a woman, or with women alone?

DUNN: No, I haven't really explored homosexual relationships.

CLARE: You've seen people who have a homosexual relationship?

DUNN: Oddly enough, the people I've been close to have been heterosexual women and men.

CLARE: Perhaps it's not so odd. The peace you describe, it seems to me, is the peace of a child surrounded by loving adults. I wonder whether one source of great comfort to you is the physical comfort of a relationship, as distinct from the sexuality of a relationship.

DUNN: I don't know. It's odd that you should say that, because it suddenly occurs to me that another time I can get in touch with that peace is if I have a child who isn't very well – not really ill, because that is obviously different – and is in bed and I can sit on the bed reading to them, being with them. The adult-child thing has given me at times tremendous sense of peace. Caring for, or being cared for, rather than a sexual relationship: it hadn't occurred to me, it isn't something that I'd thought about, but I do on the whole approach sexual relationships as something dangerous and to be wary of, something where you've got to keep your wits about you.

CLARE: Such wariness can lead to great difficulties in the sexual area. It takes a long time before someone will let their guard go. Was that true of you?

DUNN: Yes, though not fantastically so, because I think I've always been very committed to sexual life. I don't feel I'm one of those people who is particularly frightened of sex. But perhaps that's because I haven't allowed it to take me over.

CLARE: You've put it into a compartment?

DUNN: No, I don't think I've done that – I don't want to give the wrong impression. I've always been very interested in sex. I think it's funny as well as moving; it has been tremendously important to me, and I don't want to underestimate that. It has given me a tremendous amount of warmth and closeness and fun. But I do sense what you're talking about – it's as if I can't quite allow myself the full impact of its importance.

CLARE: Do you dream?

DUNN: Yes, I do. There's one of my dreams in *Steaming*, but you probably didn't hear it because people laugh! It's a serious dream that Nancy has about being given a little baby to look after, and she puts it in the spin dryer. When I remember and have time to think about the dream in the morning I really love it. I love that sense of richness that dreams give me.

CLARE: Do you have a recurrent dream?

DUNN: No, I don't.

CLARE: Your dreams are mainly pleasant?

DUNN: I do have anxiety dreams sometimes, but not a tremendous amount. I have a lot of dreams I wake up feeling really lovely from.

CLARE: Looking back, have there been moments when you thought your control would crack, that you would break down?

DUNN: Never to the extent that I've had to be hospitalised. I've certainly had a very overwhelming sense that I just cannot manage — that everything's too much. And I have that quite a lot of the time.

CLARE: What sustains you through it?

DUNN: Tremendous interest. I'm very interested in people, and I have developed friendships which give me enormous nourishment. I have also developed quite a new ability for me, to actually feel love for people — love, and delight that those people exist.

CLARE: When you went away on that big ship, did you think it was for something you'd done?

DUNN: No, I don't think I did.

CLARE: Did you have any idea why you went?

DUNN: I don't think so.

CLARE: Listening to you describe much of your life one gets a sense of your bafflement about how people lived, and what they did and what they were meant to do, what the rules were, what marriage was, what the people in Battersea were like. Whereas now I sense that you're beginning to put it all together. It sounds rather patronising.

DUNN: No, it didn't sound patronising. I think that's true. Yes, I am beginning to see more clearly, to experience other people much more deeply, and I think that's taking away quite a lot of my fear — and therefore I feel less baffled.

CLARE: It sounds as if the future will be better than the past.

DUNN: I hope so.

PROFESSOR HUGH DUDLEY

Later on, when in the course of my life, I have had occasion to meet with, in convents for instance, literally saintly examples of practical charity, they have generally had the brisk, decided, undisturbed and slightly brutal air of a busy surgeon, the face in which one can detect no commiseration, no tenderness at the sight of suffering humanity, and no fear of hurting it, the face devoid of gentleness or sympathy, the sublime face of true goodness.

MARCEL PROUST, *Swann's Way*

I wanted to interview a surgeon for reasons very similar to those that turned me towards a judge: each still wields immense personal power in these days of the committee man. When it came to choosing, there was really only one candidate. Hugh Dudley, Professor of Academic Surgery at St Mary's Hospital Medical School in London, was known to me through his occasional contributions to the fortnightly *World Medicine* in the days when it was edited by Dr Michael O'Donnell — pieces which were always stylish, witty, tinged with a refreshing trace of self-mockery, and invariably astute. If any surgeon could be persuaded to emerge from behind the mask and gown then surely he would be the one.

His writings revealed him as a man with a low threshold for fools and petty bureaucracy. Once he described his fellow doctors as 'middle-of-the-roaders' when it came to 'our ability to break loose from the shackles of everyday existence, the main features of which are flexible compromise and accommodation'. On another occasion he declared: 'Doctors are essentially disorganised people; they have spasms of obsessionalism when they are looking after patients.' He is fond of quoting Derek Dunlop's remark that what makes for durability as a clinician in medicine is 'a modicum of intelligence, a modicum of good looks and a modicum of money'. (Dunlop used to add that the best formula was to possess the first two and marry the third.) He has always been particularly critical of committee men, which must make for an interesting life at St Mary's given the academic committees which, of necessity, the professor of surgery must attend. The 'good committee man', in his view, is someone who is well equipped with appropriate social graces, and can turn a polished phrase or deliver an inoffensive quip, who somewhere in the past participated in another committee with success ('though usually no one can remember what the outcome was, if any'), and for whom 'amiability, acquiescence and inactivity' are the watchwords. He has been sharply critical of the more reactionary aspects of medical school education, and mildly despairing about the growing penchant for what he has termed 'the pseudo-surveillance of administrative prudes' within the National Health Service. In short, he is a man who does not mince his words and is not afraid to express an opinion, however unpopular.

He was born in 1925 in my own native city of Dublin, of Protestant Irish parents. Both his parents were schoolteachers; he was the youngest of a family of three, having two elder sisters. They moved to England and he was brought up in the West Riding of Yorkshire, where he attended Heath Grammar School in Halifax. Between 1942 and 1947 he read medicine at Edinburgh University, and spent a year with the British Army in Germany before briefly going into general practice in Banffshire; he then decided to specialise in surgery, and spent most of his early postgraduate years back in his Edinburgh medical school. He spent just over four years as Senior Lecturer in Surgery at Aberdeen University before being appointed the foundation professor of surgery at Monash University in Melbourne, Australia, in 1963. Ten years later he returned to London to take up his present position at St Mary's.

He is a married man, his wife having been a nurse. He has three children – a son who is a geologist and another who is a metallurgist, both living in Australia, and a daughter who runs a guest house in Orkney.

In a sense, Professor Dudley was the only one of my nine subjects in the first series who had anything to lose by participation. After all, there is no lasting embarrassment in a writer's revealing a little neurosis, no occupational danger in a comedian's describing profound periodic melancholia, no personal chagrin in an actress's confessing to stage nerves. Even a judge, particularly when he is retired, can happily claim to have had a previous incarnation as a guard for Rameses II. But there would be little kudos for a surgeon who admitted to feeling gloomy just before he enters the operating theatre or fearfully anxious as he reaches for the scalpel! Add the fact that the professor, despite his highly individual profile, is a team man, a member of an academic department, who conducts ward rounds, teaches students, and sits on committees, and a tendency on his part towards wariness is understandable. Of the other eight subjects, only Peter Marsh occupies an equivalent corporate position – and in his case, given his professional activity, the exposure, such as it is, would more than compensate for any of its less rewarding aspects.

In truth, the image of the surgeon described by Proust is, with some modifications, much as most of us would wish him to be. Of course in these holistic days we would want the fully integrated surgeon to be contemplative yet decisive, sensitive yet impassive, committed yet remote, compassionate yet phlegmatic. But if we had to choose, and he was to operate on our gall-bladders or on those of close friends or relatives, the odds are that we would settle for him to be skilful and efficient; if he were all the other things as well, that would be a bonus.

I was curious to know the extent to which Hugh Dudley was in fact 'brisk, decided, undisturbed and slightly brutal', or whether he was playing the part of the Proustian surgeon. In one way he was cool, unruffled, cautious and sceptical; but the manner in which he spoke vibrated with passion, irascibility, and a great deal of impulsive behaviour. I was curious, too, to learn something of the fascination of surgery from the inside and to discover whether it possesses a particular sensual quality, given the delicate emphasis in even the most general surgery on the subtlety of the tactile sense. And there was the issue, hanging over from Glenda Jackson's interview, of the conflict between one's professional dedication and the demands and needs of personal relationships and family tasks.

The reasons for his choice of a medical career remain shrouded in uncertainty. Perhaps the surgeon would expect the psychiatrist to speculate on the basis of insubstantial and insufficient knowledge – my suggestion that his mother's death from pneumonia when he was twelve might be a relevant factor was dealt with wryly but firmly. No matter: the question remains an interesting one, even if the answer remains elusive. And I sympathise with his ambivalence about recommending a medical career to his children.

One is struck by the influence of his apprenticeship and the suggestion that he modelled his own behaviour on the character of his shy, reserved, somewhat fearsome and taciturn Scottish surgical chief. These days there is much talk about what motivates doctors, how they can be influenced in their career choices, what kind of incentives can be laid before them. Yet there are still those, like Professor Dudley back in the early 1950s, who are influenced in the main by an individual who inspires admiration for his dedication, his humanity and his skills – which is reassuring to those, like the professor and myself, who occasionally find ourselves wondering if we do exercise any educational impact.

Finally, there is the story of the dog Dudley shot. When first told on the radio, the tale certainly caught the imagination of listeners. In this animal-loving kingdom, it must be as near as one is likely to get to having the good professor struck off the General Medical Council's register, and Professor Dudley tells us that it cost him an academic position in this country for some years. It is unlikely that a man impulsive and irascible enough to shoot a dog who was worrying his ducks would be considered unsafe with a clamp if a junior nurse started to faint over one of his patients. I knew a surgeon once, a gentle giant of a man outside the operating theatre, shy, shuffling and inarticulate, who became a raging, ill-tempered, foul-mouthed thrower of instruments the moment the patient was wheeled in, the lights were adjusted and the instruments were uncovered. His behaviour never did him any harm: but what if he had shot a dog?

More than any other, that story gives the lie to that outward appearance of calm, surgical stolidity. Professor Dudley, thankfully, is a surgeon whose emotions are all there, even though he makes a show of hiding them – in deference, no doubt, to the public's need to have its stereotypes honoured. In participating in the series, however, he indicated that his outward control did not imply a refusal to countenance self-exploration; given the results, I for one am very grateful.

ANTHONY CLARE: Professor Dudley, how do you feel about talking about yourself?

PROFESSOR HUGH DUDLEY: To say diffident would be to underestimate my feelings. I feel decidedly uneasy for two reasons: first of all, because I don't think I've very much to say; and secondly, because I'm a little bit apprehensive that you will uncover things that I didn't mean to say.

CLARE: Things you didn't mean to say because you meant to say something different, or because they were true?

DUDLEY: Both. I'm always rather inclined to go off at half cock every time I open my mouth and fail to engage the brain properly before releasing the tongue. Sometimes I say things which afterwards I regret, even though they may well be true.

CLARE: What sort of things?

DUDLEY: Often opinions about people or things which, though they sometimes cut through to the truth, can upset people or hurt them and which, if I gave more consideration to what I was saying, I would probably not have put in the same way, or not even said at all.

CLARE: That approximates to one of the stereotypes people have about the surgeon – that he's somebody who speaks his mind.

DUDLEY: I'm not sure I would agree with that. He's certainly 'action-orientated', to use the jargon phrase. He likes to get on with things, and perhaps that makes him a little brash or inclined to express himself in ways which people would prefer to be less direct.

CLARE: Are you intolerant of other people's deficiencies?

DUDLEY: Appallingly, yes – but of course it doesn't mean that those deficiencies are real. It's only the deficiencies as I see them. I'm known to be extremely intolerant and quite short-fused about other people's attitudes in a way that doesn't earn me a great number of friends.

CLARE: Is that professionally or domestically?

DUDLEY: Oh professionally, for the most part. No doubt my children have tales to tell on the domestic front, but I don't think that's all that important.

CLARE: Why not?

DUDLEY: Because on the whole my domestic life, such as it is, has been an extremely happy one: as my wife keeps telling me, I am – to use the standard, and perhaps not very accurate, word – dedicated to my professional life.

CLARE: Said by wives, that can be a double-edged remark!

DUDLEY: That sounds like a psychiatrist speaking. Do you mean that it's said not because it's true, but because the wife is upset at not having enough of her husband's time?

CLARE: It can be said for that, yes.

DUDLEY: I can assure you that isn't the case with my wife. Of course she'd like to see more of me and have a more settled domestic life, but I think she's always respected my single-mindedness in relation to my profession.

CLARE: Is it single-mindedness?

DUDLEY: I think so, though that doesn't mean I don't have a lot of interests in the penumbra that surrounds my profession; but I think it would be fair to say that I've always put my profession, and trying to do as well as I possibly could in it, in my order of priorities.

CLARE: Above your family, say?

DUDLEY: Yes. Of course it's dangerous to erect hierarchies, and you said 'above my family'. More important in perhaps temporal terms – I would agree with that. I would hope that my family did get a reasonably fair deal and I hope that my wife still does, but there's no doubt that getting on with the job has been the thing that has largely governed my life.

CLARE: Is this a feature that pre-dates medical school?

DUDLEY: I can't really remember about that, it's so long ago. I was keen to make the most of my intellectual opportunities as a schoolboy, but I was by no means a dedicated professional or a swot or anything of that kind. In fact I didn't do all that well at school: I managed to keep in the upper third of the class but nothing better than that, mainly perhaps because I was interested in other things.

CLARE: Both your parents were schoolteachers. Did that have any particular influence?

DUDLEY: It had an enormous influence on the way I grew up in terms of the depth and breadth of my knowledge. I was part of a reading household. If somebody raised a question over the dinner table, the immediate answer was to go and look it up, and go and look it up now. I developed habits of reading and of searching for knowledge at a very early and impressionable age, which became part of my life and which make it difficult sometimes for me to understand other people who don't use their time to the best advantage in terms of the acquisition of knowledge.

CLARE: Was it a highly disciplined environment?

DUDLEY: I wouldn't say that: it was a highly productive environment. Nobody said, 'You must look it up'; it was the natural thing to go away and read something if you didn't know enough about it.

CLARE: Your mother died when you were quite young.

DUDLEY: Yes, in my early teens.

CLARE: What age were you exactly?

DUDLEY: I think I was thirteen – then again, I don't think I can remember.

CLARE: Can you remember the event?

DUDLEY: Very well. This was in the pre-antibiotic era. My mother took ill with pneumonia, and I think probably – although I'm not sure about this – got pneumococcal meningitis to which she succumbed, pretty rapidly, over a period of weeks.

CLARE: So you wouldn't have been particularly prepared for it. Was it a traumatic event?

DUDLEY: Looking back on it, I suppose it was, but I don't remember it as traumatic in that I wept or anything like that. But I naturally accepted that my parents would live for ever and that they would go on providing both emotional and intellectual support, so it probably was quite traumatic.

CLARE: You're saying that as a speculation?

DUDLEY: Yes I am, because I don't really remember.

CLARE: Do you see why it was traumatic?

DUDLEY: No. I'm really using my professional knowledge, such as it is in your field, Dr Clare, to think back. I probably did depend on my mother a very considerable amount. I was the youngest of three children and a rather late arrival and I should think the trauma was fairly closely knit up with my mother – though I don't, as I say, remember any great emotional agonies.

CLARE: Does either of your two older sisters remember your response to it?

DUDLEY: We don't ever discuss it.

CLARE: Who took over your mother's role?

DUDLEY: I don't think anybody did. It may well be there could have been somebody, but I think I was fairly able to cope by myself. Perhaps that has had its effect on me subsequently.

CLARE: In what sense?

DUDLEY: I shouldn't have said that. I've let myself in for the sort of thing that I was talking about earlier on by putting forward a speculation, saying that could perhaps explain some of my, let's say, continued emotional immaturity in that I still have a quick temper. As I was saying earlier on, I tend to open my mouth too fast, or not to consider the feelings of others quite as deeply as I should.

CLARE: Something tells me that you're not absolutely convinced. You refer to it as the sort of thing that people like me might lay a lot of emphasis on, but I sense that you can't see that it was all that traumatic an event.

DUDLEY: I reckon that's fair, but I'm never very convinced about anything! Part of my training has been to encourage me to be sceptical and critical about virtually every item of life, including those things that have application to myself.

CLARE: Sometimes this kind of emphasis is given to the same experience when it's undergone by others. For example, the loss of a mother can sometimes be explained as having an enormous impact, when in fact you yourself have grave doubts that it did.

DUDLEY: That's a fairly straightforward psychoanalytic theory – that you don't know about things that have affected yourself simply because you have done the appropriate suppression or repression. If one recognises that there's some truth in psychoanalytic theory one must be prepared to believe what you're told, even though you can't necessarily appreciate it at other than an intellectual level.

CLARE: Putting it more simply than that, do you feel at times that more importance is attributed to these kinds of experiences than they warrant?

DUDLEY: That's a professional question in the sense that you are asking me to say what I believe about a particular branch of medicine. I can't answer it in an intelligent way because I really don't know enough about it to voice an opinion. I think most outgoing surgeons would be rather inclined to discount information of that kind. I would prefer to keep a reasonably open mind and say that if somebody who has thought about the matter a lot and researched it a lot really believes it to be true then I'll accept that it probably is true, even though, as I've said, one has difficulty in taking it on board emotionally.

CLARE: In your adolescence, after the death of your mother, was there any sign that you were anything other than a fairly normally healthily developing person?

DUDLEY: I don't think so; but as I say I was possibly in some ways intellectually immature. I was very keen to get on with things and to continue with my intellectual development. Whether I was good at handling the everyday things of life I'm not quite so sure. I still get into arguments with people and I'm always taking views which are perhaps a little bit away from the centre of things – not, as I think you'd agree, very typical of the ordinary medical student, except perhaps in Dublin!

CLARE: Perhaps not even there! But on this aspect of your

personality: you recall, going back some time, the argumentativeness, the taking of a slightly unpopular position.

DUDLEY: I do recall it. I wouldn't have but for the fact that I'm talking to you, which forces you, in your middle fifties, to look back. Yes, I've always been like that, and I really rather forget that I've always been like that – sometimes because it has got me into so much trouble.

CLARE: Can you remember the first time it got you into trouble?

DUDLEY: I can think of examples, but whether they would be the first time or not I've no idea. When I was a young registrar in surgery in Edinburgh I was sent to Scandinavia as a reward for some work that I'd done, on a trip round various institutions, and I came back and was asked to give a talk at one of the regular Saturday morning meetings at which all the senior surgeons are gathered together. I had the temerity to make some remarks about one aspect of the quality of Scandinavian surgery which I thought were helpful to understand what was going on, but in fact were interpreted as being very rude to our Scandinavian colleagues. Six months later I was taken aside and told about this rather than being told about it at the time – which irritated me rather, even though it may well have been deserved.

CLARE: What did you do?

DUDLEY: I didn't do anything, couldn't do anything. In the hierarchical situation in Edinburgh, I just had to accept what I was told and leave it at that.

CLARE: Did your decision to do medicine take some time, or was it an immediate decision?

DUDLEY: Well, I'm told by my elder sisters that I'd always wanted to be a doctor and that from a very early age I wanted to be a surgeon. I have no conscious memories at all of coming to that decision; it was something that always seemed quite inevitable.

CLARE: There is no medical influence in your family?

DUDLEY: None whatsoever, I'm afraid.

CLARE: One is struck by the fact that one of the things you remembered about your mother's death was its detailed cause.

DUDLEY: Looking through professional eyes I think that's what the cause was. I knew she had pneumonia.

CLARE: There's nothing to tie your mother's death with your career?

DUDLEY: I think not, no. I'm pretty certain that my intention to go into medicine antedated the event.

CLARE: What was it about medicine that attracted you? Was it surgery, even that early?

DUDLEY: I think it may well have been. I wouldn't be surprised, because I suppose I do have some of the personality attributes that tend to make people into surgeons: the idea that one wants to do things rather than to be contemplative, the desire to see the results of what you do quickly – which, as you know, is characteristic of surgery, whether the results be good or bad. These things are perhaps part of my personality, and they therefore tend to ease you towards a particular career choice.

CLARE: Had you a mechanical interest in things?

DUDLEY: Not really, no. I'm not very good with my hands; some of my colleagues would no doubt say that's true in relation to my surgery! I have no other particular skill: I like using a hammer and chisel and that, but the results are appalling.

CLARE: In your experience, is there any significant correlation between a surgical skill and a mechanical skill?

DUDLEY: I think the answer to that is no, but that may well change in the future. It has already changed for dentistry, where to be a good dentist you have to be a good craftsman and particularly perhaps a craftsman who can do things like sculpture. In surgery it has certainly not been true, but up to now surgery has been a very crude, low technology discipline.

CLARE: So the notion of your having finely tuned hands that are the envy of a jeweller, and that the insertion of the suture to close the wound is an act of some artistry is totally misplaced.

DUDLEY: Well, as you know, in medicine you should never use words like 'totally' or 'absolutely' because there are always exceptions – but largely misplaced, yes. Of course there are skills in my profession, but you can derive those skills rather than possess them. Indeed I am probably almost entirely a derivative man. I learnt how to do surgery from my masters and they taught me the adequate technical skills so that I could.

CLARE: When you went to medical school, were there other motives at work in addition to the attraction of the job itself? Was the notion of medicine of any significance – healing the sick, the vocation of medicine?

DUDLEY: I think this is very rarely the case in motivation for medicine. It's always held up as being one of the most important

things, and in the days when I used to interview students for admission
to St Mary's they always put it first because they thought it would
please the people who were interviewing them.

CLARE: Would you ask it as an interviewer?

DUDLEY: I often did, but I certainly wasn't looking for that
reply.

CLARE: What did you do if you got it?

DUDLEY: Tended not to believe it! My own feeling is that most of us
went into medicine for either reasons which are wholly unclear, like
my own, or because we saw something that we wanted to do, as
distinct from any service we wanted to give.

CLARE: But do you think the first two are better reasons than the
third?

DUDLEY: No, not at all.

CLARE: But I sense you mistrust getting the third?

DUDLEY: Only from experience, when you talk to your colleagues.
Perhaps I should ask you the question? You talk to your colleagues –
you don't really find that that was the major motive?

CLARE: What about the motive of money?

DUDLEY: I think it's very important. Money isn't everything, as one
of my favourite novelists says, but it buys nearly everything.

CLARE: And in your case was it an important motive?

DUDLEY: Not at all, except in the very short term. I went to
Edinburgh University because my father was keen that I should do so,
on the grounds that there were lots of prizes to be won. And that
helped considerably because he died when I was halfway through my
undergraduate career, and I was able to supplement the small grants
we got in those days by winning the occasional prize; but after that
money wasn't a motive. I felt, quite falsely of course, that if I went into
academic surgery and climbed the academic ladder the university
would look after me. It was a naive idea, as I'm sure you would agree,
but it was the major driving force – that if I did well and got up to, say,
professorial status I would always have enough money. I didn't really
think about money consciously at all.

CLARE: Right through your five years at Edinburgh you intended to
be a surgeon?

DUDLEY: Very early on I was confirmed in my view, which I think I'd
held before from my experiences learning anatomy, which I
thoroughly enjoyed – yes, I wanted to be a neuro-surgeon. Everybody

does, of course. Then you come down to earth and decide you'll do something slightly simpler.

CLARE: But you didn't do surgery straightaway. You had a year in the army and then you had some time in general practice.

DUDLEY: It was a very short time in general practice and it really was just filling an interval. I never had any intention of being a general practitioner, and if my principal is listening he will say that was a very good thing. I didn't have the patience or the long-term view of illness or the ability to relate with people who didn't want to agree with what I offered them that are necessary in a general practitioner.

CLARE: Did you then go back to Edinburgh and continue with your postgraduate training?

DUDLEY: Yes, I trained for nearly the next seven years in Edinburgh in the ordinary standard way that surgeons did train in those days. You were apprenticed to one person, which is quite unusual now. I was apprenticed to James Learmonth, who finally started me on my surgical career by making me his houseman, which was a very important turning-point in my career because it brought me into contact with this difficult man – who was a very hard taskmaster, who virtually never gave us any praise, who expected us to be there all the time, but I have every gratitude to him for having instilled into me some of his attitudes to surgery.

CLARE: Was he a man who bore fools badly?

DUDLEY: Yes.

CLARE: Was he taciturn, or a man of many words?

DUDLEY: Most of the time moderately taciturn; but he expressed himself well and had a great feeling for the English language – which was another thing I liked because that had also, to a certain extent, been instilled into me by my parents.

CLARE: Was he a man with many friends?

DUDLEY: I think he probably had more enemies than friends. The friends he had were very close and he had an extremely warm relationship with them, although that wasn't often expressed. I and many others who worked for him – I almost said with him, but better to say for him – found after he'd retired that he was indeed a very warm person, and dropped all this professional guard I've tried to describe to you.

CLARE: Was he a married man?

DUDLEY: Yes, a very happily married man indeed.

CLARE: Do you remember the moment he made you one of his men?
DUDLEY: It was probably when he offered me the housemanship, which was fairly early on in my clinical career. You did two or three years in clinical work as an undergraduate; and from then on he also gave me a great privilege, which I think very few other people had, of allowing me as a student to come to the Saturday morning meetings I've already mentioned. These were really for postgraduates and were closed meetings, not open ones. I was allowed to trot along to these, and began to soak up attitudes towards surgery which have stood me in good stead ever since.
CLARE: How did he indicate that you were his choice? At a meeting?
DUDLEY: He stopped one night in the middle of a ward corridor where I'd been working as a locum houseman. He'd come in, quite unusually for him, to see a sick patient – unusually because at his eminence he didn't need to do that very often. He stopped in the middle of the corridor, turned round and said, 'You'd better be my houseman' – and that was the signal that he was going to take me on.
CLARE: What is the fascination about surgery? You strip it of any kind of false glamour about the artistry of the hands and the medical vocation of saving lives and so on. You describe it as a profession, but you also make it plain that, certainly in the eyes of this man whom you clearly were influenced by, it is an almost all-consuming profession. It makes great demands in terms of time and other activities, so the reward, putting it at its most selfish, must be great. If it's not some kind of altruistic reward, and you've made it plain that it isn't, what is it? What is the sensual fascination of surgery?
DUDLEY: You've almost answered the question by what you've just said. I think it does have a sensual fascination. It is doing something which has a defined output which you can see, which makes people grateful to you in a very direct way; and as a consequence it's a fulfilling thing to do. Some surgeons, I wouldn't deny this possibility, would say it's like going to bed with a beautiful woman. You have a real climax over what you do. In addition, of course, it gives you great power, because you are the life and death man for an individual person. Surgery is always associated with risk and people recognise that risk and therefore you can see that they are subservient to you; you have the power of life and death over them in a very real way, and if you restore life then you earn their gratitude.
CLARE: Let's take the sensuality first. What sort of surgeon are you?

DUDLEY: I'm what is called a general surgeon; that means I work particularly in the abdomen – the stomach to a layman.

CLARE: Do the contents of an abdomen offer one much opportunity for sensual satisfaction?

DUDLEY: I think you're trying to twist the meaning of the word 'sensual'. You could never say that there is an intrinsic conventional beauty in the contents of the abdomen – rather the reverse in fact – but to deal with something that's wrong there, to be able to remove, say, a tumour or to change function in relation, say, to an ulcer, and to see that work and to be able to guide nature on its way to healing things smoothly and uneventfully after the procedure is, I think, the sensual satisfaction.

CLARE: It would be misleading to believe that there's any kind of physical sensation in handling the innards of the average abdomen?

DUDLEY: I think the answer to that is no, that would not be the important thing – although to be able to do this with sufficient purpose to achieve what you want to do and at the same time to possess a sufficient gentleness not to damage things is very satisfying. I would have thought that the neurosurgeon in particular gains immense satisfaction from his delightfully delicate but highly effective touch on the brain.

CLARE: You mentioned the power of the surgeon.

DUDLEY: Yes, in relation to other people: this feeling that you have control over them, I'm sure that is part of one's gratification, if one's honest about it. As one grows older, though, I think one learns to place this in much greater perspective: it's the dangerous surgeon who goes on thinking that the most important thing in the world is for him to exert his power and therefore get the patient to do exactly as he wants, which is not always in the patient's best interest.

CLARE: What is the temptation like to play to the gallery in the surgical operating room, because there often is a large team around you?

DUDLEY: When I was young there was a gallery out of which people occasionally fell! There is, of course, a great temptation, and wholly to suppress that temptation may well be wrong. The room in which we operate is called a theatre, and there is a certain theatricality about surgery. It's decisive, it's quick, it's dramatic in its effects – not as I've said before always to the benefit of the patient – and to have an element of showmanship in that may well enhance performance.

Some of the greatest surgeons were unashamed showmen, but none the worse for it.

CLARE: What about James Learmonth?

DUDLEY: No, he wasn't. He was a more workmanlike man. He enjoyed a set piece and did it very well, and was probably quite gratified if he had a big audience. I think he positively suppressed certain aspects of his showmanship, but by doing so he enhanced others. He was an autocrat, he did like to be the Chief and that in itself meant that he was a personality that stood out. He had his own particular dressing-gown outside the theatre, and insisted that people didn't sit down while he was in the room eating his lunch and things of that kind – so in a way he was a negative showman, or an academic showman.

CLARE: You were attracted by some of the elements of that discipline. Were there similarities between him and your father?

DUDLEY: None whatever. My father was a very pleasant man, a schoolteacher without ambition. He liked to keep his class in order but his method of doing it was largely, as far as I can recall, by ridiculing them in a pleasant way and by threatening them with impossible punishments, using a three-foot ruler if they misbehaved. But he certainly wasn't an autocrat.

CLARE: How did Learmonth impose his discipline?

DUDLEY: He was like the husky dog at the head of a team. He had this air of authority and he was able to impose it. In those days – and they're not all that long ago, thirty, thirty-five years ago – there was still great respect for a man of this kind, and when he said 'Jump', we all jumped.

CLARE: What about these days?

DUDLEY: I think we live in a healthier time now. Although I hated the discipline, I respected it, but I don't think we should ever want to reproduce this pattern of training. I like respect and I get very upset when I don't get the respect to which I believe I'm entitled, but I don't want the attitude any more whereby this almost gladiatorial discipline was imposed upon us.

CLARE: But with it went a single-mindedness. Is the same single-mindedness visible today?

DUDLEY: When we get old we all say that things aren't as they used to be, and I think that probably things aren't the same. There isn't necessarily as much single-mindedness as there was. Whether that's good or bad I don't know. I'm cautious about expressing an opinion because I think we can all be wrong so easily when we engage in value discussions of this kind. But I would say that there's probably less tendency to make surgery your central activity and it may be that that is bad for surgery. I can't put it stronger than that.

CLARE: It isn't one of the things that occasionally put you into a seething rage.

DUDLEY: Of course it is! It's the major thing that puts me into a seething rage! I want people to be like me and to think that surgery is the most important thing in the world. I've tried to raise the standard of my own surgery – and I don't just mean the technical side of it – my care of patients, because I think that's an important thing to do. Everybody should try to perfect themselves as much as they possibly can in the tasks they undertake in life, and when I see other people either failing to pay attention to what I've learnt and am trying to teach them, or not putting their discipline first I get very cross. It's one of my major shortcomings in man management that I show my anger all the time.

CLARE: I sense that you're ambivalent about that side of you.

DUDLEY: I'm ambivalent about pretty well every side of myself and that's almost inevitable, isn't it? If you've got a scientific training, and perhaps particularly if you've got a scientific training in our field, you distrust the veracity of any conclusions you draw, particularly about human beings.

CLARE: Have you ever exploded in such a way as to put in jeopardy your career as an academic surgeon?

DUDLEY: Not actually in relation – well it may well have happened in relation – to surgery, but I've done things which, through acting too quickly, have interfered with my professional life.

CLARE: Such as?

DUDLEY: There's the famous episode that follows me round the world. A few years ago I was introduced to an American surgeon whom I'd never met before but with whom I was going to collaborate on a book, or a series of books, and he said, 'Are you the man who shot the dog?' I'd shot a dog, my neighbours' dog, in Aberdeen many many years ago because it worried my ducks and killed some of them, in spite of the fact that we'd asked them to control it. They hadn't and, impetuously and furiously, I shot it. That didn't do my career any good.

CLARE: Why not?

DUDLEY: Well, to shoot a dog . . . 'Is he to be trusted? Is he the sort of

man we'd like to see on our professorial board, our senate of the
university?'

CLARE: Was that an option up at the time?

DUDLEY: It might have been: I can't judge. I was applying for Chairs
at that time in the United Kingdom and I had some inkling that this did
have an adverse effect, and led to my transportation to the colonies –
which I thoroughly enjoyed, and from which I gained an immense
amount.

CLARE: You were another criminal we sent off to Australia?

DUDLEY: That's right.

CLARE: Were you married at the time?

DUDLEY: Yes, I'd been married for many years.

CLARE: You married a nurse who knew something about medicine.
How did your wife cope with this display of pique?

DUDLEY: I don't really know how she's coped with all the displays of
pique that have taken place over the years. But she's enormously loyal
and long-suffering and thinks that, on the whole, I'm right.

CLARE: On the whole?

DUDLEY: Yes.

CLARE: What happens to someone who thinks – on those rare
occasions that this occurs – that you are wrong? How do they set
about changing your mind?

DUDLEY: On the whole people just disregard me or cut me out of
their circle. I try to keep a modicum of independence.

CLARE: What about the competitiveness of surgery? Are surgeons
competitive with each other?

DUDLEY: Immensely. It goes back to a certain extent, to the need to
be competitive in terms of getting patients. Whether that's inside or
outside the Health Service is irrelevant, because most surgeons like to
exercise their skills. They want to do the things they think they're good
at, and in fact to do them, because of the showmanship side, is to
display how good you are. Therefore they tend to be highly
competitive in the search for patients, and they are also, I think,
innately competitive people. This outgoing personality that likes to
take action is associated with a competitive edge.

CLARE: You once wrote of what you call the 'subtle denigration' of
the work of others which characterises the changing room conversation of surgeons and anaesthetists. Is that related to this kind of
competitiveness?

DUDLEY: I think so. I don't think it's unique to surgeons. Medicine is a gossip-ridden profession. The surgeons and anaesthetists have more opportunities because they have a locker room in which they sit around between cases and talk about each other – it's a popular sport.

CLARE: My own recollections, as a medical student, are that there was something particularly acrimonious, cutting, to use a terrible pun, about surgical conversation.

DUDLEY: I agree. It probably goes back to the feeling that you've got to be on top of the other man if you're going to practise your profession.

CLARE: Again, permitting the wildness of this metaphor, the surgeon poised over the absolutely impotent and passive body is a figure of some dramatic consequence. The patient is utterly helpless. To what extent is that particular excitement part of the surgeon's job satisfaction? I'm told that many surgeons do not think of what they have in front of them as the bits and pieces of a human body: it's much more like a machine, and they're the mechanics putting it together again and taking it apart. Is that a very crude, reductive view of surgery?

DUDLEY: No, I think that's very fair. It's a useful thing to be able to achieve in a surgeon that you shouldn't have your emotions *vis-à-vis* your effect on a human being in the forefront of your mind at the time of operation – which is, as I've tried to emphasise, a technology, something which one should do to the best of one's technical ability. I personally forget very quickly as the knife goes in that I'm dealing with Mr A or Mrs B and think rather that I'm dealing with a duodenal ulcer or a cancer of the colon.

CLARE: There are pressures at the moment from outside medicine to make the contemporary doctor more holistic, more attuned to the personal, psychological as well as social aspects of the patient – and yet here you're saying that at the moment of operation that might be quite the most inappropriate advice and that, if anything, you should be thinking more and more in terms of organs and the organism.

DUDLEY: I don't think these two views should be thought of as contradictions. There are times in all our lives when we have to concentrate on a technical skill. For you it may be how exactly to conduct an interview, or how to put together the information you obtain most effectively to get a diagnosis. For me it's how to cut and sew. I don't think that means that for the other seven-eighths of our lives or whatever fraction it may be we can't be the holistic person you refer to. I agree that if your technology dominates your thinking throughout the whole of your professional day then this will happen; you will not become a very effective person to deal with other persons. But why should we have to be the same all the time? I can't see why. After I went to Australia, and was setting up a new medical course, I thought about this quite a lot, and felt that it's too simple a view to suggest that a man's discipline necessarily governs his behaviour. As doctors we've got to be conscious of our need to do different things and I've tried very hard – probably not succeeded, but I've tried very hard – to preserve a reasonable attitude towards people. Reasonable in the sense of respecting them as other people, in spite of my technical discipline as a surgeon.

CLARE: Do you feel it is reasonable to expect a man whose major occupational demand is to free his mind of all extraneous matter and concentrate on the skin and the viscera, the blood and the vessels in front of him, to have a reasonably sophisticated management of feelings and an empathy with other people's emotions and their sensitivities?

DUDLEY: Yes, I think it is. It hasn't been emphasised as much as it should have been in our education, but I agree with the drive towards trying to be reasonably holistic in our approach. I don't like the word very much, but I like the sentiment behind it; why shouldn't we bring the same application and the same intellectual effort towards that aspect of our profession as we do towards our technical side? Some people are natural doctors – the good old-fashioned general practitioner, people like that – but you've got to work at both sides of your life if you want to be effective.

CLARE: But I've heard surgeons themselves polarise them. They say, 'Look, if you want your gall bladder out wouldn't you prefer to go to somebody who does thirty a week and doesn't give too much time to thinking about the post-operative complications, than go to a man who does three a week, but is right up-to-date on the scientific and evaluative literature?'

DUDLEY: I would want to go to both. I'd want to have the first man you described to remove the gall bladder, and the second man to look after me to make sure that if the thirty a week man has one patient in the thirty who goes wrong, it wasn't to be me! But I don't see why the two things can't to a considerable degree be combined. I resent this polarisation even though I recognise that the surgical personality is perhaps part of the cause of it. The surgeons are seen, to use your word, to be a stereotype, and we're not allowed to escape from the bounds of that stereotype. But I can't see why a reasonable or even really high technical skill can't be combined with an attitude towards people that you don't necessarily have built into you, but which you can acquire if you're prepared to work at it.

CLARE: Does this characterise a lot of what you're trying to do in your present mixture of academic work and surgery?

DUDLEY: Yes. My job is to try and produce the next generation of surgeons and I hope at least some of the next generation of academic surgeons. What I want to do is not so much to teach them the technical skills which we've talked about as to teach them attitudes – and amongst those attitudes is the idea that it is reasonable to expect them to have a modicum of technical skill *and* good attitudes towards people. I don't believe in the entirely mechanistic approach to surgery although I recognise that it's important. You're better alive in the hands of a technical expert than dead in the hands of somebody who is not so well versed in the technicalities. But there is a place for both and I don't want to be polarised in the way that you describe.

CLARE: What about the price that can be paid for single-mindedness? Following in the tradition in which you were trained, you must have spent many of your waking hours pursuing your surgical craft. Did you see much of your children when they were growing up?

DUDLEY: I thought I did – enough by my way of thinking, and probably by theirs too! Whether I gave them enough support is a different question, and one which I can't answer. Only they could say. They seem to have made a reasonable success of their lives. Whether, looking back, they felt deprived by the fact that they didn't have enough of my attention, as distinct from enough of my time, I don't know. If I was doing it again I would try harder to make a balance. I was far too driven by the ideas I had of getting on and making the best job I could of my mixed task as an academic and a surgeon, and perhaps therefore I didn't give enough of my time and thought processes to my children.

CLARE: Where did this drive come from?

DUDLEY: Partly Scottish medical education, which in those days was a subdivision of Scottish education, which has 'an urgency of purpose' built in; and partly the example set by James Learmouth, who epitomised this particular attitude; and partly, I suppose, something in my genes or whatever you like which has given me this driving urge throughout my whole life.

CLARE: Did your wife have some reservations about the impact of James Learmouth?

DUDLEY: A great deal. I think she sees very much more clearly than I how this affected the direction of my life, and maybe has some regrets for the narrowness that it imposed on myself and, by implication, on her also.

CLARE: Narrowness?

DUDLEY: Well, you can't do all the other things that people do if you're going to be single-minded about your profession.

CLARE: Did any of your three children at any time express an interest in a medical career?

DUDLEY: My daughter, who's the youngest, thought of it a little bit. I won't say I actively discouraged her, but I certainly didn't encourage her because, and I think my wife would do the same, I think if you're going to do it, you should do it properly and that means you should do it the way I've done it – and I wouldn't want necessarily to impose that on any of my children. I think they sensed this, and none of them in the end wished to go into medicine.

CLARE: But must it be done the way you did it?

DUDLEY: Probably not. I think if you have got more skills and you're fleeter of intellectual foot than I am you could probably . . .

CLARE: But that wasn't why you did it the way you did?

DUDLEY: No, you didn't let me finish. You could probably do all that I've done to the same standard and still have time to do other things as well. If you're not in the top flight you have to work very hard in order to do it well.

CLARE: But you didn't drive yourself like this because you had to, but because it satisfied you.

DUDLEY: That's true, and why does it satisfy you? How do you gain satisfaction in anything you do? It's not an easy thing to analyse, is it? I don't suggest that it has universal truth for everybody, and there are many more ways of doing surgery. For example, you might choose to do surgery as a mechanic, and make a great success of one or two operations which brought everybody flocking to you.

CLARE: But you didn't say that to your daughter when she was vaguely interested. It was the purity of the dedication that, in a sense, made you frighten her a little away.

DUDLEY: Yes, I think that would be so, because you recognise that you do lose things by being narrow, and that you may miss out on lots of exciting things in life. I wouldn't want my daughter to feel that she had to do that.

CLARE: Did your children resent what they lost out on?

DUDLEY: It's a question you'd have to ask them. They show no signs of doing so, but maybe that is because they want to be kind to the old man and not make him feel upset about the fact that they did miss out on things. I don't know. They're nice people and it may well be true that they want to protect me. But I hope and believe that they didn't really resent it; they did their own thing.

CLARE: What would your wife say? Have you talked about the price paid in that sense?

DUDLEY: A little. Not very much because there's a certain fatalism about it – it's all happened now, and what's the point in looking back over something you can't repeat? If we were doing it again, she would want it a little bit different.

CLARE: Presumably such a woman has to very much make her own life?

DUDLEY: She made her life perhaps by filling the gaps that I left in managing the family. Probably the fact that the family are so good, at least in my view they're good, is due to her.

CLARE: When you are driving yourself, do you ever sometimes think that you might break down or crack up?

DUDLEY: I've far too much pride and self-confidence to think that. In the past I could see it happening – more a breakdown in terms of being able to deliver the goods that I'm supposed to deliver than a mental breakdown of the kind you deal with. You can try to keep too many balls in the air at once, and that's always been one of my failings. I think I can take on pretty well anything and add it on to what I'm doing already. It's tantamount to being insane to believe that you can, and I nearly always fail. So I make my life very complicated and sometimes non-productive by the amount I take on and that gets me into a fizz, but not a breakdown.

CLARE: So you've never felt that your emotions were out of control?

DUDLEY: I've often had my tantrums over things which should have been trivial, as many of us do when we get tired or under a lot of stress, but no more than that.

CLARE: Do these irritabilities or occasional explosions, coupled with your tendency to suffer fools poorly, mean that you are a fairly isolated person?

DUDLEY: Yes, I suppose that's true. I have a very delightful staff who put up with a lot and who work hard to make me feel not isolated. I think some of them even like me. But yes, I do lead a fairly isolated existence in that I'm not part of the hail-fellow-well-met, back-slapping cameraderie that characterises many social groupings.

CLARE: Are you difficult to like?

DUDLEY: I should think that's probably true, yes – irascible, critical, going off at a tangent sometimes in a way that makes me pretty complicated to understand.

CLARE: Has this always been the case?

DUDLEY: I suppose it has.

CLARE: Would many people have talked about some of the things that I've talked about with you?

DUDLEY: No. Hardly any, I would think.

CLARE: Any professional colleagues?

DUDLEY: Just occasionally, in a very fragmentary way.

CLARE: What is that about a man such as yourself who knows he's irascible, a bit prickly, a bit unapproachable, a bit fearsome even, and yet can still say, 'I think some of my staff even like me'? You may be having me on – you may know perfectly well how many of your staff like you. They may all adore you, for all I know.

DUDLEY: Oh I know two . . .

CLARE: Are you curious?

DUDLEY: No, not particularly.

CLARE: You don't care what they think?

DUDLEY: I don't make it important in my life. I try to do what I think I ought to do and I sometimes fail miserably by losing my temper or becoming illogical, but I try very hard, and as long as you're trying hard I don't think it really should matter what other people think.

CLARE: Yet some people derive a good deal of what drives them on from what other people think.

DUDLEY: Yes, I suppose that's true. It's certainly true of me in a negative way! If I find that somebody is thinking ill of me, maybe for very good reasons, that upsets me a great deal and it provides a brake on my driving on. When I think I've been doing things with the best intentions and trying to get something organised which is new, different and – I believe – highly exciting, and then find that it's all wrong in the eyes of somebody else and that they think my motives are thoroughly suspect and that I'm just looking for more power, then I find that very upsetting indeed.

CLARE: What about the fact that you may, through your irascibility, hurt other people who are more sensitive than you are?

DUDLEY: That bothers me but, as you I'm sure know, it's always a retrospective phenomenon. If you really had control of the situation you would never become irascible, and that's why I admire people who have the urbanity that I lack. I get very upset about it in retrospect when I feel I have hurt somebody but by that time it's all over – and unfortunately it's not an area in which you can learn from your mistakes.

CLARE: Of course there are positive advantages to this kind of personality.

DUDLEY: I think there are. I still think that if you want to create change except on the slowest of time scales you need people like me to perturb the system, to use a physiological phrase. I have been a system perturber – which sometimes is ineffective, but sometimes is catalytic to change. It seems to be something that I either acquired very early in life or had fitted into me, and it's always been my pattern of behaviour.

CLARE: Does a personality like yours allow you to suffer regret? Do you look back and reflect sometimes on things that might have been?

DUDLEY: Yes, I do look back, and of course I've looked back a lot more as I've grown older and seen things that I profoundly regret, that I've done very badly and should have done so much better; and then I've had to say, 'Well, I did them and it's all gone now, I must try and do better' – although it's extremely difficult to succeed, particularly when you have a personality of my kind.

CLARE: One last question. How much relief does surgery allow you through cutting, opening, taking out organs? There are those who have said it has a certain sadistic quality to it.

DUDLEY: Your question is in two parts really. First, what does it do for me? And second, is it sadism? It does a tremendous amount for me that's just pure joy. I don't know quite what its springs are but it is an emotionally satisfying discipline, as I guess psychiatry may even be, though it's hard to imagine! Is it sadistic? I don't know: I would like to think not, but I'm not sufficiently versed in the roots of human behaviour to deny the possibility. It may well be. It's not true, I think, that most surgeons are sadistically inclined in other ways. I may be sometimes in my criticism of my junior staff, though when I stand behind myself and try and observe what I do, I don't see that. I see it as just a highly critical attitude – but maybe I'm deluding myself.

NEMONE LETHBRIDGE

It is a man's duty to comfort himself and wait for the natural dissolution, and not to be vexed, but to find refreshment solely in these thoughts – first, that nothing will happen to me which is not conformable to the nature of the universe; and, secondly, that I need do nothing contrary to the God and deity within me; for there is no man who can compel me to transgress.

MARCUS AURELIUS

Earlier in this collection I remarked on the fact that many of the individuals interviewed by me could be seen as outsiders, individuals conscious of the extent to which they are different from, or even at odds with, the majority of their fellow men. Such a feeling of difference can be cultivated by choice, as in the case of, say, Peter Marsh, or can be experienced with much misgivings, as described by Nell Dunn. While each of my subjects in his or her own way has helped cast some light on how in individual cases such a sense of personal isolation or distinction can arise, Nemone Lethbridge seems to bring many of the crucial factors together in her own personality and experience.

She was born in Quetta – now Pakistan – on 1 March 1932. Her early years were spent, as were those of Spike Milligan, in India. Her father, a British major-general, was later Chief of Staff in Burma and Chief of Intelligence in post-war Berlin. Her mother was an English débutante with, in Nemone's words, 'a streak of wildness in her'. At the age of nine, Nemone Lethbridge was sent to school in England, first in Dorset, then at Tudor Hall in Banbury, and then at Bath High School. After school came Somerville College, Oxford, where she studied law. She was called to the Bar in 1956 and practised there until 1962, when she revealed that for three years she had been married to Jimmy O'Connor, a Fleet Street journalist, who had spent ten years in prison for the murder of a man in Kilburn in 1942 – a murder which O'Connor always denied ever committing.

Encouraged by Nemone Lethbridge, Jimmy O'Connor turned from journalism to playwriting and had several successes, including three

Wednesday Plays for the BBC in his first year of writing. The marriage lasted twelve years, and after several false finishes it ended in divorce in 1973. This left Nemone Lethbridge with two small children and virtually no money. She in turn took up playwriting, and achieved considerable success. In 1981 she returned to the Bar, where she is once again practising the career she first took up over twenty-five years ago.

All that had been written about Nemone Lethbridge suggested a strong-willed, self-reliant individual with the outsider's suspicion of the easy and the established and a penchant, one might even say a need, for the quirky and the unexpected. In the major public decisions of her life, such as the choice of her career and her husband, she expressed herself in an unconventional manner. As she points out, a career at the Bar was unusual for a woman in the 1950s, a marriage to a convicted murderer was, as she rather relishingly retells it, a shocker for staid souls in the Inns of Court! I was curious to know whether these decisions were coincidental in their unorthodoxy, or whether they were all part of a coherent picture – that of a deliberate maverick, willing herself to challenge conventional attitudes and behaviour.

For a start, she was influenced, like David Irving, by an absent father. Major-General Lethbridge was an awesome and inspiring figure and, by virtue of his work, introduced Nemone at a tender age, some might even say a precocious age, to the horrors of the concentration camps and the agony of the Holocaust. In the interview Nemone identifies as the central effect of this exposure the fact that she could never quite lose herself in the distractions and the trifles of adolescent life; it had the effect of introducing her to adult reality before her peers knew what being an adult was. It is clear from her own account, and from what is known about her, that this did not produce a dour, humourless ascetic – rather, she thrived on the brittle, flippant style of Oxbridge and the wild enthusiasms of the undergraduates of her time. But, for her, the memories of post-war Berlin serve to ensure that there is always a flavour of melancholy in the high excitement, always a nagging reminder that however good life is it is for many people nasty and brutish and short.

It is interesting to note that in only two interviews, those with Nemone Lethbridge and Christmas Humphreys, did I discuss at any length the individual's religious beliefs. In both cases, a firm religious philosophy was adopted – Buddhism by the judge, Roman Catholicism by Nemone Lethbridge – and in both the search and choice were motivated by a need to explain, to make some sense of apparently senseless, purposeless suffering. 'There must be suffering, the heart must break,' murmured the dying wife of Judge Humphreys and Nemone Lethbridge seems to echo such a sentiment with her powerful and unequivocal insistence that she does not know anybody whom she really loves who has not suffered – 'I'm not interested in people with easy lives.'

It is not so surprising a philosophy in a woman who married a man scarred and stigmatised publicly as the perpetrator of a terrible crime – a crime that Jimmy O'Connor has always insisted he did not commit. At times it can even lead to an actual attraction to suffering – Nemone talks in the last minutes of the interview of the 'voluptuous thought' of death, and claims that she would not wish her children to have easy lives – and at times, too, it can propel individuals to take on more in the way of easing the pain and sufferings of others than they are capable of discharging. Such considerations have tended to make some people sceptical about the motives of so-called do-gooders – voluntary workers, organisers of self-help groups, and so forth. The motives of those who wish to help are questioned, in so far as they appear to stem from what are rather portentously termed 'unresolved' conflicts over personal sufferings at some earlier stage in their own lives. My own field, psychiatry, has made a significant contribution to the sceptical analysis of the motivations of altruism, and with good reason. But Sir Thomas Browne's maxim to the effect that, 'By compassion we make others' miseries our own, and so, by relieving them, we relieve ourselves also', operates under the surface in many instances; and even in the heart of the most Nietzschean of helpers – 'Compassion for a friend should conceal itself under a hard shell,' he declared in *Thus Spake Zarathustra* – some impulse, generated by a personal experience or imaginative notion of suffering, can be detected.

Did Nemone Lethbridge try to redeem the world for her understandably bitter husband? It would appear so from her testimony. Was she wise to do so? Who is to say? What seems clear is that her action is all of a piece with her philosophy of life, predictable even from the personality formed in Berlin, the 'oddball' as she describes herself at Tudor Hall school. I was struck in the interview with Nemone Lethbridge, as I was from time to time with Nell Dunn and Spike Milligan, by a profound sense on the part of my subject of the gap between the way the world is and the way it should be – that gap which tends to preoccupy us most when we are depressed. The response of some individuals to this discrepancy is to refashion the world according to their own desires – an approach expansively described by Peter Marsh. Alternatively, one can try to reshape the narrow world of one's immediate family and friends, through some new communal way of living, an approach once favoured by Nell Dunn, or less dramatically, by ensuring a different experience for one's children, an approach adopted in varying ways by Arnold Wesker, David Irving, Hugh Dudley and Nemone Lethbridge. Or again, one can try to tackle the larger world by seizing every opportunity to shout against its barbarity and insensitivity; of those interviewed, perhaps only Spike Milligan has from time to time taken on that demanding task.

There is something of the stoic's resignation in Nemone Lethbridge's philosophy of life. She still gets vexed and she still gets depressed, but there is an air of acceptance in her words which many people who from time to time suffer depression and anxiety struggle yet fail to achieve. Perhaps her early exposure to the dreadful events of Belsen has helped her to maintain a sense of proportion necessary to keep one's own sufferings and those of humanity in general in perspective. Perhaps it is the result of the years close to a man whose life was almost ruined by circumstance. Perhaps it is the knowledge that she has survived particularly difficult and depressing moments. Perhaps it is her faith. Whatever it is, it has made her particular contribution to this collection a thought-provoking and valuable one.

ANTHONY CLARE: Your life has been publicly lived, with your career, your marriage, your divorce and your life since very much open to the public gaze. Would I be right in assuming that you have no misgivings about talking about yourself in public?

NEMONE LETHBRIDGE: I do have misgivings, but at the same time I edit what I say. I have a self-editing mechanism in me. There are certain things I'd never talk about, but there's a whole area of one's life which one doesn't mind talking about at all.

CLARE: What are the misgivings?

LETHBRIDGE: I hate to hurt people, and it's very difficult to talk about the living. I'd hate, for example, to say anything that would hurt my former husband. Apart from this, it's up to me to be quick-witted enough not to answer questions that ... go into secret places. Obviously there are secret areas in one's life, but it's up to one to keep them secret.

CLARE: Does your anxiety about the secret places concern yourself or other people?

LETHBRIDGE: Both. There are certain areas of my life with which I haven't yet come to terms myself. Maybe in ten or fifteen years I shall feel different about them. But I never want to hurt living people.

CLARE: Does the same consideration affect you in talking about the dead?

LETHBRIDGE: I think one must observe a certain discretion about the recently dead. But as they recede into history I think they're fair game.

CLARE: Your father was an army officer. What sort of man was he? Was he the model of a modern major-general?

LETHBRIDGE: No. He was quite different. He was a very cultivated man, a very original man. He had a deep love of India and the Himalayas, and he loved Asia more than he loved Europe. He had a tremendous knowledge of anthropology and of the different peoples of India – this was his great interest in life.

CLARE: Was he a very intellectual man?

LETHBRIDGE: He was a very practical man, but he always read. He was never without a book. He read seriously, and he spent his life reading about Asia and the Moghul Empire and that sort of thing.

CLARE: What age was he when you were born?

LETHBRIDGE: He must have been in his thirties – I can't remember.

CLARE: Were you the first of the children?

LETHBRIDGE: No, I was the second. I had an elder sister who died.

CLARE: Quite young?

LETHBRIDGE: In infancy, yes.

CLARE: So in practical terms you were the first?

LETHBRIDGE: Yes, yes.

CLARE: What was his relationship with you? What sort of memories do you have of him?

LETHBRIDGE: Alas, because we were children in the war, he was very much an absent father through all those years. We were very proud of him, and he was a spendid figure in his gorgeous uniform, and one had a lot of prestige at school because of this glamorous creature who used to arrive occasionally. But those years were lived largely without a father. Afterwards, in a way, it was too late to know him as I would have wished, because by the time he was home my brother and I were adolescent, and I really only got to know him well in the year of his death.

CLARE: Which was?

LETHBRIDGE: He died in 1962. And in that year, the year he was suffering his last illness, I got to know him very well. I felt an awful sense of waste because I hadn't been able to do this before. He really was a wonderful man, and a very brave man.

CLARE: Was he fierce in the sense that a military man in uniform can appear fierce to a small child?

LETHBRIDGE: I found him terrifying when I was an adolescent but I think this was because he already knew that he was suffering from lung cancer. He had a major lung cancer operation ten years before his death. Those last ten years were very difficult for him, because he was living under this shadow. Although we knew it, we really didn't make allowances for his gloom, and we found him a very gloomy and terrifying figure. But when it finally hit him again and he had secondaries and he knew that his life was very short, he came to terms with it in an extraordinary way and went back to being his old self. His last year was a model of what a dying man's end should be. He showed such tremendous courage and such compassion to us and to other people. He really was the most remarkable man, a wonderful man.

CLARE: You say that he was more terrifying during your adolescence. Did that have any impact on you?

LETHBRIDGE: I suppose it meant that I didn't confide in my parents as I want my children to confide in me. I went off on my own, and did things without telling anybody. I've remained extremely independent.

CLARE: What about your mother? What sort of person was she?

LETHBRIDGE: She's a very strong personality in her own right, and a very bright lady. All her life she has read very widely. Seventy-eight now: she's never without a book, a serious book, and she's got a continual plan of reading. She loves to talk about what she's reading, and she's got a tremendous life of the intellect.

CLARE: In your descriptions of your early life, your parents come across as benign but rather distant. Bookish, very God-fearing in a non-Godly way, moral people.

LETHBRIDGE: They're very moral, but they were strongly agnostic – militant agnostics.

CLARE: Was it a very disciplined household?

LETHBRIDGE: By today's standards, certainly. It was very kind, but, my goodness, one went to bed at seven or whatever and one didn't get up again!

CLARE: What if you did?

LETHBRIDGE: I can't imagine doing such a thing! It was also very cold, so one didn't dare get out of bed. My parents never had any heat upstairs. Even in the depths of winter, one got into bed and the sheets burned like ice. We didn't have hot water bottles – we had hot bricks!

CLARE: Where were you living then?

LETHBRIDGE: This was in Somerset, where I was brought up. It was a great ritual: the bricks were heated in the bottom oven of the Aga cooker and wrapped in pieces of blanket and put in the beds. Then one went into bed in this icy room and cuddled one's brick.

CLARE: How was discipline enforced?

LETHBRIDGE: I think we were very obedient. I can't remember being punished.

CLARE: How many were there in your family?

LETHBRIDGE: There was myself and my brother, we were very close in age. And I've got a sister who's much younger.

CLARE: I imagine you to have been a high-spirited sort of person, who wouldn't have brooked too much discipline.

LETHBRIDGE: No – but I absolutely adored my mother, and we had a very close relationship.

CLARE: Do you see a lot of yourself in her?

LETHBRIDGE: I would like to. I admire her very much. She's a very gentle person. She's an intellectual person. And she has a great love of the country and of gardens and of beauty, poetry. This side of her I would like to develop in myself, I can see this. But the pagan monkey in me doesn't come from her. That came down the chimney, I think!

CLARE: Pagan monkey?

LETHBRIDGE: Yes.

CLARE: Go on.

LETHBRIDGE: My worldly side has nothing to do with her at all. In many ways she led a very sheltered life, in that she married very young to an extremely good man who looked after her and she's not been exposed to the world in the way that I have, because women of her generation weren't. So she's kept that inviolate quality which is impossible for people of my generation, because our lives are very much more difficult.

CLARE: Are you still close?

LETHBRIDGE: Yes.

CLARE: Was there a time when you were far from close?

LETHBRIDGE: There was a time, yes, when we grew apart, but we never lost touch. She's a marvellous letter writer, and since I was nine I don't think I've been through a week without at least two letters from her.

CLARE: When you say you grew apart, do you mean that distance divided you, or more substantial things?

LETHBRIDGE: My whole way of life was very strange to her and, I think, painful.

CLARE: When was this?

LETHBRIDGE: Really from the time I went to Oxford until I had the children. The children were the start of a great reconciliation.

CLARE: You've described yourself as miserably unhappy at school.

LETHBRIDGE: I was terribly homesick and I missed my mother very much. And I missed my animals and my home. I loved my home.

CLARE: What about friends at school?

LETHBRIDGE: There was a plus side. I've formed certain friendships which I've kept. That is the good part of boarding school.

CLARE: Were you a mixer at school, or a loner?

LETHBRIDGE: I was a mixer, but at the same time – it sounds pompous – I really was more serious from about the age of twelve than most of my contemporaries. The great watershed of my life, I can now see – it took me years to realise how important it was – was going to Germany as a small girl, after the war.

CLARE: What age were you?

LETHBRIDGE: Twelve. It was a shattering experience suddenly to be precipitated from a country life in England, the very isolated, almost Edwardian life we lived, very cut-off in the depths of Somerset, going very rarely to London, just going to school in Oxfordshire. My movement was very restricted, simply between two English counties. Suddenly arriving in Berlin immediately after the war was like another world. And, after that, going back to school where all my friends were still talking about gymkhanas. They were mostly horse-mad, and it was gymkhanas and gymkhanas and gymkhanas!

CLARE: How long were you in Berlin?

LETHBRIDGE: My father's headquarters were actually in Westphalia, but he used to go up periodically, once every three weeks or something.

CLARE: And he'd take you with him?

LETHBRIDGE: Yes.

CLARE: What are your memories?

LETHBRIDGE: First of the extraordinary beauty of that landscape – Brueghel-like landscapes, great flat rolling snow-fields and dark skies. But then of complete devastation and starving people. My father was Chief of Intelligence, Rhine Army, at that time, and every day they were finding new horrors and atrocities and opening up new concentration camps. He never felt that he should hide this from his children, so we knew all about it. It was like living with ghosts. And then to get back to school and hear people talking about nothing but ponies.

CLARE: Did it frighten you? You wrote, 'We were aware of the ghosts around the table, of Belsen and Treblinka, of the generals hanging from meathooks while the SS filmed their agony.'

LETHBRIDGE: Oh of course it disturbed me, yes. Certainly.

CLARE: In what sense?

LETHBRIDGE: It made me unbelievably restless. I just couldn't settle down and be content with my lot again. Because I felt there was so much to be done in the world, I wanted to go into politics. I felt the solution to this was a political one, and I developed an absolute passion for politics.

CLARE: When you say that it moved you to see the solution in political terms, was this a highly idealistic political notion? Were you a Marxist?

LETHBRIDGE: I thought Communism was the answer.

CLARE: You weren't religious then?

LETHBRIDGE: No.

CLARE: You were like your parents.

LETHBRIDGE: That's right.

CLARE: So what did you do in your early teens about this political impulse?

LETHBRIDGE: I became a Young Communist. I was the only Young Communist at my school, Tudor Hall. It was partly a sort of bloodymindedness, because it annoyed people so much.

CLARE: But it was your first role as an outsider?

LETHBRIDGE: Yes. I suddenly *got* communism like people get born-again Christianity – I just fell in love with the idea.

CLARE: And what was the response of those around you?

LETHBRIDGE: They always regarded me as a bit of a lunatic anyway, I think. I was always the oddball. I've always been an outsider and it doesn't worry me at all.

CLARE: Your school friends would see no discontinuity between you as you were then and as you are now?

LETHBRIDGE: No, they still think I'm a lunatic, I think.

CLARE: Because?

LETHBRIDGE: I'm always out of step, but it doesn't worry me at all.

CLARE: And it didn't worry you as an adolescent?

LETHBRIDGE: No, I rather liked it. I know I had an awful streak of 'enfant terrible' in me.

CLARE: You were never lonely? You didn't feel that it must be reassuring to be part of something?

LETHBRIDGE: I used to get fits of Keatsian melancholy, but this was rather delicious. I used to read the romantic poets or look at the autumn leaves.

CLARE: When you went up to Somerville College, Oxford, what were you looking forward to about university life?

LETHBRIDGE: I suppose I thought it would be all Brideshead. I read Evelyn Waugh avidly and of course it *was* Brideshead. That book is so accurate in its description of Oxford. Marvellous.

CLARE: What about your political ambitions? Had they died?

LETHBRIDGE: Well, I fell out of love with communism very quickly.

CLARE: Was there any event that caused that, or was it just a gradual disaffection?

LETHBRIDGE: I think it was the Berlin Wall and world events.

CLARE: In Oxford you were not a political person?

LETHBRIDGE: I was: I joined the Liberal Party and I've been in the Liberal Party ever since.

CLARE: You mentioned that around that time your mother and your lifestyle moved apart, that she found it difficult to understand. Why? What was your lifestyle?

LETHBRIDGE: I was very wild and, of course, immediately discontented with my home. The whole quiet tenor of English country life I suddenly found very boring.

CLARE: When you say 'very wild', what was being 'very wild' like in Oxford in the 1950s?

LETHBRIDGE: Oh gosh, climbing in, dances, dances, dances. Climbing in late at night up lampposts, really silly things.

CLARE: Was it a very exciting time sexually?

LETHBRIDGE: It was very strange, because there were so few girls and so many chaps. I think we became terribly spoilt, because we were so courted and taken out.

CLARE: When did you discover that you were attractive?

LETHBRIDGE: It must have been when I first went up to Oxford. It was a very heady experience, suddenly to turn from ugly duckling into a semi-swan.

CLARE: Was there anybody special with whom you became romantically involved? Or even sexually involved?

LETHBRIDGE: I carried a candle for years for an older man. From the time I was about sixteen, and I adored this man.

CLARE: Did you know him personally?

LETHBRIDGE: Yes – and I still know him.

CLARE: Did that relationship dominate your period at Oxford?

LETHBRIDGE: In a way it did. It meant that I never married at that stage: I was firmly set and thinking about this one person.

CLARE: You thought you might marry him?

LETHBRIDGE: I thought I might, yes.

CLARE: Was he at the university?

LETHBRIDGE: No.

CLARE: While you were at university it was like being engaged to somebody outside?

LETHBRIDGE: Yes.

CLARE: Did that serve to protect you?

LETHBRIDGE: I think it did, yes.

CLARE: Would colleagues and contemporaries have known about him?

LETHBRIDGE: Oh yes – I used to boast about him like crazy.

CLARE: How much of it was fantasy, and how much reality?

LETHBRIDGE: Oh it was real. He's had four or five wives, and we still adore each other.

CLARE: So you proceeded through Oxford having a Brideshead time. Was there any conflict between that kind of life and your idealism? What had happened to your memories of Berlin?

LETHBRIDGE: Well I didn't realise until I started writing a piece for television how important they were to me. I suppose they did, to a certain extent, go into the back of my mind. It was only when I started to think about this period that I realised that they were absolutely crucial.

CLARE: The remark was made, I think in Brideshead, that for a whole generation Oxford was the childhood that the students didn't have when they were children. Would that apply to you?

LETHBRIDGE: I think so, because our childhood was really very serious. It was very constricted. Living deep in the country, there was hardly ever any petrol, so we weren't mobile. We really did live almost a Jane Austen life.

CLARE: There wasn't much fun?

LETHBRIDGE: No, but we didn't miss it because we'd never had it. The great enjoyment, the thing that brought me more happiness in my childhood than anything else, was my pet animals. I had a lot of pet animals, and I can remember every one of them and their names. My rabbit, Cellophane, and various things like that. I had a pet rat.

CLARE: When did you develop the desire for a religious belief?

LETHBRIDGE: I think this came with Oxford, and it started as a kind of romantic Brideshead thing. I was very drawn to the Catholic Church for completely the wrong reasons – its beauty and its mystery, and I always loved Latin. I love the music, and that was the door I went through.

CLARE: When did you formally join the Roman Catholic Church?

LETHBRIDGE: After I came down from Oxford. My parents didn't care for it at all because it went right against their sort of Victorian free-thinking, agnostic philosophy. And they really thought it was full of Jesuits with thumbscrews.

CLARE: What was it that you felt Roman Catholicism explained that the free-thinking attitude to life didn't? Was it again tied up with Berlin?

LETHBRIDGE: It must have been, yes. I wanted to find a way of justifying suffering and of making sense of lives that were wasted. I couldn't see the point of these people who died so terribly, with their promise unfulfilled. No free-thinking philosophy could provide an answer to this.

CLARE: It was what – too tidy?

LETHBRIDGE: No, it didn't start to explain it. You could build a very rational, personal life and a very happy life and an orderly, disciplined, good life on it: but you couldn't explain why thousands of people had to die like this, why babies have to die of meningitis and that sort of thing.

CLARE: Did you at any stage have a personal experience that reinforced the more impersonal experiences of Berlin?

LETHBRIDGE: I didn't.

CLARE: Any tragic loss or any catastrophe?

LETHBRIDGE: Later, yes.

CLARE: But you'd already joined by then?

LETHBRIDGE: Yes, and later in my life I lost my two best Oxford friends, at about the age of thirty, of separate causes. It was very strange and gave the whole era, the whole period a kind of unreal, Arcadian quality because there was nobody left I could talk to about it. It seemed as though it had never happened. After we came down I shared a house in London with both these girls, and they both died within a very short period. It really was most strange.

CLARE: What age were you then?

LETHBRIDGE: We were all the same age – about thirty.

CLARE: You were at the Bar at that stage?

LETHBRIDGE: Yes.

CLARE: It was a very masculine world.

LETHBRIDGE: Yes it *was* a very masculine world. But, in a way, one had the edge just because one *was* a woman.

CLARE: How much did you use the fact that you were a woman, and a very attractive woman?

LETHBRIDGE: As much as I could. I'd no scruples at all.

CLARE: Did you come across people who would demean your intellectual skills by referring to the fact that you were an attractive woman?

LETHBRIDGE: This always used to irritate me. I hated being patronised. It really annoys me very much.

CLARE: Did it happen much at the Bar?

LETHBRIDGE: Yes. I remember it being said that women could never succeed at the Bar because they've got awful, squeaky little voices. At the same time it was said that a woman would never read the news – it was impossible, it was inconceivable that this little squeaky voice could read the news.

CLARE: That presumably served as a challenge?

LETHBRIDGE: Yes.

CLARE: You spent seven years at the Bar. How successful were you?

LETHBRIDGE: Oh, I worked, which was quite difficult in those days for girls – so few of them managed to get any work at all.

CLARE: And what branch of law did you specialise in?

LETHBRIDGE: Crime.

CLARE: Was that a choice, or what was available?

LETHBRIDGE: There was work available at that time, and there were a few solicitors who didn't mind instructing women. Now it's quite different, but there was terrific prejudice then.

CLARE: Was there additional prejudice about crime, rather like forensic medicine – that it was a subject not particularly suitable for a woman?

LETHBRIDGE: Oddly enough, I think the two fields where women first made their impact were crime and divorce. I don't really know much about it, but I think they found it much harder to make their way in the rather classier areas such as conveyancing.

CLARE: You met your husband in your career. How did that happen?

LETHBRIDGE: He was a great drinking chum of a member of my chambers, Lionel Thompson.

CLARE: At this stage your future husband was writing.

LETHBRIDGE: He was working in Fleet Street, for Kemsley.

CLARE: And he was also a great character.

LETHBRIDGE: Oh yes. A very, very amusing man, a tremendous raconteur and spellbindingly funny.

CLARE: You'd never met anyone quite like this before?

LETHBRIDGE: No. And I remember very clearly the evening I met him. I went into a pub with Lionel Thompson to watch a television programme. I didn't own a television set at that time, and Jimmy was there and Lionel said to me, 'I want you to meet the most fascinating man in London.' Jimmy was holding court, he loved to hold court with a lot of people round him. I did find him completely enthralling.

CLARE: Was he very Irish? I know he was born in Paddington, but I assume it was an Irish family.

LETHBRIDGE: Yes, by blood, pure Irish. I suppose in many ways he is. He looks Irish, and he has these great Celtic swings of temperament.

CLARE: And alcohol?

LETHBRIDGE: Yes.

CLARE: Were you instantly drawn to him?

LETHBRIDGE: Yes, I was instantly fascinated.

CLARE: How much was that bound up with his past?

LETHBRIDGE: Of course it was bound up with his past. But I can never see anybody as existing in one moment of time – I look at everybody that way.

CLARE: But his past was an unusual one.

LETHBRIDGE: Yes, it was.

CLARE: To what extent does somebody with a past like that serve to warn a girl off, given that he'd been accused of a violent crime. Did you at any stage ever believe that he'd committed it?

LETHBRIDGE: No. No he hadn't.

CLARE: So in that sense he was another outsider, a man who'd suffered greatly . . .

LETHBRIDGE: Yes. He interested me because he'd suffered, which made him very much more interesting – I always find people who've suffered more interesting than people who've had easy lives. And I also felt that he'd suffered an enormous injustice, which I still feel.

CLARE: He had suffered a great deal in his early childhood, quite apart from this other trauma?

LETHBRIDGE: He had, yes. He had a very hard childhood. He came from extreme poverty, and he had a Dickensian childhood.

CLARE: Was he a very argumentative man?

LETHBRIDGE: Yes, he is. He still is. But alas, as he's got older, the shadows have drawn in and he's become less amusing and more tragic.

CLARE: Melancholic?

LETHBRIDGE: Yes, he is melancholic. But he's got good reason to be.

CLARE: Was he aggressive when you knew him?

LETHBRIDGE: No, this was not one of the things that struck me.

CLARE: When he drank?

LETHBRIDGE: Well at that time he didn't show his drinking. He could carry it very well. He has enormous physical stamina and nobody ever knew how much he put away. Certainly I didn't because he was never drunk.

CLARE: Really?

LETHBRIDGE: No.

CLARE: His father drank heavily.

LETHBRIDGE: Yes.

CLARE: He talked about that?

LETHBRIDGE: Yes.

CLARE: When did you decide to marry him? How long after you'd met him?

LETHBRIDGE: About a year or so.

CLARE: Who did know?

LETHBRIDGE: Only a very small circle of friends.

CLARE: Your mother?

LETHBRIDGE: Not to start with.

CLARE: Was your father alive then?

LETHBRIDGE: He was, yes. Nobody in my family knew straight-away.

CLARE: Why was that?

LETHBRIDGE: I was such a moral coward, I didn't know how to tell them. I knew they'd be worried sick. And I thought, which I think now was misguided, that it would be easier for them if I could present them with a *fait accompli*, and be able to say, 'Now look, I've been married for so many months, and it's all right, there's nothing to worry about.' I think this was wrong, that one should level with people. But at the time I thought it would cause less anxiety if I did it that way.

CLARE: When did you tell your mother?

LETHBRIDGE: In the end, I had to tell her because my younger sister came up to London and was going to live with me. I felt it would be wrong to involve her in my deception, so I had to come clean.

CLARE: You hadn't told her either?

LETHBRIDGE: I told her first. And then I thought it would be absolutely wrong to make her involved in this.

CLARE: How much younger was your sister?

LETHBRIDGE: She's nearly nine years younger than me.

CLARE: Is she like you at all?

LETHBRIDGE: No, she's quite different.

CLARE: What did she make of your decision?

LETHBRIDGE: She welcomed it. She was very fond of Jimmy, and still is.

CLARE: How long after you married did you tell your close family?

LETHBRIDGE: A matter of a few months.

CLARE: But it was much more than that before you told the world.

LETHBRIDGE: We didn't tell the world. We wanted to keep it under wraps, because we knew there'd be horrendous publicity and that sort of thing. We didn't tell anybody – in fact we deliberately got married in Dublin so there wouldn't be anything in Somerset House.

CLARE: Was he a Catholic?

LETHBRIDGE: Yes. But you can't hide things from Fleet Street for ever. We managed for three years, which was something of a triumph.

CLARE: Which of you was the better known? Your husband, with his Fleet Street connections?

LETHBRIDGE: He was very well known in Fleet Street, yes. He'd worked on *Picture Post* and he worked for Kemsley and he was a great London character, one of the sights of London, I think.

CLARE: When it was all revealed, your career took a dive.

LETHBRIDGE: I couldn't get a place in chambers because of the embarrassment caused by the publicity.

CLARE: Your husband had served ten years in jail?

LETHBRIDGE: Eleven. His conviction was in 1941.

CLARE: So he was out in the early Fifties. We're talking now about the early Sixties. He was well known in Fleet Street. He was a writer. Was he a playwright then?

LETHBRIDGE: While he was in prison he'd done a drama course with Ruskin College, Oxford, and he'd started writing seriously while he was in jail.

CLARE: What made it impossible for you to continue practising at the Bar?

LETHBRIDGE: Simply the lack of chambers. The head of my own particular set didn't want to be tarred with my brush, so he refused to accept my rent. It was hard enough for women in those days to get chambers at all, and I couldn't find another set.

CLARE: What did you do then?

LETHBRIDGE: We bought some land in Greece, so we built a house. Jimmy did a script in Hollywood of the Great Train Robbery, and took the money to Greece, so we had plenty of funds. We built a marvellous house on an island and thought we'd live there happily ever after.

CLARE: Then what happened?

LETHBRIDGE: Well, you can go to one of these earthly paradises and you think all your problems have gone, but about six months later they all came creeping back. One's problems are the same in Southend as in the South Seas.

CLARE: And what were the problems that crept back?

LETHBRIDGE: The principal problem was that I wasn't sufficiently employed. I was very energetic and very restless. It wasn't enough just to live in a beautiful place. I had no children and I was just running around chasing my own tail.

CLARE: Did you plan to have children?

LETHBRIDGE: I always wanted children, yes. But I had great difficulty in having them.

CLARE: So what did you do?

LETHBRIDGE: Jimmy had a marvellous period. He wrote a lot of plays for the BBC and he was acclaimed and awarded. So we spent a lot of time going backwards and forwards, having plays in rehearsal. Then I started to write myself, and life seemed interesting and productive. But in television fashions change, and the great days of the single play disappeared. There really wasn't the outlet for serious writers by the beginning of the Seventies that there had been in the Sixties. The Sixties was a golden period for television. But then it all changed, and suddenly there wasn't enough work. It is the most crippling, awful thing, to be insufficiently employed.

CLARE: That coincided with increasing strains in your marriage?

LETHBRIDGE: These things contribute one to the other.

CLARE: When was your first child born?

LETHBRIDGE: In 1970.

CLARE: Was that a time of great stress for you?

LETHBRIDGE: It was a very strange time, because I spent the whole of the pregnancy in hospital.

CLARE: Why?

LETHBRIDGE: Because I miscarry so easily. It really was a very strange limbo period.

CLARE: You had a son.

LETHBRIDGE: Yes, my son Ragnor. I had the most terrible puerperal depression. I went completely out of my mind.

CLARE: How long did it last?

LETHBRIDGE: It took a number of years to pull right out. I was acutely depressed for nearly a year.

CLARE: Was this the lowest point in your life?

LETHBRIDGE: Yes.

CLARE: Did you ever make an attempt to end it?

LETHBRIDGE: I couldn't think about anything else – I became absolutely obsessed with the thought of suicide.

CLARE: This was quite unlike you.

LETHBRIDGE: Yes, but it was there.

CLARE: Before that, would you have said that you had a melancholic tendency?

LETHBRIDGE: Not strongly, mildly. It's easy to be wise after the event, but one can see straws in the wind.

CLARE: When this happened, were you in hospital for quite some time?

LETHBRIDGE: No – because of Ragnor, I was in hospital for a time, six weeks or so.

CLARE: What do you think got you through it?

LETHBRIDGE: Good friends, I think, and good family; the fact that I'd had a very happy childhood, and I knew that happiness was possible. I think if I had *not* been very happy at certain periods of my life, I couldn't have coped with it. But I never lost the knowledge that happiness existed.

CLARE: Do you think about that experience in terms of its ever happening again, or is it something you feel you've put right behind you?

LETHBRIDGE: It's never quite behind. I can see straws in the wind sometimes.

CLARE: In the way you feel?

LETHBRIDGE: Yes. When everybody starts to annoy me, and I want to burst into tears in the street, I know I must watch out.

CLARE: What do you do?

LETHBRIDGE: I don't have to do anything, really. I just tell myself to watch it.

CLARE: What treatments did you have then?

LETHBRIDGE: Drugs, drugs.

CLARE: Do you think they helped?

LETHBRIDGE: One doesn't know how one would have been without them. In the end, I just threw them all down the lavatory because they have such unpleasant side effects. In the end I think you've got to argue your way through it in your own mind.

CLARE: You had a second child, two years later. Did you have anything like this then?

LETHBRIDGE: No, no.

CLARE: Do you understand why you had this depressive illness after the first birth?

LETHBRIDGE: I don't. One can see certain contributory factors, but to understand it . . .

CLARE: What were these factors?

LETHBRIDGE: Well, I was unhappy in my own life. What I didn't realise at the time is that I would much rather be a driver than a passenger in my own life. The most depressing thing is having to be a passenger.

CLARE: And you were a passenger then in what sense?

LETHBRIDGE: Having been in hospital for so long, it's awfully difficult to cope with the real world when you come out. Even though I hadn't been ill I'd just been lying up. I found it frightening to cross the street, and I suppose I'd become institutionalised. He was an awfully delicate baby, and I didn't know how to cope with his constant illnesses. I found him very, very difficult.

CLARE: Have you used that experience, in relation to other people who've gone through it?

LETHBRIDGE: I really got it out of myself by writing a play. I wrote it out of myself.

CLARE: *Baby Blues*?

LETHBRIDGE: Yes. Then I did try to set up groups for people who've been through similar experiences, which actually worked very well. But I no longer have anything to do with them, because dealing with depressed people is so draining – I don't think you can do it, unless you're doing it professionally, for more than a limited period of time.

CLARE: In that play, men don't figure very much or very well.

LETHBRIDGE: No, they don't.

CLARE: In fact, they're rather a rotten lot.

LETHBRIDGE: Yes, I know. I was rather unfair.

CLARE: Perhaps not! What *is* your feeling about men?

LETHBRIDGE: I don't have a generalised feeling now – they're individuals.

CLARE: You did then?

LETHBRIDGE: I got a bit paranoid at the time. It's not a very good play, but it was very therapeutic for me. After I'd written it, I felt much better.

CLARE: There's a lot of you in it.

LETHBRIDGE: Yes.

CLARE: Your marriage was breaking up then. You once said, 'Some experiences are so traumatic that they do leave you marked. And Jimmy is very warped.'

LETHBRIDGE: The experience of being in the death cell – I don't think you recover from this. You certainly don't come out the same man as you went in.

CLARE: I know it's very difficult for you to sum up such an experience, but – insofar as it affected you – what did that death cell experience do to your husband?

LETHBRIDGE: He never really walked out into the daylight. He still dreams about it. He still wakes shrieking. It's a terrible thing to do to a human being.

CLARE: Did it affect his relationship with you?

LETHBRIDGE: It affected his relationship with the world.

CLARE: What about you?

LETHBRIDGE: I was just part of the world. It is much stronger, so much more vivid than anything that ever happens after.

CLARE: Was it something you could understand?

LETHBRIDGE: I can understand it now, but I used to feel it was so strange that the rest of his life, including our marriage, seemed to be like a dream to him. He was fixated with this one appalling event.

CLARE: Even then? Even during your marriage?

LETHBRIDGE: Yes.

CLARE: You were, and he was, a Roman Catholic. Did getting a divorce cause a lot of pain to you?

LETHBRIDGE: Well it did. If I'd not been a Catholic, I would have done it before. But I felt I must try at all costs to maintain this marriage.

CLARE: At its lowest ebb, was it a very acrimonious, fractious marriage?

LETHBRIDGE: Yes.

CLARE: Painful?

LETHBRIDGE: Yes. But – and this is the plus side – now that we have not lived under the same roof for ten years or more, we do have a very good relationship. I now regard Jimmy as a dear friend.

CLARE: You had to cope with people saying, or implying, that they told you so. How did you cope with it?

LETHBRIDGE: I said, 'Shut up', or, 'Mind your own business.'

CLARE: Did it shake your confidence in yourself, that it had come apart?

LETHBRIDGE: Yes. The hardest thing to come to terms with is one's loss of self-esteem. I felt a non-person for a long time.

CLARE: How did you recover from what must have been a very grey period? What sort of reserves did you call on?

LETHBRIDGE: Energy, really. I've got a lot of energy.

CLARE: Physical energy?

LETHBRIDGE: Physical and mental energy. When I finally found myself living in the East End of London with two little children, I made a conscious decision: 'At this point either one lives or one dies.' And I just thought, 'I'll live, and I'll plunge myself into everything that I can.'

CLARE: It didn't shake your faith in your idealism? You said once: 'In a moment of high hope and idealism and a common cause in the fight to abolish the death penalty, I married Jimmy O'Connor.' But the crusade came to a very bitter and sad end.

LETHBRIDGE: Yes ... well no, it didn't. It didn't because I still regard Jimmy as my husband, I'm still Catholic. The fact that we cannot live together is a great pity. But it doesn't make me not a Catholic. The Pope in Rome doesn't say that two married people have to live in intolerable conditions. What he does say is we're still married. Although I've been through a civil divorce, I shan't remarry.

CLARE: You won't?

LETHBRIDGE: No, I shan't. I've no wish to.

CLARE: When you say some experiences are so traumatic they do leave you marked, you were referring to him. What about yourself? You've had some pretty traumatic experiences?

LETHBRIDGE: They should leave you marked. If they didn't leave you marked, you'd be an insensitive blob of plastic.

CLARE: Some people might feel that a better word than 'marked' would be 'distorted'. That's why people are frightened of traumatic experiences.

LETHBRIDGE: Yes, it's either make or break. But I don't know anybody whom I really love and respect who has not in some way suffered much. I'm not interested in people with easy lives.

CLARE: Does anything frighten you?

LETHBRIDGE: Yes – the thought of my children being run over.

CLARE: Does anything about you frighten you?

LETHBRIDGE: I get afraid of running out of energy sometimes. There seems so much to do.

CLARE: Do you have regrets?

LETHBRIDGE: I have regrets about my own neglect of friends – that sort of thing. I have plenty to reproach myself with, but I don't resent the hard things that fate has brought.

CLARE: Is there anything that you were exposed to you would make every effort to avoid in relation to your own children?

LETHBRIDGE: Not exactly. But I did consciously decide that I wanted them to be more street-wise than we were. Our childhood was very, very happy, but we weren't really given much practical equipment with which to face the world. Because they've been brought up in the East End, I hope they're street-wise. Sometimes I think they're over-street-wise, but I think they'll have better survival equipment than I did. I wouldn't wish them to have easy lives, no.

CLARE: In the sense that you had an easy life, what were you unprotected against?

LETHBRIDGE: Treachery. I couldn't believe that people wouldn't be honourable, like my parents.

CLARE: Can you remember the first betrayal?

LETHBRIDGE: The whole business of having to leave the Bar the first time round. I felt an acute sense of treachery, and I couldn't believe that so many people I thought my friends could behave in such a shoddy manner. I think that hurt more than almost anything.

CLARE: It still does?

LETHBRIDGE: No, I've become very philosophical about it.

CLARE: Are there people you wouldn't speak to?

LETHBRIDGE: No, no, no. We have an absolute rule in my household that we don't let the sun go down on our wrath.

CLARE: In that sense your children will be wiser?

LETHBRIDGE: Yes. They live much more in the world than I ever did as a young thing. They play in the street and they're right in the world.

CLARE: What do you want to do that's still undone?

LETHBRIDGE: I want to bring up my children. I'd like to live long enough to get them to manhood, and get them set. After that I don't mind. I'd be happy to die, I'm not afraid of it.

CLARE: But not yet?

LETHBRIDGE: No – I've got a lot of unfinished business. But I find it a rather voluptuous thought.

JUDGE CHRISTMAS HUMPHREYS

Just as miraculous cures are brought about by doctors who are themselves suffering from fatal diseases, great issues of life and death are decided by Judges who, in their daily lives, can't make up their minds when to play out their trumps and whose existence is entirely in the hands of resolute wives or implacable sisters.

JOHN MORTIMER, *Clinging to the Wreckage*

Psychiatrists, by public reputation, are prone to ambiguity, imprecision and opacity and appear to flourish in that no man's land situated between guesswork and certainty. In contrast, lawyers take on some of the implacable majesty of their profession. Clarity, verbal precision, intellectual dexterity, formidable powers of cross-examination and an awesome certainty – such are the qualities which, from time to time, we attribute to those who wield the fearful power which resides in the very core of the judicial system. Conventional wisdom dictates that as the judge dons his wig and gown he discards his personal prejudices, his blind faiths and emotional biases and becomes the detached dispenser of abstract justice. If there is a medical counterpart, it must be the surgeon, cool as the steel he plies, detached from the warm humanity upon which he operates. When I came to select subjects to interview, my list quickly included a judge and a surgeon, for the mainsprings of decisiveness, authority and power interest me. So too am I intrigued by the act – is it of the will? – whereby emotional, irrational, impulsive and human man adopts a position that is almost God-like in its disinterested appraisal of the activities of his fellows.

The judge chosen and agreeable to be interviewed was no ordinary member of Her Majesty's judiciary. In addition to having been an Old Bailey judge for eight years, Travers Christmas Humphreys founded the British Buddhist Society, and for the better part of his long life was a recognised international expert on Buddhist philosophy and belief.

Christmas Humphreys was born in London on 15 January 1901. In her day book his mother logged laconically his advent: 'Hairdresser 10.30. Baby arrived 2.20.' It was a matter-of-fact style which her son inherited. His letter accepting my invitation offered me the advice that forty minutes would be too long for most interviewees – most people could say everything that needed saying about themselves in twenty. I took great pride in showing him that, despite his prediction, he himself had a great deal to say over two hours – and we were still talking then. If he acquired his terse style from his mother, he inherited a legal bent from his father. Travers Humphreys was a junior counsel for the defence of Oscar Wilde, and later became one of the great criminal judges. His son was educated at Malvern College before going up to Trinity Hall, Cambridge in 1919 to study law. He was called to the Bar in 1924, became a leading Treasury counsel, attended the War Crimes tribunal in Japan, and was a prosecuting counsel at a number of famous trials, including that of Craig and Bentley for the murder of a policeman. His cross-examination played a crucial part in the guilty verdict which caused Ruth Ellis to go to the gallows, the last woman to be executed in Britain.

He married in 1927, and the marriage lasted until the death of his wife in 1975. Together they founded the Buddhist Society, and over the years both he and his wife travelled extensively throughout the world, learning about and teaching Buddhist values. In his lifetime, he wrote twenty-two books on Buddhism, in addition to books on law, other oriental religions and poetry; his autobiography, *Both Sides of the Circle*, was published in 1976.

I refer to Christmas Humphreys in the past tense because in 1983, at the age of eighty-two, Judge Christmas Humphreys died. I had not seen him since the day in February 1982 when he gave the interview which is republished here; but I know he felt it painted an accurate picture of him, and one that he was quite willing to have portrayed to the world. On his death, his own Buddhist friends requested permission to reprint it in their magazine.

It was not the easiest of interviews. The Judge was the very epitome of briskness, never using two words when one would do. He was resiliently unpsychological – but in fairness he had warned me, sending me a lengthy and detailed manuscript summarising himself and ending: 'I note no emotional reaction to crises of any kind, being blown through my house, theft of car and burglary, and loss of friends, only at my deprivation of their presence for a while. Have I submerged my emotions ten fathoms down? If so they can stay there. Meanwhile at least I can't be hurt.'

It is not uncommon to find that individuals who aspire to a certain invulnerability, a studied emotional impregnability, have been hurt in the past, and hurt badly. What lay behind Christmas Humphrey's cool, unemotional, detached attitude? His background, more than that of anyone else I interviewed, was archetypally English, his genes impregnated with English tradition, precedent and lineage, his schooling a classic one of public school and Oxbridge, his manners impeccable and formal, his bearing that of a tall, thin military officer and his social behaviour at once dignified and distant. His family could trace itself back to the mid-16th century and was linked with the Saddlers' Livery Company, of which Christmas Humphreys was Master; all of which might well explain his style and attitudes.

But there was a traumatic event in his past, to which the Judge returned repeatedly when explaining the path his own life took, his Buddhist conversion and his fatalistic attitude towards death. His brother was killed in the First World War, and that event appears to have exercised a remarkable impact on the adolescent still at school and still struggling to evolve his own philosophy and his own identity. At the present time, there is much interest in and concern about the phenomenon of conversion, much public discussion of movements like the Moonies, Exegesis, charismatic born-again Christian sects and Scientology. A common feature of sudden conversion is a mystical experience, yet little in the Judge's character or bearing, at least not sixty years on, suggested that he was given to transcendental states. Yet, a sudden, insight-laden experience is precisely what Christmas Humphreys described, one of those 'moments of sentimental and mystical experience' described by William James, 'that carry an enormous sense of inner authority and illumination with them when they come'. James went on to add that they come seldom, do not come to everyone 'and the rest of life makes no connection with them or tends to contradict them more than it confirms them'. In the case of Humphreys the rest of life was changed and changed utterly.

Or was it? Might it not have merely been a case of someone of a certain frame of mind, a particular mental set, an idiosyncratic personality type seeking and finding a system of belief more intellectually suited to him than the prevailing Judaeo-Christian system? He was not a joiner though he was part of a clubbable profession, a member of a Liveried Company and an enthusiastic traveller; and, temperamentally at least, he seemed more suited to the less personal, cosmically-oriented philosophy of Buddha than that resting on the individualistic creed derived from the life and teachings of Christ.

It was only with regard to personal issues that the Judge's imperturbability wavered and a slight irritability showed through. With his death died the Humphreys line. We talked of that eventuality towards the end of the interview. He did not have children, and there were sound reasons which he proffered. But the question provoked from him a sudden, and for him, emotional discussion of children in terms not dissimilar to those used by David Irving in describing the impact of his own children on his life's work. Without contesting the Judge's views on overpopulation, I sense in his vehemence a distaste for the kind of emotional demand and even contact which children represent. 'My house', declared Humphreys proudly, 'was a home of complete peace.'

The lack of children certainly meant that his life quest was unencumbered by practical considerations such as, 'Where will they go to school?' and, 'Is the house big enough?' Doubtless such considerations were at the back of my mind when I questioned him on his experience of suffering. I found it curious and compelling that all his comments on suffering invariably returned to the theme of his brother's death. Even our discussion of his wife's death was marked not by a sense of loss so much as an air of another stage reached, another cycle completed in the great, never-ending cosmic odyssey. 'There must be suffering, the heart must break,' murmured his wife on her death-bed. Her words did seem to strike an antithetical chord to the harmonious composition so meticulously put together by her Buddhist husband. Listeners and friends of mine have commented on the aloof, almost chilling way that Christmas Humphreys discussed his wife's death, his matter-of-fact acceptance of the end. Of course, such a response would be all of a piece with his stated, fatalistic philosophy and its conviction in the process of reincarnation. But on hearing the interview again, and reading it, I am not so sure that one would be wise to make such a judgement. Ten fathoms down, where Humphreys buried his emotions, he did not erase or eliminate them. For me the entire interview illuminated the way in which individuals find the philosophy which fits their temperament and the manner in which temperament and philosophy then reinforce and strengthen each other. Buddhism helped the Judge to cope with the pain of bereavement in his adolescence and in his old age. I suspect it helped him to cope with the knowledge that a great family lineage would die with him though, resolute to the last, he insisted that such a fact caused him no pain from the outset. Perhaps the price paid for this emotional serenity was a certain isolation but, given his position as a judge this could not have been exorbitant or limiting.

Finally, there is the Buddhist judge sitting in judgement on his fellows. His belief in reincarnation, illustrated by some typically quirky examples, might move some to wonder about the Judge's sanity, but such beliefs, it has to be said, are widely held in various cultures, including our own, and lack the essential characteristics of the morbid delusion. There is no evidence that his deterministic view of man and behaviour greatly affected his judicial performance; indeed, he was widely regarded as a benign judge, and such controversy as there was largely related to the leniency rather than the severity of his sentencing. Having said that, I still wonder at a view of the world which can cope with the horrors of Dachau and Belsen by seeing them as the understandable results of lives lived in an earlier incarnation. In one sense, of course, it is a comforting and a comfortable belief. Order and purpose are inserted into life, with the additional bonus that one is relieved of the moral imperative of doing very much to change life's remorseless course. After all, there will always be a next time, another life in which to obtain a fairer share of the good things of life.

More worrying is his simple insistence on the unreliability of defence witnesses and the basic solidity of those called for the prosecution. The image of the judge as detached and unbiased takes something of a knock at this stage – but I hardly believe that many who really know the reality of the courtroom and the judicial process will raise any eyebrows. The remote, rational and unbiased judge is one of life's fictions believed in very largely because believing in the alternative, while more sensible and more grounded in reality, is too demanding, too ambiguous, too worrying.

There are similarities between Christmas Humphreys's serene, Buddhist-inspired acceptance of death, his own and that of others, and, say, Malcolm Muggeridge's regularly stated desire to die. The serenity is interesting in that it stands in sharp contrast to the notion that religious belief encourages neurotic symptoms, repressed desires, unfulfilled needs and stunted personality growth. Freud contended that religion was the universal neurosis, and such a view has had an enormous influence. Yet throughout his life Christmas Humphreys illustrated the strength that is to be had from a firm religious conviction, the assistance afforded by faith in surviving setbacks, negotiating loss, accepting even death itself. Neurosis it may be, but of a kind that is not taken to doctors, results in no long-standing consumption of psychotropic drugs and absorbs no scarce, skilled medical resources. Doubtless there is a price and often it is paid, not by the firm believer so much as by those who live in the shadow of such beliefs. In the case of Christmas Humphreys, however, it is difficult to advance the case that his firm, unwavering, distinctive philosophy exercised a damaging personal influence on anyone.

When I interviewed Christmas Humphreys he told me he expected to live for several years yet for he had still much to do. In the event, he died within eighteen months. Shortly after his death, a close colleague in the Buddhist Society wrote to me and, in the course of his letter, he expressed the view that the Judge had appeared to virtually everyone who knew him an austere, remote and remarkably self-sufficient man. Did Buddhism shape him or did he find in Buddhism the philosophy of life which perfectly suited his temperament and personality? I tend to think the latter. I did not sense in his account of his life much change in his character. Even before his conversion to Buddhism he describes himself as someone who did not react strongly to things. The Buddhist way of life complemented his detached posture. It did not create it.

ANTHONY CLARE: Judge Humphreys, given that your faith, Buddhism, emphasises the illusion of the self, I anticipate that we may have some problems in persuading you to talk fairly exclusively about your own self. Do you enjoy talking about yourself?

JUDGE HUMPHREYS: No, but I'm quite prepared to if it helps anybody else to learn the lessons that I have learnt in eighty-one years.

CLARE: They've been pretty good years?

HUMPHREYS: I've thoroughly enjoyed almost every minute of the entire time.

CLARE: And talking about them?

HUMPHREYS: Yes, if it helps other people; but I'm not the type that wants to chatter about myself.

CLARE: As you recount them in your autobiography, the very early years of your life were very happy.

HUMPHREYS: Perfectly happy. I never had any unhappiness that I remember as a child. My parents loved me and I loved them. I had a very happy personal family life.

CLARE: Was it a wealthy family?

HUMPHREYS: No. My father was a barrister, the son of a lawyer. Those lawyers go back many hundreds of years. The Saddlers' Company in the City, of which I'm a member, goes back 250 years, and certainly 200 years of that involves a succession of lawyers, although my father was the first to be a judge.

CLARE: Did your family have a nanny?

HUMPHREYS: Certainly I had a nanny – I loved my nanny – and then I had governesses. One of them was a marvellous pianist and I can see myself now in a little white jersey curled up on the sofa with my teddy bears, listening to her playing Chopin; and today I think I know almost the entire repertoire of Chopin by heart, although I can't read a note of music.

CLARE: What was your mother like?

HUMPHREYS: My mother was half-Belgian, half-Yorkshire and she was a woman of great charm socially, who during the First World War suddenly surprised everyone by producing and founding the Belgian Red Cross in England – and that became of enormous help to what remained of Belgium.

CLARE: Was your family a very emotional family, or was it a fairly pragmatic, busy one?

HUMPHREYS: Pragmatic, if you want to choose between the two terms.

CLARE: How would you describe it?

HUMPHREYS: Normal, happy, call it upper-middle-class if there is such a thing nowadays – my father working hard at the Bar, my mother with many interests, and myself as an extremely happy child at a private school, a public school and then Cambridge University.

CLARE: Of course your adolescence coincided with the First World War.

HUMPHREYS: Yes, and that was unbelievably horrible. Nowadays it's difficult to make a younger generation understand what it meant – that every other woman in the street wore total black, that one million young men of England died over the Channel in France, that it was not a question of whether you had lost a relative but whom you had lost, and if you were young, how long you were likely to survive.

CLARE: The way we've talked suggests that there was a sharp

contrast for you, as a growing person, between a stable, happy, contented family life and this terrible occurrence.

HUMPHREYS: I got to my public school in 1915 or so, when the War had started, and it was in 1917 that my beloved only brother was killed. That to me was an appalling shock.

CLARE: What age was he?

HUMPHREYS: He was four years older: he was killed when he was seventeen, I was thirteen or fourteen.

CLARE: How close had you been as brothers?

HUMPHREYS: Not all that, because being four years older he was always one step ahead. He was at school ahead of me, for example. No, it hit me very badly in terms of religion.

CLARE: I'm interested to know the extent to which you had a relationship with him. Brothers tend to fight a bit.

HUMPHREYS: Very close. Whenever we met he, being the older brother, would try to help me with the problems of a younger boy.

CLARE: Were there many people in the house, or was it a fairly close, small-knit family?

HUMPHREYS: No, there were plenty of visitors coming for tea and later on also for supper or dinner; and, yes, my mother kept open house to quite a lot of relations of one sort or another and friends.

CLARE: Do you remember your brother going to the front?

HUMPHREYS: Yes, I remember him coming back on leave, and I remember him going back from leave.

CLARE: Did he have a uniform?

HUMPHREYS: In his uniform as a sub-lieutenant in the King's Royal Rifles.

CLARE: Were you alike as boys?

HUMPHREYS: I never knew him well enough, because four years is a very big gap between boys to know their innermost minds. He was always a few steps ahead.

CLARE: But his death seemed to change everything?

HUMPHREYS: It changed everything for me. It was like a blow in the face. You see at that school where I was at, Malvern, hardly a week went by, every other week at least, and some boy would be sent for by the housemaster, and told quietly in his study, 'John, I'm sorry I've got bad news for you, I've just had a telegram from your mother to say that so and so and so and so, your brother, your father, whoever it is, has been killed. Now you must be brave, etc.' I for one remember being quite stunned and not believing it, the whole mind rejected the possibility. I remember going up to school and people, older boys, sort of patting you on the shoulder, 'Sorry old chap, I hear the bad news, etc. etc.', and answering, 'It's all right, it's all a mistake, it can't be true'; totally rejecting the possibility that my beloved brother should have been killed. I think perhaps the circumstances affected one. After all, war is war and there were bloody battles going on. He was standing at the parapet, I think, somewhere near Ypres with an orderly, and everything was perfectly quiet, and a stray shell came over and blew him to pieces, and the orderly was untouched. Somehow that made it worse.

CLARE: And then what happened to you?

HUMPHREYS: I had up to that time been a sincere, practising, happy Christian for the Church of England.

CLARE: Your parents had been devout?

HUMPHREYS: Yes, I led the choir when I was at my private school – perhaps the happiest days of my life when I was doing that. I went to Malvern, so I went up to church or the big chapel on Sunday mornings before breakfast for Communion. I was totally happy in it, and I suppose Jesus was a sort of super boy scout in my mind, to be followed and loved and, if one could, imitated. And then this blow. I think it was mixed in my mind with some statement at the time. Some expressed horror in the press – 'Have we really got to a stage when our bishops are blessing our tanks as they go into battle, knowing that the German bishops of the same Christian faith and with the same God are blessing their tanks as they go into battle to kill each other?' That hit me particularly. I said, 'There's something wrong here', and I think almost immediately, almost before I left school (I came down rather early), I started reading as widely as I could, to find some other religion which had different ideas.

CLARE: What particularly were you looking for?

HUMPHREYS: Some way of life which would not be so grossly unjust and, as I would realise later, not so tied to what is called the theist concept, that is to say to God as being an almighty marvellous particular person, who judged and who forgave or didn't forgive, and so on and so on. I was already beginning to develop deeply the concept of total cosmic law, as I later called it.

CLARE: Had you at that stage accepted the death of your brother?

HUMPHREYS: I accepted. When the war ended I happened to be in

Piccadilly Circus. Extraordinary things were happening. People were going almost insane with the emotional relief – a woman standing on the curb at the corner with a Union Jack wrapped round her just standing there quite quietly crying, a man standing on a taxi with two other men on the taxi roof holding his legs while he was shooting off a revolver into the air. I found myself standing on a table in a restaurant somewhere, drinking a glass of champagne with my arm round a waitress, and I went home and solemnly told my father, 'Dad have you heard that the war's over?' And my parents were sitting quietly, not rejoicing: they were thinking of Dick, my brother, who had not come home.

CLARE: What was the impact on them of your brother's death?

HUMPHREYS: Very bad. Obviously my father adored my eldest brother, as often happens in a family like that. I think my mother preferred me. I think that's almost natural. They took it very hard, and therefore it became obvious what I was going to do in life. I'd gone up to Cambridge and obviously it would be the law.

CLARE: Do you remember the feeling then? Was there anger about his death?

HUMPHREYS: No, I never have been someone who reacts with strong feelings. There was, well, horror at the news. I don't know how else to put it.

CLARE: To what extent were the feelings you had about the Christian failure partly feelings of anger that this should be allowed?

HUMPHREYS: Yes . . . what's wrong with a religion that allows that to go on?

CLARE: Your parents stayed Christians?

HUMPHREYS: My father was never an obvious Christian. He didn't go to church. My mother did.

CLARE: You say that when you found yourself the only son in this family, it became apparent that the law would be for you because this was a family tradition. Had you any leanings in that direction yourself?

HUMPHREYS: I hadn't thought about it at that time. If anything, I was interested in becoming a schoolmaster. I enjoyed school and I liked the idea of teaching and I liked good teachers and I saw bad teaching. I began to have some idea, involving another boy whose parents could have afforded to help us, of starting a school as soon as we could; but when it became obvious that I should go into law, I took law at Cambridge and that was that.

CLARE: Had any teacher in your schooling been influential?

HUMPHREYS: I don't think so, but I liked them all, kept in touch with most of them.

CLARE: So when you went up to Cambridge it was to do law. What was your university life like?

HUMPHREYS: Perfectly happy, but I remember looking at the older boys who had come back from the war, seeing a group of them sitting in a circle on the lawn of Trinity Hall, Cambridge, picking daisies and almost silent and dazed. They hadn't woken up from the fact that this ghastly horror was over and that life was now before them and some of them aged twenty-two looked older men, as indeed they were, and I aged eighteen was almost a child in their presence.

CLARE: The impression given of the universities in the early Twenties is of happy, gay, sociable, gregarious places with people living out a sort of adolescence. Was it like that for you?

HUMPHREYS: No, because always I think round one were those who themselves had suffered and had been wounded and lost their beloveds. All of us had still, I think, some lingering sense of loss. On the other hand I was utterly happy at Cambridge, and I had plenty of friends. I found the Lodge of the Theosophical Society, and that interested me. That seemed to tell me more about religion generally. And I had found a book on Buddhism which is dated in its book plate as 1918, so I'd read that when I got up to Cambridge – and when I read it I said, 'Well, if that's Buddhism, then I'm a Buddhist.'

CLARE: Other people were seeking their solutions in political terms – indeed, you joined all three political parties.

HUMPHREYS: Only in order to go to the union to listen to the debates. As a joke I said, 'I don't care tuppence about any sort of politics but it's wonderful to hear great men, all the greatest men of the year came up.'

CLARE: It's a little unusual to find a lawyer totally uninterested in politics.

HUMPHREYS: I'm sorry: then I'm an exception. I couldn't be less interested.

CLARE: Did you have many friends at Cambridge?

HUMPHREYS: Yes, lots.

CLARE: Girl friends?

HUMPHREYS: No, don't you remember, there were no girls there. Indeed in my innocence I remember for May week – you know what I mean by that? – asking some girl up for dancing and . . . – well, where's she going to stay? I said, 'Actually there's an extra room in my lodgings, I'm told,' and somebody said, 'Don't be funny.' I said, 'Why not?' I honestly didn't understand why a girl shouldn't come and stay in a spare room in my lodgings!

CLARE: Were you particularly naive?

HUMPHREYS: Yes – I don't think there was quite so much of the immediacy of the sexual interest in friendships. I think one could have a great many boy and girl friends without that necessarily being part of it.

CLARE: When did you become interested?

HUMPHREYS: Probably when I met my wife, and we said, 'Hello, you again', and then we immediately talked about marriage. I said, 'Don't be silly, I haven't been called to the Bar yet.' I had just been called to the Bar, and we had to wait three years before I had the enormous income of £600 a year on which to get married.

CLARE: I note in your autobiography that around this time you had your horoscope read and you were struck by two elements in it. The horoscope said that in the matter of earned income you have nothing to fear . . .

HUMPHREYS: Yes, I haven't.

CLARE: . . . and you didn't then either. The other element intrigued me a little more. It said, 'Your troubles with the opposite sex will end with marriage' – a reversal of the usual rule. What troubles?

HUMPHREYS: I suppose I'd been squabbling. Yes, I may have had some friendship that went wrong, I don't remember, because the moment I met my wife – she was in the background all the time – it was quite obvious we were going to get married, and she helped me out of any squabble I was having with another girl.

CLARE: Apart from the disaster of your brother's death, I don't sense in your account any great emotional turmoil in your adolescence – or indeed in your early twenties.

HUMPHREYS: No, there wasn't.

CLARE: Even before then?

HUMPHREYS: Thoroughly enjoying everything.

CLARE: Even before your discovery of Buddhism you came across as being relatively content and at peace.

HUMPHREYS: Yes – I call it 'life-is-fun', and I'm saying so today, and every bit of it is fun.

CLARE: But it is dreadful.

HUMPHREYS: Of course it is dreadful. Of course the suffering is perfectly intolerable. But it's fun in my particular sense of the term, getting on with helping to get rid of it, that is the purpose of Buddhism after all, as Buddha said, 'One thing I teach – suffering and the end of suffering.'

CLARE: The account you gave of your mother fits that. She comes across as somebody who got about and did things. Is that the sort of woman she was?

HUMPHREYS: Yes. So was my father.

CLARE: Brisk?

HUMPHREYS: Yes.

CLARE: Like you?

HUMPHREYS: Yes. Vivacious, society woman.

CLARE: Not given too much to retrospective regret?

HUMPHREYS: No, nor was my father, nor was I.

CLARE: Did the death of your brother shake them in any way – did it come as a blow that shook the foundations?

HUMPHREYS: Only as a blow to the father losing his beloved son, and the mother losing a beloved son.

CLARE: So the search that you describe is not conducted by somebody lost, in pain, seeking solace?

HUMPHREYS: Lost in spiritual pain. I wanted life to be sensible, reasonable, to see the purpose of it, I wanted to see the journey ahead, how I should do it, or rather how I and my wife to be would do it, what we were going to do together; and therefore I wanted a religion that would help one to do it – religion being in my belief one of the many ways to the goal of every human being, indeed of all life, which is a return to the totality from which we came.

CLARE: You also wrote a curious poem when you were nineteen, I won't recite it all but you say – 'few enemies I had, and fewer friends, and no regrets for what has gone before', 'who leans upon the name of friendship lends to hostile fortune so much power the more' . . .

HUMPHREYS: '. . . saw naught but the workings of a perfect Law . . .' I'd already found the law of Karma, the Cosmic Law.

CLARE: But you were nineteen!

HUMPHREYS: Yes, but I'd read that book, you see, when I was seventeen – *Buddha and the Gospel of Buddhism.*

CLARE: Where did you get it?

HUMPHREYS: I found it wandering up and down Great Russell Street, all those bookshops there, trying books on this and that – Hinduism, the religions of the east. I found it and read it, and I've got it at home, with a book plate in with that date.

CLARE: And when you read it, did you have an immediate realisation that this was the answer?

HUMPHREYS: Just like that: 'That's right, that's true, that's for me.'

CLARE: A flash?

HUMPHREYS: A deep content, yes. Satisfaction, good, that's it.

CLARE: No doubts since?

HUMPHREYS: None at all.

CLARE: How do you explain that?

HUMPHREYS: By the Buddhist doctrine of a rebirth.

CLARE: But not everyone who reads that book will have the same experiences as you.

HUMPHREYS: No. On the other hand they may be impressed with it – it's a very good book on Buddhism, if they want Buddhism. Clearly I did.

CLARE: Have you ever had a sensation like that with anything else?

HUMPHREYS: Some other religion do you mean? No, it was as if I was being shown all about this life as learned from previous lives.

CLARE: Have you ever had that sensation with another person?

HUMPHREYS: No. My wife and I were as we regarded each other, each one half of a whole; we had lots of men friends, women friends, we adored each other. People have written apparently saying that they used to watch us looking at each other, well into life.

CLARE: Did your wife have an experience like yours? Was there a moment of revelation for her?

HUMPHREYS: She was older and had fought in the First World War in the Fannies, the First Aid Nursing. In fact she was decorated with a medal for picking up wounded under fire. She was quite fearless, Irish.

CLARE: Has anybody ever misunderstood the nature of your character and seen you as an emotionally cold person?

HUMPHREYS: Quite possibly.

CLARE: No one has ever said so?

HUMPHREYS: You see it perhaps in my enormous conceit – I don't know. That's their business. That's my stoicism – perhaps like Marcus Aurelius, if you like, when somebody came and complained to him, 'Master, it is perfectly intolerable the way this man reviles me and abuses me', and so on, to which the answer was, 'That's his business.' I rather take that line myself. If somebody says, 'Somebody was being very rude about you the other day', I say, 'I'm sorry, that's his business.' He may have been right, I don't know.

CLARE: When did you meet your wife? Can you remember meeting her for the first time?

HUMPHREYS: Yes, I can. I was taken to have tea with her by a mutual friend and we sort of looked at each other. Nothing happened then, but quite rapidly I was going back alone, and very rapidly we were almost saying, 'Hello, you again.' It was that sort – it wasn't emotional, it wasn't sexual, it was friendship, the intimacy of union of two parts of a whole, as we felt it. After that we did everything together, for fifty years. Colleagues. Co-workers.

CLARE: You didn't have children?

HUMPHREYS: No. She couldn't because her inside had been pulled to pieces by carrying heavy stretchers. They weren't supposed to do that. She had picked up the end of a stretcher with a heavy man on it, and had come back from the war in an awful condition. An osteopath took years to get her right, but she couldn't have children.

CLARE: How did you feel about that?

HUMPHREYS: Not the slightest worry, never worried me. I think I should have been almost annoyed if we had, because they would have got in the way of my life. My life was a day's work outside and coming back in the evening to get on with the work which already had become my *dharma*, as we Buddhists say – my duty, my job in life.

CLARE: But you're a man who places a heavy stress on tradition; and one of the traditions of your family, going back hundreds of years, is the Saddlers and the law. There's a man bearing your name, Christmas Humphreys, back in the 1750s, yet your autobiography ends with your being the last of your family line, living in North London.

HUMPHREYS: Yes, I haven't the slightest desire for children nevertheless.

CLARE: Why not?

HUMPHREYS: I see the way children even today cripple and confine the family – they stop them doing this, they make a nuisance of themselves, later on all sorts of squabbles and arguments and fightings. We never had that in my house. My house was a home of complete peace. And, incidentally, if I've got any political leanings it would be that the troubles of the world are too many people. If something could be done to reduce the number of children being born and the population of the world came down by about thirty per cent – practically all these troubles would disappear. But I'm not going to advertise that!

CLARE: But tell me: how would I know what caused you pain?

HUMPHREYS: What caused me pain? Failure to do what I was trying to do.

CLARE: But you've never failed to do what you wanted to do.

HUMPHREYS: Of course I have, because what I'm trying to do is too enormous. It is contained in the object of the Buddhist Society: to publish and make known the basic principles of Buddhism, and to encourage the application of those principles. I can't tell 50 million people all about Buddhism, though I do my best.

CLARE: Children would have interrupted all of that?

HUMPHREYS: Yes.

CLARE: How did your wife feel about it?

HUMPHREYS: She never suggested that she minded when it was quite clear that she couldn't have children.

CLARE: What age was she when she married you?

HUMPHREYS: She was ten years older – I was twenty-six, she was thirty-six. It makes a difference, of course. She was a silversmith by profession – she had her daily job and I had mine in the law.

CLARE: When you married, were your parents alive?

HUMPHREYS: Yes.

CLARE: Would your father have wanted a grandson?

HUMPHREYS: I don't know, I never asked him. I never discussed it. It was quite obvious to him early on that by her age and by her condition there wouldn't be any grandchildren. He never suggested he wanted them.

CLARE: And looking back, you say, 'No regrets.'

HUMPHREYS: No, none.

CLARE: Would you say you were lucky?

HUMPHREYS: No such thing as luck. No such thing as good or bad fortune. I agree with St Paul: 'Be not deceived, God is not mocked – as ye sow, so shall ye also reap.'

CLARE: When you've sat in court and you've seen before you a young man whose family was shattered, whose circumstances were much worse than yours, who had committed some crime which in turn further embarrassed and perhaps even wrecked the family, perhaps some sexual crime – how would you cope with the disparity between your experience, your life, your standards and those of this young man?

HUMPHREYS: Our previous lives. I had built up myself to be what I am, good, bad or indifferent. He had built up himself to be whatever he was, good, bad, or indifferent. I would therefore help him. I couldn't openly do it in court, but I never hate any single human thing that lives.

CLARE: You mean he's responsible for what he does and did?

HUMPHREYS: He is totally responsible, absolutely responsible. No God intervenes. The law is complete. The law has no exceptions any more than the law of gravity. So each man makes himself what he is and has made himself what he is and is now making himself what he will be, in many many lives to come.

CLARE: There is in law a notion of diminished responsibility.

HUMPHREYS: All right, but there's none that I know of in the cosmos. Gravity doesn't do this or that, more or less: gravity's perfect, complete, lovely.

CLARE: But how can you say that someone who was in a concentration camp in the last war was responsible for where they were?

HUMPHREYS: Why were they in that concentration camp? Because of what they had done in lives gone by. Why has the man committed murder? Because he's come to a state of mind in which he could do it, as many other people don't do it – but could do it when driven by the same pressure of circumstance. When I ceased to be a judge and was on television I was asked about Buddhism and about the law. 'Mr Humphreys, do you take your Buddhism into court with you?' I said, 'Yes. The man in the dock is me, because to me the whole of humanity is one, millions of forms of the same one life. Life is one, we are all brothers. Why don't we behave like it?'

CLARE: Within this understanding, where is evil?

HUMPHREYS: Evil is caused by man's not understanding the basic laws of life. Therefore he is concerned with self with a small 's' – 'I, I, I, I, I, I want this, I don't want that, you're in my way, get out of my way, if necessary I have to kill you.' The whole of his life turns around his own necessities, desires, hopes, fears – or his family, or maybe his village. Finally it's his nation, and he's prepared to die for his nation.

CLARE: Some would say that what you've just described is a rather chilling philosophy.

HUMPHREYS: Yes it is, it sounds so cold to begin with. But don't forget that out of the vast field of Buddhism came what I believe to be the greatest contribution to religion which any religion has produced – the doctrine of a being whose whole being is wisdom. And wisdom means love, total love, combined with total law. There is a saying – 'Love is the fulfilling of the law.'

CLARE: Can I take you back to the event that precipitated you into Buddhism – the death of your brother. I know, because you've described it elsewhere and you've hinted at it here, that his death illustrated for you the bankruptcy of the Christian explanation of suffering.

HUMPHREYS: The Christian explanation of suffering to the extent that it turns on theism. I've never said one word against Christianity as a religion for millions of people, but the one thing I cannot stomach about theism is the concept of almighty, absolute, total, unnameable God as a person who can do this, that or the other at His whim or will.

CLARE: So how does Buddhism explain your brother's death?

HUMPHREYS: By saying that he had so lived in previous lives that the time came when he would be unreasonably, suddenly killed. I can't imagine what those causes would be, but it was right that he should die at that time, in that place, in that way.

CLARE: And that consoles?

HUMPHREYS: I don't say it consoles, but it explains.

CLARE: And of course he will live again, so in a sense of course his death is only a passing phase.

HUMPHREYS: That's why, to a Buddhist, death doesn't awfully matter. We all die sometime, I say periodically.

CLARE: Which also means that you've lived before.

HUMPHREYS: Many, many lives – and I remember several. Thousands of people remember their past lives: only in the East is it commonplace to remember.

CLARE: What do you remember?

HUMPHREYS: I remember Rome so well that when I was reading Roman Law I came across a name and I jumped in my seat – Gaius Aquilius, that was me. But he only got into the textbooks because he'd invented some minor mode of proving something or other, whatever it was.

CLARE: How did you know it was you?

HUMPHREYS: I jumped in my seat when I heard that name. As soon as I got to Rome as a visitor I went straight into the Forum, and felt at home. I remember Egypt. I had a girl friend, a very close girl friend of a great many years, in fact until quite recently, and she remembered an incident between the two of us. A great many people believe.

CLARE: What was the incident?

HUMPHREYS: I was awfully pleased with myself, with my gold armour. I think I was in the bodyguard of Rameses II, and I had been misbehaving myself, alas, with somebody who was a virgin in some temple and the penalty of that was death. And she remembers me, her lover, being carried past her in some public place on some great occasion on the steps of a temple, on the bier, having been tortured to death. She remembers going up to the High Priest and winding her long hair round his neck to try and kill him . . . Well, needless to say – bonk! Somebody just struck her down and killed her!

CLARE: Some people find this impossible to believe.

HUMPHREYS: I don't mind what anybody believes. I know what I believe: as Jung would say, 'I also *know* some things.' You remember his last broadcast on television?

CLARE: When asked about God?

HUMPHREYS: Do you believe in God? *I know.*

CLARE: But Jung believed in a god – he was a theist in that sense.

HUMPHREYS: So do I, but my concept of the god is totally, totally impersonal.

CLARE: Have you ever been struck by the fact that some people place more store by personal relationships than others? That you have not necessarily found a great deal of your satisfactions in life through close personal relationships?

HUMPHREYS: No. I have lots and lots of friends and I'm sorry when they go and I'm sorry if they die or are killed, but because of my beliefs I'm not worried about death, anybody else's or mine, in that sense.

CLARE: Have you ever been depressed?

HUMPHREYS: I don't think so. I think the whole of life is fun. I don't mean it's funny, heaven knows I think I've got a deeper sense of the suffering of mankind at large than most people. The last time I was televising I had the best part of a hundred letters, and the stories they tell you of the suffering are perfectly ghastly. 'Can you help?' they ask. And I will often write back and begin with one sentence: 'You have got to begin, my dear, by accepting everything that you've told me.' I remember one woman writing back. She said, 'I didn't bother to read the rest of your letter: thank you, that's the word I wanted, accept it as right.' So I come back to my friend Marcus Aurelius: 'All that happens, happens right' – look round and you'll find it so, he wrote in his diary.

CLARE: But doesn't it lead to fatalism?

HUMPHREYS: Fatalism only in the sense that if I have put so many causes into operation, nothing on earth, God's earth or anybody's earth, is going to stop something happening sooner or later unless I can put into operation new causes to neutralise those ones.

CLARE: When your wife died, what did that do to you?

HUMPHREYS: It happened to be slow, and therefore I was ready. We said goodbye, and that was that.

CLARE: But her mind went a little, and that can be very distressing. There was mention of that in your autobiography.

HUMPHREYS: I went twice a week for four years to the nursing home where she was, to hold her hand.

CLARE: Was that painful?

HUMPHREYS: Yes, I suppose so, but it was my way of helping her to take what was coming.

CLARE: Her last words were, 'There must be suffering, the heart must break.'

HUMPHREYS: Yes, that was when her mind went rather suddenly, before she went into the nursing home. That was her message to me – that she knew the mind had suddenly cracked, gone. To all intents and purposes there was nothing left there in that body.

CLARE: It's a striking statement. I sense that that is not how you see life. There must be suffering, the heart must break, but you're talking about acceptance.

HUMPHREYS: No, the heart must break because none of us can take suffering and be utterly unmoved. You're a horrible person, there's something wrong with you, if you are not moved by the suffering of others. The heart must break with your beloved, or others. The heart must break, some people say, when you merely read in the papers of another million people killed unnecessarily in some religious war.

CLARE: Again one cannot divorce such considerations from your overall philosophy. You said of this death, and you had been married for forty-eight years, 'Here for me was no real parting, only a needful separation before reunion in some new job which hand-in-hand we share in our usual blend of love and laughter, just settle down and do.' The problem with that, and I don't want to sound irreverent, is that it makes life sound like periodic spells of gardening.

HUMPHREYS: All right – rather a good term!

CLARE: It's quite opposite, though, to the notion of the heartbreak of life, of losing your brother or your wife . . .

HUMPHREYS: Not heartbreak: wounding to a boy of sixteen, still hurting. Yes, I was hurt to hear.

CLARE: Do you ever wonder at the extent to which Buddhist belief came at a time when you needed something?

HUMPHREYS: That was my *karma*. Just when it was necessary, when I was ready for it, that book came into my hands. It changed my life, to doing what I was meant to do.

CLARE: Did you feel at home in Buddhist societies?

HUMPHREYS: Totally, in the temples, totally.

CLARE: You've been in Thailand, Japan, Burma, on the borders of Tibet: did you ever feel more at home in those countries than in Britain?

HUMPHREYS: I was always perfectly clearly English in a sense that I didn't cease to feel myself as English looking at foreigners. But I was totally at home: as Kim would say in Kipling's *Kim*, 'I waggled my toes in the dust and felt at home' in India, which after all is the home of Buddhism in one sense, and in the monasteries of the Tibetans.

CLARE: Were you ever tempted to stay?

HUMPHREYS: No, my duty is here, nothing would take me from London.

CLARE: What was this duty?

HUMPHREYS: To publish and make known the basic principles of Buddhism for the West.

CLARE: With a view that one day . . .

HUMPHREYS: That they needed it. If you understand and really apply Buddhism it kills all mourning, all fear of death, all the horror of death: that in itself is worth doing. It kills the injustice of suffering. It kills all blame. You don't blame somebody else for doing what he did that's your fault – you are to blame and so on. It's so wonderful, I find. It gives such an extraordinary balance, a reasonable, joyous life, living according to law, according to love, that I'd like to tell other people about it.

CLARE: But those societies in which Buddhism flourishes seem to have no less of their fill of human disasters than those in which it doesn't.

HUMPHREYS: When you say human disasters, I've found that all the Buddhists I saw in Buddhist countries are a much more naturally friendly people.

CLARE: Whereas here you don't think people are naturally friendly?

HUMPHREYS: I think the English would be if the government would let them alone. That's my view of politics. I make a joke that if I had power, I would abolish politics. Leave your village to look after itself, leave your town to look after itself. A great deal of the policy that's meant to help people is totally selfish, it's merely to help that party. I'm not interested in any party.

CLARE: What do you think would be the result of such a policy?

HUMPHREYS: I don't mind. That's their business. They will suffer the consequences of their actions – I shan't be alive to know about it.

CLARE: The difference between you and a non-Buddhist is that everything that happens is as it is.

HUMPHREYS: Everything happens right – Marcus Aurelius.

CLARE: So you can be neither an optimist nor a pessimist, just a realist.

HUMPHREYS: That's right. Realist in the sense that it happened because it ought to happen. Now it has happened, what shall I do about it? What is right for me to do?

CLARE: That brings us to the post-war period. You became a prosecuting counsel, and you were involved in some spectacular and famous trials. Capital punishment was still on the statute book. How did you feel about that? Why were you always a prosecutor?

HUMPHREYS: I wasn't. At the Old Bailey, six of us were the Prosecuting Counsel. Between us we did the cases for the prosecution of the Director of Public Prosecutions. At times I defended, and when I became a Queen's Counsellor I ceased to be a Public Prosecutor and became a totally defending counsel.

CLARE: Did you have any particular preferences, one way or the other?

HUMPHREYS: Yes, always prosecuting.

CLARE: Why?

HUMPHREYS: Because ninety-nine per cent of the people who go into the witness box for the prosecution are telling the truth, or trying to, and something like that percentage of those who go into the witness box for the defence are lying. And I like to prove the truth. I like to support the police, for whom I have enormous admiration. I like to support people who, against their will, come in to say what they are quite certain had happened, and I'm prepared to believe them. I was totally fair, I hope, with the jury. I believe I was called a fair judge.

CLARE: Gentle.

HUMPHREYS: All right, a gentle judge. But I always preferred to prosecute rather than lend my ability, my brain, my will to persuading a jury that black is white.

CLARE: Is that what you think a lot of defending is?

HUMPHREYS: Of course it is. No one in the whole court doubts for one moment that that man is guilty, and the jury can say 'Guilty' just like that.

CLARE: In your time you must have seen some spectacular miscarriages of justice?

HUMPHREYS: I only remember one in which I was personally concerned, out of all the murder trials I did. There was precisely one in which, in my view, the verdict was totally wrong. In other cases I'm proud to say that where I was not certain that the murder verdict would be right, I managed to get that man off from the prosecution end of the line, by my final speech.

CLARE: You were involved as prosecuting counsel in the Craig-Bentley case where, because of a difference in age, the older, less guilty man was hung and the younger and more guilty one was not.

HUMPHREYS: Yes, but the sentence had nothing to do with me. I thought that was perfectly horrible. One boy was actually under arrest at the time. He only shouted, 'Go have him, Chris,' or something like that, and the other boy went and murdered. Yes, of course I watched miscarriages of justice. Our justice is not perfect, but I believe it's the best in the world. I tell you this: that when we arrived in New York or Washington and had a meeting of eleven nations who were going to prosecute the Japanese in those post-war trials, the first thing we had to decide was what law we were going to collectively apply in order to do justice to the Japanese, and I'm told that within twenty-two minutes – somebody timed it – it had been universally agreed it would be English Common Law, since it was the world's finest.

CLARE: Had you been offered a High Court judgeship at the time, would you have accepted it?

HUMPHREYS: If it had been at the time of the death penalty, I rather doubt it. I don't think I could ever have brought myself to sentence a fellow human being to be hanged. I don't know, I was not offered one.

CLARE: But you could prosecute?

HUMPHREYS: Certainly.

CLARE: Knowing that your skill would actually bring a hanging about?

HUMPHREYS: No: knowing that I had a job to do, to put the facts as fairly as possible before the jury.

CLARE: And they would then be responsible?

HUMPHREYS: It was then for the judge to address the jury on the prosecution and defence, for the jury to decide, and for the judge to sentence. I'd done my job and I sat down.

CLARE: The belief I have most difficulty with in Buddhist philosophy is this notion that everything is, in some sense, right.

HUMPHREYS: Take the law of gravity: are there any exceptions to it? It's part of nature's law. Aren't the astronomers now coming round to seeing a total cosmic law? And the vast movement of all these solar systems; somebody was saying that our solar system we're so proud of is probably placed in the outer suburbs of the Milky Way – in other words, some tuppenny-halfpenny little thing that doesn't matter. Isn't our idea of time and space and of all these vast universes under the control of this vast, perfect, total, complete law, isn't that reasonable? I love it. I'm perfectly happy with it.

CLARE: To be a grain of sand in this vast cosmic universe?

HUMPHREYS: Certainly, to be a drop of water in the sea.

CLARE: This is a very different way of looking at life from that of millions of your fellow countrymen here in Britain.

HUMPHREYS: Of course it is. That's the difficulty of bringing Buddhism to Europe – that it has many concepts, which are totally different from our own.

CLARE: Do you have many non-Buddhist friends?

HUMPHREYS: Plenty.

CLARE: What do they make of you?

HUMPHREYS: I don't know. They just know that I'm interested in Buddhism, and they probably are not very interested in any religion. But I have plenty of Catholic friends.

CLARE: You're not just interested in it: it actually consumes your whole life.

HUMPHREYS: I don't say 'consumes', no. It is the law by which I live.

CLARE: But nothing is untouched by it.

HUMPHREYS: How could it be, if it's true? Truth is truth.

CLARE: The feature of Buddhism that strikes me is its detachment. It is outside the hurly-burly. Its emphasis is almost other-worldly.

HUMPHREYS: Yes, I'll take that. Other-worldliness in the sense that worldliness is self. I want this, I want that, I don't want this, is selfish, that's the world. Right.

CLARE: I'll press you a little about that because, in a sense, your life was easy, it fitted this model very simply. By and large your early life – compared certainly to the early lives of many people I see – was relatively content. It was happy. You had a relationship with a woman that lasted forty-eight years and, as far as I can make out, was contented.

HUMPHREYS: I've had a very happy life.

CLARE: You didn't have the responsibilities, the demands, the frustrations and the emotional strain of children. You travelled widely. You were not financially impoverished in any way. You had a career in which you fulfilled yourself. You saw and met many famous people. You had a notion of considerable achievement while you emphasised the illusion of self. You expressed it at every available opportunity. In what way did Buddhism have to meet any important psychological need for you?

HUMPHREYS: None, because I've been a Buddhist before in past lives. Good Lord, I didn't come to Buddhism for the first time in this life! How could I? How could I read a book, as a boy almost, and start lecturing on it quite soon, on totally different ideas almost unknown to the West in 1920? There weren't thirty books on Buddhism in 1920. I was giving lectures on Buddhism all over the place – 'It's wonderful stuff, listen, chaps!

CLARE: But you don't have to conjure up the notion that you'd known it all before.

HUMPHREYS: All right, I'm just conjuring up a notion. To me it is so basically true that I'd almost join Jung in saying 'I know'. I cannot conceive *karma* and rebirth not being true. I mean that.

CLARE: You wrote to me about this interview, and you said an interesting thing. Right at the end of your letter you referred to your emotions, and you said: 'They appear buried ten fathoms down. If so, they can stay there. Meanwhile at least I can't be hurt.' What did you mean by that?

HUMPHREYS: People often say, 'That really was horrible, I really felt very hurt by that, by what that man said.' I'm not. They can be as rude as they like about me, it can't hurt my feelings. I don't care two hoots what anybody says about me, unless they are telling me something I should have done – 'My God, yes, you're right, I wish I had, sorry.' If they prove I've been wrong or unfair or unjust and so on, yes; but I can't be hurt in the sense that most people feel hurt, wounded in their feelings. I say I haven't got any feelings, put them in the dustbin.

CLARE: Were you always like that?

HUMPHREYS: I think so. I can't remember any time when I was hurt. I might have felt I'd been wrongly treated, 'damned unfair' I might say, that's another matter – but I wouldn't go back to try and hurt that chap because he'd hurt me in that sense.

CLARE: You make it sound as if being hurt is absolutely unacceptable, a dreadful thing to be avoided.

HUMPHREYS: Yes, because it arises from ignorance. You don't understand the nature of the self, the nature of the almighty self, the absolute oneness of all life, in ten billion forms, of which I am one very complicated one and you are a complicated other.

CLARE: Sometimes being hurt can be helpful.

HUMPHREYS: Perhaps I'm wrong with your definition of being hurt, annoyed at what somebody else says. I don't feel anger at anything anybody says or does.

CLARE: When you see other people in emotional states of various kinds, what do you make of it?

HUMPHREYS: 'Can I help you?' – that's my answer. There are a hundred ways of helping. You can help by touch: when somebody's suffered a terrible loss, you instinctively put a hand on the shoulder. You can telephone – 'My dear, I'm so sorry to hear this.' You can write. Sometimes you're quite wrong. You think a man is emotionally worried; he's not, he's physically ill, and so on. Often your trying to help is clumsy, but are you trying to help, is that your ideal in life? To help as many people in as many ways to the one goal, the Buddha's goal, the end of suffering.

CLARE: You don't achieve this goal in a lifetime?

HUMPHREYS: Not in ten, not in a hundred. It's a cycle – birth, growth, decay, death round and round, what the Tibetans call the wheel of life.

CLARE: How do you feel about death?

HUMPHREYS: That it is quite inevitable, though it doesn't worry me in the least. That the only thing that concerns me is whether I've arranged my will and the appallingly complicated condition of my affairs. Otherwise I don't mind. In fact I've already got a provisional date in my mind.

CLARE: And it is?

HUMPHREYS: I shan't tell you that – several years yet. In other words, when I think I have done as much as I can do in this life towards my ideal, and I'm beginning to fail mentally and physically and so on and not doing it as well, I'll get out of the way.

CLARE: What do you think is your worst fault?

HUMPHREYS: Most of my worst faults, as other people regard them, I regard as virtues! I think perhaps a failure in true leadership, by being a little too cool and calm as to what is obviously the right thing to do. I see it, so I march towards it, and I may give the impression of being didactic, dogmatic and too pleased with myself in knowing what was right. Perhaps I am.

CLARE: You believe you will be back after death. Have you any notion in this life what you may be in another one?

HUMPHREYS: I've got a semi-serious notion of what I would like to do, and that is to spend a life in a more introvert way, to use a psychological term, to have more time for the meditation and deep thinking which I'm coming to now in old age. I'm finding re-reading books that I haven't read for many years terribly exciting. I'm now seeing them much more keenly, much more clearly, much more on a higher plane, and I'd love to get into a quiet corner and do that for a whole life. In other words, a retreat.

PETER MARSH

If a performance is to come off, the witnesses by and large must be able to believe that the performers are sincere. This is the structural place of sincerity in the drama of events. Performers may be sincere – or be insincere but sincerely convinced of their own sincerity – but this kind of affection for one's part is not necessary for its convincing performance.

ERVING GOFFMAN, *The Presentation of Self in Everyday Life*

Advertising is defined as making something publicly known with a view to increasing its appeal. It is an activity of particular interest to the psychiatrist in that it highlights, even exploits, the conflict, delight and difficulty we all experience distinguishing fact from fantasy. I am frequently consulted by people who feel far from desirable, who lack the means to project their personalities in such a way that others might find them socially agreeable companions, and who feel frightened and self-conscious about their seeming lack of any clear personal identity. Much of modern advertising quite deliberately plays on such preoccupations; all manner of things, from beer to fast cars, kitchens to cameras, are marketed in terms of the impact they will have on buyers. The world of advertising substitutes its own reality, its own particular world in which lounges are always clean and orderly, gardens trimmed and colourful, families harmonious and nuclear, and conversation preoccupied with need and the satisfaction of need.

But advertising does more than merely create a world of fantasy and artfully substitute for the real world. It subtly creates stereotypes – the successful businessman, the brilliant doctor, the reliable banker, the debonair actor – by fusing selected social characteristics, moral attitudes, habits of behaviour as well as modes of speech and dress. It provides a readily available guide to social roles. Indeed, the use of popular actors, television performers and sportsmen in advertisements blurs further the already shady line between the reality of the worlds these individuals actually inhabit and the world of the advertisement into which, for a modest or sizeable fee, they agree to step.

When I decided to interview someone from the world of

advertising, my producer, Michael Ember, suggested Peter Marsh. The driving force behind one of Europe's fastest-growing agencies, Peter Marsh's biography read like a script publicising a self-made millionaire. He was born in 1931 in Hull. His father was a brass finisher and turner, and Peter Marsh was brought up in a strong socialist and Methodist tradition. After working as, among many other things, a librarian and an actor, he entered advertising via the BBC and a TV commercials production company in Manchester. In 1966, with Rodney Allen and Mike Brady, he formed Allen, Brady and Marsh and the company began with the Cyril Lord carpet company account (which was later to prove a near-catastrophe when the company went bankrupt). Since that time, lucrative contracts for advertising companies, such as British Rail, the Midland Bank and Woolworth's have been won and have rocketed ABM into the Top Ten advertising companies in this country.

But what makes Peter Marsh particularly interesting is that the methods employed in refashioning, say, the image of British Rail appear to have been employed by him in refashioning Peter Marsh. For Marsh has turned his back on Hull, his working-class roots, his socialist and Methodist birthrights as resolutely and as firmly as Arnold Wesker cherishes and cultivates his own roots in East End Stepney. Over the years, Marsh has expressed regret at having been born working-class, regarding himself in Hull as a 'cuckoo in the nest'; and since then, his success has acquired an entrepreneurial, unashamedly capitalistic business image utterly at odds with the political and philosophical values of his parental home. The marketing of Marsh is carried out with an assiduous eye to detail, from the neatly pressed suits, the monocle, the gold cuff-links and the silver-knobbed cane to the baronial mansion, the elaborate dinner parties and the aura of money and success which he explicitly aims to exude. His energetic selling of himself is quite unashamed and carefully orchestrated.

And in these activities Peter Marsh exemplifies the notion, most persuasively described and analysed by the American sociologist Erving Goffman, that how we are seen by others, how 'sincere', 'straight', 'upfront' we are thought to be in our social dealings, is largely determined by our 'performance' – defined by Goffman as the activity of an individual which occurs during a period marked by his continuous presence before a particular set of observers, and which has some influence on the observers. The way we project ourselves involves a performance infused by signs, which dramatically highlight and confirm certain aspects of our 'selves' which we wish to be accepted as intrinsic to our characters. Most of us are given clues, hints and stage directions, in childhood and we build on and develop these in such a way that our adult performances are 'natural', spontaneous and of a piece. Every now and again, an individual's early upbringing will be disrupted, as in the case of Nell Dunn, and the part, so to speak, will not be learned. The result is a certain kind of perplexity and confusion in adult life, as the individual experiences the recurrent feeling that he or she does not know quite what the appropriate behaviour, responses, even feelings are in given situations. For the most part, however, the process of developing a persona, equipped with opinions, values, appropriate dress sense and speech, is a steady one.

But there are individuals who utterly reject the script which life has given them at the outset and write their own. A celebrated public example was Brendan Bracken who began life in the small Irish market town of Templemore in north Tipperary of Roman Catholic and Republican stock and clawed his way into some of the most exclusive preserves of English social and political life by the age of twenty-five, becoming an Englishman on the way. Peter Marsh's transformation, while not quite in that class, has many striking similarities. Like Bracken, Marsh appears to have wanted desperately to escape from the class into which he was born. Like Bracken, Marsh has no great desire to be reminded of his personal past. I suspect that Marsh, like Bracken, was not a popular schoolboy, being regarded as too assertive and selfish – a school contemporary of Marsh remembers him in precisely this way. Bracken, according to Charles Lysaght's perceptive biography, assiduously learned the ways and values of an English upper class to which he did not belong but to which he passionately aspired and into which he to some extent penetrated. Marsh throughout the interview emphasises the extent to which he too has had to learn the stage directions, the lines and the cues which people born and educated into the world of big business, wealth, property and power have long absorbed into their very marrows.

In this context, it is interesting to see how often theatrical metaphors are used, and Peter Marsh's brief but curiously important involvement with the stage cited. All the world is not a stage, declared

Goffman – adding, however, that the crucial ways in which it isn't are not easy to specify. Much of Peter Marsh's life takes place on a stage, and there are appropriate stage directions to be followed. 'If you wish to be treated first-class, act first-class' – so the early and by no means rich Peter Marsh travelled first-class rather than save money because the experience of first-class was what he wanted, and not the money. The most attentive care is paid to such matters as the clothes he wears, the prints on his walls, the music in his stereo cassette, because, in a way that is more true for him than for many others, small manifestations of personal taste and inclination define him, place him, declare him before the world.

Once I said to a patient who had an unenviable reputation for speaking her mind, and thereby rendering herself an extremely lonely person, 'Why don't you just keep your thoughts to yourself and act more sociably?' She looked appalled and objected that what I was suggesting was tantamount to deception. In one sense she was right. There is an assumption that there is a congruity between what we are and how we behave. Yet Marsh turns the direction of that relationship around. Where my patient insists that what she is determines how she behaves, Peter Marsh suggests that how he behaves determines what he is. He behaves as a thrusting, dynamic, successful, aggressive entrepreneur and people believe that that is what what he is 'inside'. It is the classic advertising strategy: tell them that Guinness is good for them and, by God, it will be.

Like the advertisement, Peter Marsh's life is an exaggerated version of most people's lives. The problem is that whereas most people are not continually conscious of being in a play, declaiming lines and integrating with the other players, Peter Marsh is. The price, as he explains himself, is that life is like a compulsive dynamo which ceaselessly whirrs and in which the fear of failure rather than the satisfactions of success provides the remorseless impetus. Losing control is also feared, for the very good reason that since this is a play he must always be prepared and in control: 'There can't be asides if there are no lines in the first place.' And is there a place for spontaneity?

In the opening interview of this series, I asked Glenda Jackson whether the performance on stage borrowed from emotions and passions off-stage. She doubted that this happened, pointing out that on-stage all is scripted and everyone knows what everyone else is going to say. Hence life on-stage is very much more predictable, safe and manageable than life off-stage. Peter Marsh's response to the unpredictability and insecurity of life off-stage is to turn it into a play, with himself as the leading player and the director and those with whom life brings him into contact as his fellow artistes. Our argument about the inordinate lengths to which he goes in planning social events, dinner parties and intimate lunches can only be understood in the context of this particular view of life. In his anxiety to ensure that his world view is the accepted one, Peter Marsh imposes his persona on his world to a far greater extent than any of the other eight individuals interviewed. This may explain why he is the only successful businessman among them!

In an article in *Punch* (characteristically written on the subject of success), Peter Marsh referred to Sir Peter Hall's admission that he constantly lived in fear that one day 'they' would find him out and that his success, standing, reputation and ability would all disappear. Whether Sir Peter ever said any such thing is neither here nor there – it made an impact on Peter Marsh. In one sense, he has nothing to fear, for he has revealed a great deal already about how he has made himself – enough to keep most people happy that they 'know' the kind of person he is. In another sense, however, his fear is understandable, in that his whole existence is built around not merely a self-made persona, but the destruction and elimination of an earlier persona which, every now and again, intrudes. In my interview, there are curious omissions: there is not much about his father and his father's death but a great deal about his mother, surprisingly little about his siblings although they are all living, a brief reference to a marriage that failed (but more than a suggestion here that the Peter Marsh who was involved might have been closer to Hull and Hull values than the contemporary entrepreneurial businessman, in that his first wife was the redoubtable Pat Phoenix of Elsie Tanner fame). But what makes the interview with Peter Marsh fascinating is the way in which, far more frankly than most, he confidently describes the enormity of what he has done in erecting a new Marsh, when most of us are content to make a few minor alterations to the self with which life equipped us at the starting-gate. But then Marsh would point to audacity as yet further proof that, as he puts it, the talents and capabilities that he has 'are there and innate and would have emerged anyway'. In that same *Punch* article he wrote: 'I believe that success is as inevitable to certain people as the sun rising in the East and setting in the West.' Yet this remarkably deterministic view has to be contrasted with his free-market philosophy and his apparent belief in the need for many more people to hold his view of life, power, achievement, money and status. So why the occasional emphasis on the innateness of his success? Permitting myself a rare speculation, I feel that Peter Marsh cannot bear to believe that the secret to his success is indeed to be found back in the now-despised hearth in Hull. It may owe something to an ambitious, proud and over-possessive mother; and to some other, more crucial experience which has sown powerful seeds of a fear of failure which Marsh admits now keeps him awake at night and presses him upwards and onwards when logic and another world view might suggest that he stay his hand. I doubt if it is quite as fatalistic as he would have it but, given the importance to him of ensuring that the new Peter Marsh has no sense of any debt to be paid to the old, I understand why he prefers to see it that way.

ANTHONY CLARE: Peter Marsh, how do you feel talking about the real you?

PETER MARSH: It's very pleasing to one's vanity. There must be a slight touch of apprehension when one gets underneath the tinsel on top to find the real tinsel underneath. I would say pleasure tinged with a slight amount of apprehension.

CLARE: In a sense, interviewing you is a little different from most of the other interviews in this series. Advertising and psychiatry are at opposite ends, one might say of a time spectrum. I'm interested in the past; you, as I sense from many of the things you've said and written, are interested in the present and the future. You accentuate the positive, you are about achievement. I'm interested more in terms of, not so much the flaws, but certainly the problems that people have overcome and are in the process of overcoming. What is in it for you? Why should you bother with this kind of activity?

MARSH: First of all, if you take the business itself, there are roughly 3000 people of any consequence in the advertising business – by that I mean management, creative people etc. So you're operating among an élite that is quick-witted, humane, very conscious of the world around them, and creative. It's a very exciting environment in which to work. I think also – and I certainly fall into this category – that all good advertising people are either conscious or unconscious seekers after stress. Adrenalin is a fix that you're totally addicted to, and the whole of your life is committed to winning battles. I had a dinner at my house last evening for a very important client at which we made a presentation. What we were seeking to do was change an attitude of mind by gathering facts together and using persuasion and logic and research. At the end, because you've succeeded in that communication process, you get this great feeling of satisfaction, and then you have dinner. It's calling into play not only intellectual and emotional capabilities, but that magic ingredient known as personality.

CLARE: What has that got to do with looking at yourself?

MARSH: I think we've all of us got to find a niche in which we feel comfortable and I, like many people, accidentally found myself in advertising.

CLARE: So why bother to go through this kind of exercise if you are comfortable?

MARSH: This interview? This is part of the ego enlargement. One loves being talked to, one loves being talked about – and clearly you feel you have something that may be of interest to say, because you certainly learn a lot as you go along. Also, anybody who succeeds is part of a small élite minority. I am a great élitist and therefore it's not incompatible or inconsistent that you and I should be talking across the microphone – you learn something and I learn something.

CLARE: You would be confident, by and large, about what would emerge?

MARSH: Yes, yes, yes. Less so in this form of interview. If one takes the title 'In the Psychiatrist's Chair': you're clearly seeking to get behind the public persona – which one will go into almost by a knee jerk reaction – to find what lies behind the pain, the problems, and the disadvantages. That's why I took the challenge on, because clearly this is a more rewarding interview and, by implication, a more dangerous one – for the simple reason that if you seek what lies behind, one is revealing things possibly that one would not reveal in public that one would privately.

CLARE: Is it fair to say that you would normally not have very much time for this kind of navel examination?

MARSH: No, I think the very nature of the job that I do is concerned with human behaviour attitudes – we do a massive amount of research and therefore . . .

CLARE: I meant as an end in itself. You're mentioning the business spin-offs and the professional advantages; I mean as an activity in its own right.

MARSH: I believe in it totally.

CLARE: Why?

MARSH: Because I started life as an actor, and an actor to be good must be an acute observer of human behaviour and attitudes, and you've also got to read character. Part of my job is to read character and therefore that little twitch of the nostril, that thinning of the lips, that slight move of the mouth can tell you an enormous amount about people – I'm very interested in this sort of thing.

CLARE: Do you find yourself reflecting a lot on your own past?

MARSH: Occasionally, but I think certain things you just learn from and take lessons out of. I believe, for example, that any man has got to cut the umbilical cord with his mother at some stage, and once you've learned that yourself you observe it in other people. I was with a chap the other day of fifty-six who still phones his mother every day. He's got a problem!

CLARE: Is your mother still alive?

MARSH: No, she's dead.

CLARE: Was it difficult to cut the cord with her?

MARSH: It was more a process of attrition than one moment when the mighty knife descended. If you've got any intelligence, there's a video tape in your mind that's recording events and happenings even though you're unconscious of it. I've noticed girls at around the age of puberty, about twelve, they really assess their mother as a woman and they may say, 'Gosh, she's an old fraud' – and this is when you see the mother then trying to reject the daughter and denigrate her to the husband. This hasn't happened in my family, I hasten to add, but this is my observation. I think men mature more slowly than women and have a dependence on the mother to a certain age: it's in the teens that you begin to look at her with rather more beady eyes.

CLARE: What sort of woman was she?

MARSH: I think she had a lot of my characteristics. She had a very large fund of personality. She was very musical, had a high energy quotient, was very single-minded. Regrettably she was a sort of emotional vampire, really.

CLARE: In what sense?

MARSH: In the sense that if you are a pretty boy, as I was, and a talented boy, as I was, in a working-class environment you do stick out like a new sixpence. She got an enormous amount of reflected pleasure and glory out of my achievements. What you learn over a period of time is that it's a one-way relationship. She is taking out, but not putting much in. If you look at human relationships, you learn as time goes on that certain people didn't get on with either or both of their parents, and they learn to judge their parents.

CLARE: Was there a moment that you can recall that sort of realisation dawning?

MARSH: Difficult to isolate one. It was more like the colours of a spectrum or a rainbow – one starts to blend into another. You start observing things for example, that she's not a very good housewife, that the place is not as tidy as you would like it, that there's an emotional harp being played.

CLARE: Do you think it left a scar?

MARSH: Oh yes, inevitably.

CLARE: What sort of scar?

MARSH: I think the learning process in the family is innate and unconscious, and if you then have got to create your own family you look back on what you've experienced and say, 'Gosh, I'm learning things here which I should have absorbed by a process of osmosis.' Re my relationship with children, I had to learn how to be a father because I don't think my mother handled it terribly well.

CLARE: What about your relationship with women?

MARSH: Going back to puberty and so on, I think all energetic men have a high sexual quotient, or a high sexual capability. So no great problems.

CLARE: One of the problems of being a pretty boy is that a lot of attention is received mainly from older people, usually older women, and it becomes easy for the boy in question to get attention without having to make too much effort. A certain relationship with women can develop – a power relationship, in a way.

MARSH: Yes, I think that attention thing is very debilitating, though pleasant at the time. It's distorting, and if I could have an action replay of my life I would certainly try to eliminate that content, because you become too conscious of yourself and too self-conscious. I think you've made a very penetrating point. Certainly from older women there is flattery and involvement, and that can lead to involvements of a sore, personal and deep nature.

CLARE: Did, and does, this ability to manipulate people give you a certain pleasure?

MARSH: Yes. All successful people have got to be like that. 'Manipulate' sounds pejorative. You've got to lead, and lead by example . . .

CLARE: I was being deliberately pejorative because I am getting at something on the border of shamefulness. Manipulation is a skill you know you have, and that in itself gives a certain pleasure. Was this something you realised you had early on?

MARSH: Absolutely, yes. Early on you recognise it by some reaction that has occurred rather than by some process that you have entered into. It's only by retrospective examination that you say, 'There is a process there.' It's known as charm – and that again is death, because you start consciously applying it.

CLARE: Did anyone – a girl friend or anyone close to you – accuse you of being a manipulative man?

MARSH: No, no, no. I mean one saw by their reaction – but women tend not to have that clinical attitude of mind.

CLARE: What sort of reaction do you mean?

MARSH: The person who analyses me most precisely and really carves the slices off the salami so delicately is my own wife. She has a penetrating mind and will hold me up for examination in a most healthy way and tell me what my motivations are. She's absolutely a hundred per cent accurate, but she's the only woman I've ever met who's been able to do that.

CLARE: But before she came along?

MARSH: Well one didn't have this depth of relationship – this is what comes of twenty-five years of marriage.

CLARE: Another price that the pretty boy pays is that those around him don't like it very much – his peers, for example – and it can lead to a certain kind of alienation.

MARSH: Yes but if you're born into the working-class environment that I was – there are gradations in the working class: there's the upper working class, there's the middle working class, and there's the – ugh! I came in the upper end of the working class – you are still out of phase with your environment, and so people recognise you as such. It's rather like if you go to Nepal and they choose that little girl who's going to be the princess – she's part of the community, but separate from it. You're very conscious that you're separate from it.

CLARE: It wasn't an environment you liked very much?

MARSH: No, I disliked it intensely because all my aspirations lay outside it.

CLARE: But we're talking about you now as quite a small boy!

MARSH: Yes. At the age of ten I really became hyperconscious of it, and I consciously improved my accent.

CLARE: Why?

MARSH: Because I wanted to escape from this environment in which I felt desperately uncomfortable, and of which I did not feel part.

CLARE: You didn't like the Hull accent? Your father spoke with it?

MARSH: No, he spoke with a sort of Peterborough accent, not a Hull accent. The Hull accent is a very ugly one. Neither of my parents spoke with a very ugly accent.

CLARE: But it wasn't your father's accent that you adopted?

MARSH: No, no, no, no, no, no! My aspirations lay totally outside my family, totally outside it.

CLARE: But you were experimenting with an accent as early as ten?

MARSH: Oh yes, yes, yes.

CLARE: So in early adolescence you were already distancing yourself from your schoolfriends?

MARSH: Yes, absolutely, absolutely.

CLARE: How did they respond to that?

MARSH: They recognised you as something different. I went to a Grammar School at eleven, and if you're a leading light in the dramatic society, if you are a boy soprano with a rather good soprano voice, which I had, if all your activities are related to music and the arts, by definition you're separate; and so the voice translation is a natural part, because if you learn singing your accent by definition must become more pure.

CLARE: Did you have any friends?

MARSH: Yes, yes.

CLARE: Do you still have any from those times?

MARSH: Yes, but there's a great distance now between us. I'm actually going to have dinner in two weeks' time with a school friend. He's an Air Vice-Marshal and he's a guy who sort of leapt out of the environment. By definition there must be very few people you could keep in touch with because you were separate from them – and you must be separate from them, you can't help it.

CLARE: Do you go back often?

MARSH: No, no, no.

CLARE: When you do, do you see anything there that evokes an emotional response in you?

MARSH: You can't ever escape your roots or your background, so I will respond to Northern figures of speech, Northern attitudes, to seeing that brown water of the River Humber and that fair nithers you as it comes off the river and those craggy faces. It's part of your heritage, you can't escape it.

CLARE: At that time you also seem to have been struggling to free yourself from some kind of disorder or chaos. What was that?

MARSH: Anybody who's lived in a disordered household . . . You have a sense of order, which is really putting a personality together. You'll over-react to some extent, in sense of personal appearance, organisation etc. I've seen it in many other people.

CLARE: Was it an emotional disorder in your family home?

MARSH: A combination. The physical disorder, which there was to some extent, was also reflected, I think, in an emotional disorder. Therefore you put that right in your own environment.

CLARE: Does this mean that you have a highly developed intolerance of disorder?

MARSH: Absolutely. You become intolerant – it's a reflex action you've had to develop yourself, rather than having precedents to guide you. You have to learn to go to bed early. You have to learn to pace yourself. I used to put my trousers in a trouser-press at the age of ten because I wanted to look smart – and that again is a way of trying to create some personality with no guide-lines. You will over-react: you become intolerant, and that is an aspect of character many successful people have. If you had them in this chair, you'd find that they were responding rather violently against certain things which disturbed them as a child. I started to sleep badly from about the age of ten, and this was again a sense of disquiet – I am fortunately able to exist on about three to four hours' sleep a night.

CLARE: Disquiet and unhappiness?

MARSH: Yes – disquiet equates to unhappiness.

CLARE: When you think back as you're doing now, do you feel some of those emotions?

MARSH: Laterally but not deeply. It's like if you open a school exercise book and you see that big unformed writing – you can recognise it, but it is distant from you.

CLARE: So the main residue of that time is a certain anger?

MARSH: I suppose deep down it could relate to the intolerance.

CLARE: Is that anger charged by other people recalling similar backgrounds more positively?

MARSH: No, no, no, no – but anger and aggression will be released if there is something, like disorder, which related back to that time. You will respond more quickly to it than anybody who did not have that problem.

CLARE: You had a brother: what age is he?

MARSH: He is in his early thirties.

CLARE: And a sister who was older than you. By many years?

MARSH: About three years, three or four years.

CLARE: What about your relationship with her?

MARSH: Well, these are distanced.

CLARE: Did she change her accent?

MARSH: No.

CLARE: What did she make of your transformation?

MARSH: It's like if you have a footballer born in the family – the family react and change their approach.

CLARE: No, it's not quite, because in doing what you were doing, whether you wanted to or not, you were making a fairly public judgement about Hull and the accent and the lifestyle and the values and so on. It's not just a specific talent with which you are born: it's a whole new way of life that has been adopted and that does affect those who haven't taken a similar step, those who are from within the same family.

MARSH: But, Anthony, you're seeing that with the clarity of retrospect, sitting in this studio in London W.1. If we go back to my childhood there was I, as a child, singing, acting, performing, giving sermons from day one.

CLARE: But your sister would have had feelings about it?

MARSH: Yes, but I never discussed them with her, so it's very difficult to know what the feelings were. I can remember the canon at the local church saying, 'That boy will go far' – and this again was something you got used to people saying.

CLARE: What I'm trying to get at is what you thought the impact of such a statement was on other members of your family?

MARSH: I've never considered it. I'm too preoccupied with myself.

CLARE: Is that what they said about you?

MARSH: No, no, no – that's what I'm saying about myself.

CLARE: You're not saying that as if it's a statement about everyday.

MARSH: No, I'm saying that if you have got to make that social and economic leap it's a major act of energy, will and commitment because you have no precedents to guide you, no culture you can plug into, nobody that can help you. By definition, you become tunnel-visioned – literally.

CLARE: You say you had nobody to help you – but you had a sister three years older than you?

MARSH: Yes, yes, yes – but they're not in the same intellectual or aspirational mould. That is a matter of fact. Children react without rationalisation – they just react to the environment they're in.

CLARE: But I'm talking about emotional support, not intellectual or aspirational.

MARSH: You can have emotional support but if there is no dialogue that you can conduct that will be meaningful because maybe you find it as a child difficult to have that sort of dialogue, you'll use emotional support and you'll respond to it, it's not much more than that.

CLARE: What does your sister do?

MARSH: She is retired.

CLARE: And your brother?

MARSH: He's a social worker.

CLARE: A social worker – now that's a very different activity to yours!

MARSH: Don't get me on to social workers!

CLARE: Why not?

MARSH: If you're in the free enterprise part of the economy and you have to sign enormous tax cheques as I do, and you actually set up a company as we did, three men and one girl in one office, you realise money doesn't come from anywhere, you've got to make it happen, and you're putting everything on the line including your house, your family, your respectability – then you do look a little charily on the amount of the national pound that goes on things like Social Services etc. You find it's gone up to fifty per cent, and no economy can sustain that degree of public investment.

CLARE: What would your brother say to that?

MARSH: I've no idea – he must do what he has to do.

CLARE: These are not things you've ever discussed?

MARSH: No, no, no.

CLARE: I sense no great emotional bond between you and your siblings?

MARSH: No – but there is fifteen years' difference. I'd actually left home, so it's rather difficult to have a sibling relationship when you're not siblings in that sense.

CLARE: And your father?

MARSH: My father died when he was fifty-eight.

CLARE: What was the relationship between you and your father?

MARSH: Very good, very good. You have this knowledge when you get older – you look back and say, 'Gosh, I wish he was here now.' All people say that, it's not isolated to me. He was a very God-fearing man a good trade union man, a good Labour Party supporter – his life revolved around the word 'good'.

CLARE: You have more positive memories of him than of your mother?

MARSH: Yes, yes, yes. Because you respond very positively to good things, everyone does.

CLARE: But somehow he didn't have the same manipulative qualities as your mother in relation to you?

MARSH: No. I think many men do not have the same manipulative qualities as women, because that's the way they achieve their ends. That is why this Women's Lib is a load of nonsense. If we go to my father, I have a memory of him during the war – I was a child during the war – and he was on war work and would be working ten, twelve hours a day, so he had very little time to do other than rest, recuperate then go back to work again. I have memories of him taking me to the Methodist chapel and singing the hymns and so on and so forth, and he supported his mother, who was in very difficult straightened circumstances. One reacts to a very good man.

CLARE: A feminist might well say that the reason your mother invested so many emotional needs of her own in you was that she had nothing else.

MARSH: That is a hypothesis.

CLARE: And what do you think of it?

MARSH: I would dispute it totally.

CLARE: Why? What else had she besides the talented Peter Marsh?

MARSH: I find it difficult to answer that totally because you're not in a position of being with your peers when you talk about your mother and your father, because the age isn't the same, the emotional experiences aren't the same, the background isn't the same. This is where parents are judged fairly or unfairly – and I in my turn will be judged by my children fairly or unfairly.

CLARE: But make a guess – because you were very important to her.

MARSH: Yes, but one of my beliefs, and this is something I've got very strongly from my own wife, is that when you're looking at children you're looking at the only form of immortality you have, and what you put into them is not for return – it's so that they will pass that on to their children. I do believe in these things. I do not believe that anything was put into me in that sense by my mother to be passed on. I think it was taken out, and I'm intelligent enough to realise that.

CLARE: What was she taking out of you?

MARSH: Satisfaction, satisfaction. And it is not uncommon, it is not uncommon.

CLARE: You mean you would have been paraded around.

MARSH: Yes.

CLARE: Exploited?

MARSH: Yes.

CLARE: Shown off?

MARSH: Yes, yes.

CLARE: And, in a paradoxical way, you therefore owe your major abilities to her.

MARSH: It depends what you mean by owe. The innate capabilities I have would have emerged anyway.

CLARE: Why do you say that?

MARSH: Because it's programmed into you.

CLARE: But that's as hypothetical as the objection you made earlier.

MARSH: No, no, no. It isn't hypothetical. I have observed, and I am absolutely fascinated by, successful people.

CLARE: Yes, but I'm talking about you.

MARSH: If I could relate it back to me – because you're saying it is hypothetical – I'm trying to defeat your hypothetical statement.

CLARE: You won't be able to prove that your talents are innate: that has defied the scientists, and continues to do so. What you might be able to do is point to an ancestor who had similar abilities.

MARSH: No: I want to point to people I have met. You say, 'Where does their success come from?' and you realise there's an 'X' factor in successful people that will make them succeed in spite of their environment because there's this energy – and all successful people have an energy quotient higher than the norm.

CLARE: There's a very respected school of thought which says that one of the common features is a powerful mother.

MARSH: Well, it could be.

CLARE: But you're very reluctant to concede that.

MARSH: Maybe. All I'm trying to put is another case which says that success could flow from innate qualities, where you do it in spite of and not because of – which is a reasonable hypothesis.

CLARE: It's a reasonable one, and the reason that you are fond of it, it seems to me, is that it has certain emotional advantages. It frees you of any debt. You are your own man. You can leave this background freely. It owes you nothing, you owe it nothing. But on the other hand if there's something in the hypothesis which suggests that your mother's ability to portray you as a great performer, to hawk you round as an actor, to admire your singing voice and generally tell the world that 'This boy Peter Marsh is really quite something, and he's mine' may be related directly to what you now are, a great public performer. That seems to distress you.

MARSH: No, it doesn't. If we take Menuhin's parents, particularly his mother, Ivor Novello's mother, and Noel Coward's mother, they consciously used every artifice within their capability to extend and develop the career of their son. O.K.? Now if you extended it to my case, I would say, 'Fine.' If that particular situation pertained, I would be agreeing and nodding my head vigorously. Certainly I went into the Choir School at York, certainly I was put in touch with a theatrical agency: but none of those positive things occurred, it was all passive and it was all taking in. If we take John Osborne, and he was in the theatre at the same time as I was, he has looked at his mother and has come to the conclusion that perhaps she didn't do as much as she could have done to help him along his way. He's been quite honest about this. I am making an intellectual distinction between the Noel Cowards, the Ivor Novellos and their mothers, and the way they positively provided mechanisms to progress their sons' careers, and those that don't. I must make this distinction.

CLARE: You are very fond of Menuhin as a comparison. Why?

MARSH: I think because he's a very noted fellow and had a talent which was demonstrated at an early age, about seven – and if it swims into your consciousness you use it as an analogy.

CLARE: But his talent is a specific one. What is the equivalent talent that you have?

MARSH: I've never thought about it in those terms. I certainly haven't got a prime talent as strong as his.

CLARE: But I am struck that when you look for comparisons you usually draw musical ones, and particularly that one.

MARSH: Yes, but I did mention Ivor Novello and Noel Coward: they had a more diffuse talent. John Osborne is a playwright. I've written plays, but I haven't written as good plays.

CLARE: But Yehudi Menuhin recurs. I've seen it time and again.

MARSH: I'd find it difficult to explain, other than he's a convenient analogy.

CLARE: When we were talking about where these talents originated or how they were encouraged, perhaps we should have specified what talents we were talking about.

MARSH: Yes. Again, these things happen in spite of and not because of. If you've got a singing voice, you've got a singing voice, if you've got a sense of pitch, you've got a sense of pitch, if you've got a sense of rhythm, you've got a sense of rhythm, and to you it's as natural as anything.

CLARE: But what are your talents?

MARSH: I can remember my first day at school as a child when I was five years old. They immediately cast me as King Cole, would you believe, and I walked around saying, 'Rub a Dub Drum, Rub a Dub Drum, Today's Monday come come come . . .' They hadn't been brainwashed or anything, but they said, 'Oh here's a boy, I think he'd be rather good' and so . . . What I'm seeking to explain is that you're positioned that way and you start doing it naturally without even thinking about it. You're the one who is asked to read to the class, you're the one who's asked to make up a story, you're the one that's asked to sing, you know you're asked to do it because they're responding to what they perceived in you; all you're delivering is what is natural to you, and you haven't even thought about it.

CLARE: Despite your earlier portrayal of your background, it actually cultivated you. You were constantly picked up. In another environment, where maybe there were many Peter Marshes all jostling with each other, you might not have emerged.

MARSH: No – I believe a peer group produces excellence because it produces a comparison and it produces energy and it would bring out even better things in you.

CLARE: What it doesn't produce is your sense of exclusiveness.

MARSH: Maybe not. Given the chance to have been born in a comfortable middle-class home and, as a result, having had less injection to succeed, I'd have opted for being born into the middle class – let me make that quite clear.

CLARE: Let's subject that to dispassionate scrutiny. Your emerging from Hull and your building yourself into a new person is directly related to your current success. One could not, in a sense, be easily thought of without the other. When you say that you would have preferred not to have had to come into this life in that way, we're not just talking about your past: we're talking about your present. Are you saying that what you are now involved in – the driving yourself, the achieving and so on – is not something you would have wanted?

MARSH: That's a very good question! What I am doing now I find a perfect fulfilment for what preceded it, and the whole of my actions and activity have been fuelled by that original source, which is what we were talking about. If I'd been born in a middle-class environment the same capabilities would have still been there – the energy, the drive, the musical capabilities, the organisational capabilities – and they would have been channelled into a meaningful territory, perhaps with less pain in arriving there in the first place.

CLARE: But you must meet people who come from this middle-class background that you might have preferred, people who had a lot more advantages than you, who have a fair amount of talent, and you must secretly – or perhaps not so secretly – say how little they have made of it?

MARSH: I have a motto hanging on my wall which says, 'Nothing in the world succeeds like persistence.' It goes on to say: 'Education will not allow you to succeed, the world is full of educated derelicts.' I believe that whatever environment you have, if you're designed to be a failure you'll be a failure, and that's a fact of life. You cannot programme into people that which they don't have.

CLARE: It's interesting, that recurrent image you have of programming. Yet at the same time as we discuss this you point to different influences which, taken together, appear every bit as powerful as these genes inside you. If I concede, for a second, the idea of an innate talent, what are the influences in society that make that talent flower or wither? Your familiar portrayal of your background suggests that it was not particularly conducive to the flowering: yet, as you describe it, it was in fact very conducive!

MARSH: If you were born in the South rather than the North and the London theatres were available to you and the London agents and the art galleries and so on and so forth, you would be much better off because you would accept that sort of metropolitan life as a natural part of your culture, as opposed to living in Hull where there's one theatre and you'll go once a year to the New Theatre to see the pantomime, where there's only one art gallery and there are no theatrical agents. In spite of that limited input you might succeed. If you translate that person to the London environment, where those things are freely available, you'll flower more quickly, more comprehensively and with greater depth. So I'm saying it's in spite of and not because of. You're saying it's because of; I'm saying it's in spite of. Given a different cultural input one would have done it even more quickly, and perhaps better.

CLARE: What are the aspects of you that you are less taken with?

MARSH: Less taken with? I would say intolerance. Take my own children: they have been in social contact with people from the first moment they could comprehend anything. We used to take my daughter into restaurants at four months old. So they found the social communication thing not anything they think about. It just happens. Whereas if you've got to come up through the social ladder, the first time you go into a major first-class hotel it's an emotional barrier you go through. How do you conduct yourself at a cocktail party, how do you arrange a dinner party? Now if those have been programmed as part of your environment you absorb them, *you* don't need to programme them, and if they haven't you've got to programme them. If anybody could find another way I'd be delighted to hear of it, but it doesn't exist. That will lead to a certain intolerance on occasions. You will not tolerate bad organisation or sloppy behaviour; sometimes you will not tolerate disagreement, because you are convinced and know that you are right.

CLARE: What are you like as an adversary?

MARSH: Rather difficult, I would say. I wouldn't like to be against me.

CLARE: Can you enlarge on that?

MARSH: Merely that you are committed to winning, and by that I don't mean indiscriminately or the subjugation of real values, I don't mean that at all – you actually choose the ground, and that ground has got to be fair and honest, because one thing I do believe in very strongly is a Christian ethic; I believe in these moral values very strongly, so it's got to be consistent with that. But having said that, watch out, because I will win anything that is worth winning.

CLARE: Does it ever disturb you the extent to which winning obsesses you?

MARSH: No, it's a fundamental part of the character – you've just got to respond to what you are.

CLARE: Is it a twenty-four-hour preoccupation?

MARSH: Yes, oh yes.

CLARE: So you sleep badly. Is that something you regret?

MARSH: Yes, but you regard it as part of the price. There's a price to be paid for everything. If you're a first-class athlete there's the pain barrier, or if you're a first-class opera singer. I just regard this as one of the hazards that one collects along the way. For instance, I was making notes at 3 o'clock this morning.

CLARE: But someone like you has an impact on those immediately around them. You've mentioned your wife, who clearly is quite a remarkable person. What about your children?

MARSH: They are remarkable in their own way, and I think they draw that principle from my wife, who has created the home, the love, that they need very desperately. By that I mean all children desperately need love, not that there's a deficiency in my situation.

CLARE: But is a father such as you a formidable figure to have in a house?

MARSH: Very much so, and that's why she has acted as the filter on occasions between the force of my own requirements and the effect on them.

CLARE: Because of this intolerance we talked about in relation to organisation.

MARSH: It comes out in the family, absolutely. If you look at the whole history of successful fathers – I won't name any on the air, but there are a great number of very successful politicians, business leaders, musicians, who had difficulties with their children of a massive order.

CLARE: What is the main intolerance that comes out in relation to your children?

MARSH: I suppose expecting them to behave as automatons in certain situations. But you learn to recognise this.

CLARE: What situations?

MARSH: Treating a home a bit like an office, and therefore expecting them to react in the same way as people in an office, which clearly they're not – you learn that over a period of time. I find this has been a most enriching part of my development. I'm going with my son tomorrow to Queen's Park Rangers and we're going to sit there and discuss the match afterwards and go for a walk and so on: I think this is part of the learning process that goes on until finally we meet the great reaper in the sky – and even then we're learning something, because you learn what that mighty transition is like. Children, I've discovered from other marriages, suffered in some way or other because of a job or because parents have had to move around and so on. It's not a unique thing, and I don't think that mine have suffered any more than one would reasonably expect, because of the very solid home background we have.

CLARE: What about failure: are you intolerant of that too?

MARSH: I'm only intolerant, I would suggest, if that failure was self-induced and predictable and arose out of a character weakness rather than an act of God. If a tile drops on someone's head and his performance is affected as a result, there's enormous compassion there. I spend a lot of time trying to deal with matters of that nature, but if somebody is a soak, a drunk, is not using their capability, that is different.

CLARE: You are your own boss and a lot of other people's, and that's the way you like it. In fact there's very little in your life that you would willingly delegate to others.

MARSH: My wife – I don't control my home life. I delegate to her dramatically.

CLARE: How much do you put your work aside when you go home?

MARSH: To the extent that I am capable of, and that varies according to the day and the week.

CLARE: When you go on holidays, do you put aside your work?

MARSH: Not totally, but this is where my wife is marvellous: she helps me to turn off, and I will discuss certain things with her that she will give me advice on.

CLARE: But ultimately she subscribes to your ethic?

MARSH: The hard work ethic?

CLARE: Not only the hard work ethic but, in a sense, Peter Marsh Enterprises, which includes the domestic environment as well.

MARSH: No, she keeps our domestic life very separate because we are very private people. This is why we escape at the weekends and so on. She obviously subscribes to what I am doing, the way that I'm doing it, what our aims and objectives are and we have a great compatibility in what we believe are the right things and what we believe are the wrong things: that's the essence of a marvellous marriage, and no good man can make a good business without a good woman.

CLARE: But we're talking really about the extent to which you not only control your life but ensure that almost every element in it is programmed, to use your word. It extends to minutiae. For example, a dinner party will be planned some weeks ahead. It may involve only six people, yet menus will be sent out, and people will be instructed how to come.

MARSH: Not instructed: given the appropriate information so they can maximise their enjoyment in the evening.

CLARE: Supposing they don't follow the requirements?

MARSH: You're posing a hypothesis which doesn't exist. People who want to come to a dinner party will tend to be senior business people, or politicians, or whatever; and they respond to good organisation because the alternative is cock-up and chaos. That's why you write and confirm, you say what the dress is and have a place setting worked out.

CLARE: Don't say 'you' because I don't do any of those . . .

MARSH: I do certainly, and other people do. I'm not isolated in this.

CLARE: When you start to discuss something that you do, you use the word 'you'; you address me as if I'm doing it. You control the world to the extent that when *you* do something you assume everyone does it that way.

MARSH: No, I don't.

CLARE: We've just had linguistic evidence!

MARSH: No: you're taking the linguistic evidence and then extrapolating it to an absurd degree!

CLARE: But people don't send out dinner party instructions on what to wear and detailed menus well in advance even with a highly organised social life, and you know they don't!

MARSH: Can I correct you on the facts? What people do is to send out an invitation and say what the dress is, because if it's black tie and you turn up in a lounge suit you're going to feel a little awkward and that is a concern for your guests.

CLARE: For an ordinary lunch party?

MARSH: No, no! Dinner parties. Certain dinner parties are black tie.

CLARE: But you specify dress for lunch parties too!

MARSH: Not for lunch parties – you'd say it was informal because you don't want people left in a state of confusion. Particularly women, they want to know whether to wear a long dress or a short dress or whatever. It's not a requirement I've created, it's something you respond to. As far as the menus are concerned, these are the mess arrangements that you make as a host to make sure everything is in the right place at the right time. There's nothing unique about this – you're seeking to build a sort of context out of normal efficient social behaviour.

CLARE: And you run your domestic and your social life with the same degree of personal control as your business?

MARSH: Absolutely, and people love it.

CLARE: I'm not in a position to comment whether they love it or not: what I'm intrigued by is the reason you do so, which is the same reason as you run your business in the way you do – because the alternative, as far as you can see, is the enormous awesome spectre of, in your word, 'chaos'.

MARSH: Absolutely.

CLARE: Chaos! Chaos for you covers everything from the collapse of your empire to a lady ringing up asking whether she should wear a long dress rather than a short!

MARSH: This is an umbrella word – I wouldn't call that chaos! Let's go back to this. You recognise the ease and comfort that comes from a well-prepared evening. If there is a long walk up the drive, you've got to think, 'My God, supposing it rains that night, what happens to our guests?' So umbrellas are provided. The people arrive, particularly your wife with her long dress and her hair just been done beautifully. If she has got to walk up the drive in the rain her evening will be ruined, so a little bit of thought and care has provided the umbrella to give that social comfort to your wife – it's your wife I'm worried about, Anthony, not my own! It's rather like planning a night at the theatre. If you don't meticulously plan, and everything's in the right place at the right time, the actors will bump into each other, they'll fall over the set, when they reach for the gun it won't be in the desk, when they try and fire it, if it is there, there won't be a cap in for the bang to go off. Life happens to be like that, and if you see the alternative – which I have seen – of chaos, particularly when large sums of money hang on this and you're presenting for a large billing client of several million pounds, if you don't plan it meticulously you are lessening your chances of winning. It's like the F.A. Cup – you only get one chance of winning!

CLARE: But in the full flood of that I'm rendered almost speechless – which those who know me will recognise as an unusual state of affairs! Can I just put to you that there is a price – that recurring theme – to be paid for that: that if you plan so that every eventuality is taken care of, there is no spontaneity.

MARSH: Absolute rubbish.

CLARE: Well the only person who can be spontaneous is you.

MARSH: Shall I tell you something? It's rather like farce in the theatre: if you plan it and rehearse it beautifully it gives you the opportunity to extemporise and be spontaneous according to the situation, because you're totally confident of your lines, your moves, your wardrobe and everything. You can only be spontaneous when you've got the framework that gives you that ease of mind to be spontaneous; it gives you the opportunity to be able to deal with the unexpected and turn it to great advantage, so that people are not discomforted. Without that planning you cannot be spontaneous. I am a perfectionist and I am an achiever and people that are blessed or cursed, however you care to regard it, with those particular qualities will on occasion look at something and get severely discomforted by even an abstract exercise. That's a fact of life. You cannot prevent your mind working, and you look at something and say, 'My God, that's badly done!'

CLARE: Does something that jars or interrupts that sense of order irritate you?

MARSH: Definitely, yes. Absolutely.

CLARE: Even me challenging it?

MARSH: On occasions, yes – of course.

CLARE: I am struck by the fact that the other image you use to describe life is of a play with people in roles. I have no doubt at all what your role is.

MARSH: Absolutely! Upstage centre, upstage centre!

CLARE: You've two roles then, because you're also the director!

MARSH: Could well be, could well be!

CLARE: That won't do. 'Could well be': in fact the occasions you've described are set pieces, and you write the scripts and by and large do the producing.

MARSH: I wouldn't dispute that, I wouldn't dispute that.

CLARE: Do you delegate much?

MARSH: As far as possible. But delegation can mean abdication on occasion.

CLARE: If you were to go on leave would you cut the phones and go off to Acapulco, or would you stay in touch?

MARSH: Stay in touch.

CLARE: You'd still be making crucial decisions?

MARSH: We are a fast-moving business – it's rather like the Prime Minister, she doesn't cut the phones off when she goes because suddenly the Falklands may be invaded. Our business moves as quickly as that, and I've got to respond to and be responsible for those sorts of key crucial decisions.

CLARE: I hypothesise that there is one area where you are not the controller, where you're an obedient follower, and that is domestically.

MARSH: In many respects certainly I am – I wouldn't dispute that for one moment.

CLARE: For example, who organises the holidays?

MARSH: My wife, brilliantly. She will clear it with me but she organises it brilliantly. I do, however, complain vigorously if there's something I don't like about it – and very unfairly. And I will be told I'm complaining very unfairly.

CLARE: What about aspects of your life you regret? You were married once before: is that something you regret?

MARSH: This was over twenty-five years ago: it's like the child's exercise book analogy – you recognise it, but it's not part of you.

CLARE: Had you become the new Peter Marsh by then, with a different accent and golden jewellery and the monocle?

MARSH: Not the golden jewellery. I couldn't afford it in those days!

CLARE: But you were on your way? It wasn't as a Hull boy that you were married the first time?

MARSH: It's so long ago, it's difficult to make a reasonable judgement on it. If you move into the world that I'm in, it's so dramatically different and so compelling and so all-embracing – it is a wonderfully satisfying world because it covers every aspect of the arts and music, of business behaviour, of social attitude, travel, whatever – that it's difficult to look back to Hull, it's so far ago.

CLARE: Did it last long?

MARSH: Not very long, no – about eighteen months I think.

CLARE: Looking back, does that suggest that you have a flaw, and that you've got to be on guard about it?

MARSH: I think everybody is conscious of things they're better at rather than things they're worse at, but you will take account of whatever you're good at and try and do it as well as possible, and if there's anything you're bad at, if you're smart you'll either not do it or you'll get somebody else to deal with it. Like my wife organising the holidays – she's much better at it than I am, and therefore she will do it brilliantly. She's also much more intuitive about people than I am, and therefore I will take her judgement about people.

CLARE: Are you ambitious for your children?

MARSH: Yes, yes.

CLARE: Anything you would like your son to be?

MARSH: No, it's not defined in those terms at all. All I'm ambitious for is that they are successful, given their own targets. The problems we've had have been so minimal. They don't drink, they haven't been into drugs or anything and there are no problems. But I wouldn't like them to be the drop-outs I've seen. That would cause me great anxiety.

CLARE: Supposing your son were to become what your brother is, a social worker?

MARSH: I would try to dissuade him against that fruitless area of activity. If, however, he had sufficient reason and belief and was going to achieve something, then fine. In the final analysis he would have to make up his own mind, but I do think that you can give capsule wisdom on occasion that can be useful.

CLARE: Would you want him to be like you?

MARSH: He couldn't be like me because he didn't come from the same background. He will move with greater ease and therefore he will do it in his own way. You can't reproduce what people have done, ever. You just can't do it.

CLARE: Would you say you're a happy man?

MARSH: The glib answer is yes, because you are doing what you want to do. I think if you asked Sebastian Coe if he was a happy man he would hesitate and then say yes. In order to get your happiness you've got to accept the necessary pain and problem that goes with it – so, yes, I am.

CLARE: Do you ever feel driven from inside?

MARSH: Yes, all the time, all the time.

CLARE: Do you ever wish that you could take time out?

MARSH: If I wished to take time out that would show that my inner drive was changing its direction or losing it's momentum, so I would plan accordingly, because I'm rich enough now to be able to say, 'Right, let's change direction.'

CLARE: You are rich enough, are you not, to sit on a tropical beach, put your feet up, listen to your favourite music and say, 'To hell with all this'?

MARSH: Ultimately yes.

CLARE: People may wonder why someone in your position doesn't do precisely that?

MARSH: That's why they're sitting at home rather than being interviewed by you: because they don't understand.

CLARE: What don't they understand? That what drives you must always drive you?

MARSH: The drive is programmed into you and that's a fact of life. It's not unique to me, it's common to people that are successful in these terms.

CLARE: The one thing you cannot control is turning it off. You cannot do that. There are moments, presumably, in the small hours of those sleepless nights when you wish that you could?

MARSH: Oh yes – but it's temporary, and you know it's temporary.

CLARE: Do you ever feel that you might be losing control?

MARSH: Once you felt that you'd take steps accordingly to make sure that you didn't.

CLARE: Do you ever get depressed? Do you ever wonder, 'Why am I doing all this?'

MARSH: You get depressed, everybody gets depressed on occasions, and one of the things you learn is that depression is temporary and you walk through it. There's no disaster that would faze me, because eventually you know you'll get through it.

CLARE: So you look forward with a considerable amount of confidence?

MARSH: Yes, because I find that when you think you've reached the destination you haven't: it's just a Clapham Junction along the way.

CLARE: You could look me square in the face and say that you have no fears of cracking up?

MARSH: No – I have no fears.

CLARE: Why not?

MARSH: Because I take steps to ensure that I will not crack up. I know the tensile strength of my character, I know the tensile strength of my physique and I will be able to judge if that physique is beginning to run down, I will be able to judge my own capability of dealing with a situation. If that occurs I will take steps.

CLARE: But don't some great people crack?

MARSH: I've seen men crack, and this is why we go back to the very secure domestic base, this total confidence that I have in my domestic security and the love and warmth of family that I escape into. I do not, other than in the pursuit of my job, flog myself physically – no nightclubbing, I'm not out boozing, I'm not out drugging. I'm physically strong, and I'm husbanding that. I'm looking at my own control panel, and don't forget I've had stress for so long now I can recognise it. I know when I'm getting very tired, I know when I'm getting very fraught, I know when I'm over-reacting to a situation, even though that may not prevent the over-reaction. You're looking at something you've acutely observed over a great number of years; you've also acutely observed other people over a great number of years, and you know when people are going to crack. You can read it, very, very specifically.

CLARE: So in that sense you are very much the master of your fate.

MARSH: You've got to be.

CLARE: Do you see yourself as a likeable man?

MARSH: In some respects, yes. Yes I do.

CLARE: Are there things about you that you feel people find very difficult to cope with?

MARSH: You become totally intolerant of anything except achievement.

CLARE: It's like a drug.

MARSH: It is, like a drug, lovely.

CLARE: You're hooked.

MARSH: Absolutely, it's very exciting.

CLARE: When the time comes for a withdrawal, how will you cope?

MARSH: I'm coping now. You must be able to. The people who can't fail are another failure and I couldn't bear to fail at that either.

SPIKE MILLIGAN

I'll change my state with any wretch,
Thou canst from gaol or dunghill fetch;
My pain's past cure, another hell,
I may not in this torment dwell!
Now desperate, I hate my life,
Lend me a halter or a knife.
All my griefs to this are jolly,
Naught so sweet as Melancholy.

ROBERT BURTON, *The Anatomy of Melancholy*

There are almost as many theories of humour as there are Irish jokes –
and almost as few that are convincing. There is something rather dull
about people when they try to explain why certain things make us
laugh. Sigmund Freud, in a book which stands apart from the rest of
his writings by being a study of normal rather than pathological
psychology, did attempt to provide an explanation. He distinguished
between what he termed tendentious jokes, which serve a sexual or
aggressive purpose, and innocent jokes, in which the humour depends
only on the mental activity associated with the joke technique,
whether it be an incongruity, word play or representation by the
opposite. Tendentious jokes, so this theory goes, make possible the
expression and partial satisfaction of sexual or hostile impulses in the
face of an obstacle that opposes direct expression of the impulses.
Whatever the merits or otherwise of Freud's view of jokes, his theory
emphasises the relationship between aggression and humour, a
relationship upon which professional and amateur psychologists have
speculated regarding humour itself and those, the clowns and the
comedians, whose task it is to generate it.

From the viewpoint of Jungian psychology, the clown is seen as an
archetype, ritually expressing in an appropriately controlled though
seemingly uncontrolled fashion, the repressed aspects of a given
society. The clown, and his verbally articulate counterpart the
comedian, handle something which is not quite proper, something
even a little shocking. As L. H. Charles, an analyst of American

humour, observed, the comic plays with fire – but he is not the fire, and the moment he identifies with the fire he is no longer funny. The fine, delicate sense of mastery that characterises the consummate comedian is lost, and the comic becomes ineffective, pathetic, even disgusting. That balance reflects the control which the comedian demonstrates over a tabooed phenomenon. The comedian, too, subverts man's serious schemes of control and domination. Lurking behind the comedian's mask is often a moralist anxious to redress what he sees to be a distorted, repressed or unbalanced set of values in society. One of the oldest and most revered ideas about the comic figure is that the outward performance, posture and manic behaviour belie the real individual, and that hidden not too far under the greasepaint and the laughter is a sad, melancholic Pagliaccio with a highly developed sensitivity to the world's injustices and barbarities and an overpowering desire to shout his rage. There have been a number of comic performers whose private lives appear to have been far from joyous – one thinks of Chaplin, Keaton, Sellers, Hancock – but we remain puzzled at the enigma represented by the coexistence of a comic gift and a melancholic spirit.

This enigma is personified in Spike Milligan, a man whose manic punning, deliriously fertile imagination and quirky, anarchic sense of the absurd fuelled the rise of the Goons, arguably the most innovative comic series in the history of British radio. At the same time, he has suffered from recurrent periods of such corrosive depression as to have required a number of admissions to psychiatric hospitals.

He was born Terence Alan Milligan on 16 April 1918 in India. His father was a soldier in the British Army. Both his parents were Roman Catholics, so the young Milligan was educated by the Christian Brothers in Poona. He spent the first eleven years of his life in India before he, his brother Desmond, and his parents moved to Lewisham in South London in 1933.

In the years before the outbreak of the Second World War, he began to work as a singer and a jazz trumpeter. During the war he served as a Lance-Bombardier in the Royal Artillery (where he got the nickname 'Spike') but was blown up by a shell in the Italian campaign and had to be invalided out of the army. After the war he made his début on radio and in 1951 his career as a comedian began in earnest with a radio series, 'Crazy People', which eventually became 'The Goon Show' and brought him considerable fame.

Round this time, in the early 1950s, he suffered a series of mental breakdowns and his first marriage broke up. In 1962, he married again, co-wrote two highly successful plays, *The Bed Bug* and *The Bed-Sitting Room* with John Antrobus, and was a supporter of the arts initiative, Centre 42, directed by Arnold Wesker. In 1970, he made a film entitled *The Other Spike*, in which he relived his experiences in psychiatric hospitals. In 1977 his second wife died tragically of cancer, and in 1982 he married for a third time, to Shelagh Sinclair. He has three daughters and a son.

Over the years Spike Milligan has displayed an extraordinary constellation of talents as a novelist, poet, actor and playwright; but it is as a comedian or, as he makes plain in this interview, as a clown that he is best known and regarded. In the past he has, from time to time, reflected on the relationship between his personality, his mental instability and his comic gifts, but until I met him I had no consistent picture of how he related them together. Sometimes he seemed to attribute his mental illness to his wartime injury. Yet there is a substantial gap of almost ten years between that injury and his first hospital admission. Again, in his writings there is more than a suggestion that his shy, sensitive, even abrasive personality may have actually pre-dated the war injury, and that other factors, such as his family background and his departure from India, may have played a crucial part in his subsequent ill health.

Spike Milligan has already written and spoken a fair amount about his mental breakdowns, and he has identified himself as a sufferer from manic-depressive illness. As befits the name, this illness is characterised by a severe disturbance in mood which results in the afflicted person's suffering profound depression which in turn often gives way to an equally profound elation with a subsequent swing back to depression and so on. When depressed, the individual experiences a severe melancholia and a sense of absolute despair and wretchedness which, if particularly desolate, can result in suicide. When manic, the individual experiences a marked elation which varies from enhanced liveliness (so-called hypomania) to violent, uncontrollable excitement. Aggression, anger, pressure of speech, distractibility and impaired concentration go to form the typical clinical presentation. There is, in addition, a flight of ideas, so-called because there are often only the slightest and most tenuous links between the ideas expressed – the sound of a word may produce a pun, or a rhyme lead to a complete and sudden change in the direction of thought. The elation of mood, the incongruity of the thoughts expressed and the infectious quality of the patient's manic feeling can be quite hilarious – in the early stages of mania, patients can be extremely amusing and verbally adroit.

Spike Milligan's particular brand of comedy relies very heavily on word puns, rhymes and other verbal gymnastics. In the interview he gives a couple of examples – 'I read the accounts of your life in India.' 'You mean you found the accounts? God, I thought I'd burned them'; 'Your mother was highly strung?' 'She was hanging from a rope from the ceiling' – and he provokes the question, raised in the interview, of the extent to which his constitutional propensity to hypomanic and manic illnesses underwrites his comic gift.

For most sufferers, mania plays havoc with their public and private lives, ruins their careers and severely taxes families and friends. One of the most terrible examples is that of the late poet, Robert Lowell, as chronicled in his biography by Ian Hamilton. While Spike Milligan seems to have achieved fame and a reputation as a great comic genius by virtue of his manic swings, he too has paid an enormous price in terms of the toll taken of his own health and his relationship with those close to him.

The other, perhaps related, feature of his personality to be discussed at some length is his sensitivity. He provides dramatic examples from his childhood and his early adult life in support of his being vulnerable to the world's horrors and easily wounded by its barbarity and cruelty. This sensitivity fuels his anti-vivisection and anti-blood-sports activities, and stirs great gouts of anger from within his soul. But, and this is not uncommon in sensitive individuals, he has a reputation of being less than tolerant towards the flaws and inadequacies of others. He seems to find it difficult to acknowledge that, wittingly or unwittingly, he causes pain to others. Obsessed with the absolute horror of pain itself, he finds it very hard to face the fact that he can cause it in others.

So it would seem Spike Milligan confirms the assumption that within a great comic there is often a deep well of pain, anger, passion. A striking facet of the interview is the extent to which he wishes to turn away from the adult world to that of the child. The child's world beckons him, and he has shown his instinctive understanding of that world in a number of extremely funny books written for children. He has an immediate sense of the child's love of the absurd, and an immediate empathy with the relative lack of complexity, the directness and the honesty of children. For some people, such as Judge Christmas Humphreys, it is the unsatisfactory aspects of children – their noise, their demands, their egocentricity – which predominate. Spike Milligan will have none of this, and shamelessly idealises the innocence and the goodness of children. Quite why is explored with regard to his own childhood, and his tendency to idealise the early years in India (in contrast to the grey, pre-war years in suburban London). It is interesting to note that although he is a much-travelled man, he has never returned to India. It remains the India of his childhood, while the rest of the world has the unsatisfactory aura of adult life bestowed upon it by the grown-up Spike. Like Groucho Marx, he prefers the company of children to that of most of the grown-up people he knows, and is clearly more affected by their opinion of his work than by that of more mature critics. It may be that his liking for the black and white life, and his irritation with complexity, ambiguity and imperfection, turn him towards children and childhood, for whom life is, or certainly seems, more straightforward, feelings are, or should be, more directly expressed, and for whom there is less caution, less guile, and less reserve.

People like Spike Milligan can make heavy demands on the patience and the support of those around them. Their search for perfection, their irritation with what they see as the second-rate and the inadequate, their apparent self-preoccupation can precipitate others into a black or white response – an utter rejection of what is seen to be childish self-centredness, or sympathetic and understanding support for a gifted genius.

'He's an extraordinarily sane person,' remarked Michael Bentine of his fellow-Goon, adding, 'It's nonsense he's a nut. A nut isn't a shrewd businessman, a nut can't write a television series, a nut can't take up issues and see them through, and anyone must be nutty who thinks he is.' I take it that Mr Bentine uses the word 'nut' to mean a mentally ill person, which suggests that he has a somewhat limited idea of what mental illness is. As Spike Milligan makes plain, in this interview and elsewhere, it is not only perfectly possible for someone in the throes of a severe mental illness to write a radio series (quite apart from one for television), but he has done it. And Bentine was with him at the time! He has, it is true, his way of coping, by withdrawing into isolation. To that extent, while he cannot stop his illness recurring he exercises some control over its course. To my suggestion that it is something over which he exercises more control than he is prepared to admit, his response was terse, to put it mildly. It is worth noting that hypomanic and manic illnesses are often not recognised as illnesses by those immediately surrounding the sufferer. Few of Lowell's friends realised how ill the poet was during manic episodes, and put down his extraordinary behaviour to fatigue, personal eccentricity, genius or drink. Spike Milligan has had similar experiences, and to this day there are those who insist that he has never truly been ill. As with so much in this interview, the reader can make up his own mind.

'The adult world', Spike Milligan told W. J. Weatherby in 1961, is 'so neurotic and automatic, it's a bore – and I think most kids feel the same. You can write a book for children only if you are a child yourself.' If Milligan is a child he is an enormously talented, inventive, stimulating, and gifted one, and a child which this adult world can scarce do without. Whether each can cope with the other is one of those questions I never asked him!

ANTHONY CLARE: How do you feel about talking about yourself?

SPIKE MILLIGAN: I suppose deep down it's nice.

CLARE: Are you given to musing about yourself, looking at your achievements, at what's brought you to where you are?

MILLIGAN: I'm very much a Hamlet, a melancholic actually. I can't get to sleep at night without trying to think of terrible things like when my first marriage broke up and I watched the haunting face of my children who'd lost their mother, and I never quite got over that. I can't get over it, it's left a scar. And I can't wait to keep up with trying to love them enough to make up for all that, for those shortcomings.

CLARE: Were you always a melancholic person? What about your early childhood?

MILLIGAN: I seemed a pretty melancholic person, yes. I seem to have been a loner and I think I actually took to comedy to break the monotonous relief away from myself, which was always down.

CLARE: Your accounts of the first years in India . . .

MILLIGAN: You mean you found the accounts? God, I thought I'd burnt them.

CLARE: . . . they're always positive, pastoral recollections. You seemed, for once, to look fairly positively at things.

MILLIGAN: My childhood was like a litmus paper in the sun: it recorded very well, and I appreciated it very well.

CLARE: Were you happy?

MILLIGAN: Do you know, I don't know. I think I must have been. I don't think I was quite happy – I wet the bed a lot which is usually a sign of psychological unhappiness.

CLARE: What is your first memory?

MILLIGAN: My first memory? It's totally abstract. It's looking through a glass porthole and seeing a yacht on a very blue sea. The second memory was falling down a Victorian staircase to the bottom.

CLARE: Was the first related to travelling to England?

MILLIGAN: I think it must have been, yes.

CLARE: But you went back to India?

MILLIGAN: We went back to India, yes. We came out from India in 1918, 1919, on a ship which I remember had a drunken Scotch master. We went aground on some rocks in the Red Sea at three in the morning and it took us six months' hiking through various countries to get to England. That might be the period when I saw this glass porthole, yes – in which case it's a very early memory for one year, isn't it?

CLARE: You must have gone back to India and lived there up to the age of . . .

MILLIGAN: Between India and Burma up to the age of thirteen or fourteen, yes – all the very formative years.

CLARE: But you don't think they were happy?

MILLIGAN: I don't think so no, I don't think I was happy. My father was away a lot, he was a soldier, and he was away a lot from home. My mother was very highly strung and not cruel but used to beat me sometimes quite violently, and I think there was this resentment that I didn't have anybody to go to. I thought when you got beaten by your mother you went to your father and *vice versa*. I don't know – it's a mystery. I'd like to be put to sleep one day and asked about it.

CLARE: When you say your mother was highly strung, what sort of woman was she?

MILLIGAN: She was hanging from a rope from the ceiling. No, that's a joke, no, she was highly strung. I suppose she was having no sexual intercourse with my Dad. She was a Catholic, she could not go around with men. I suppose there was a lot of tension in that case.

CLARE: Was she given to depressions?

MILLIGAN: No, she seemed stabilised at an hysterical level.

CLARE: Were you frightened of her?

MILLIGAN: A little bit yes, a little bit yes, I was.

CLARE: You had a brother?

MILLIGAN: No, she had a brother, she had the brother!

CLARE: Quite! I will rephrase that. She had a second son?

MILLIGAN: Yes, she did. Desmond Patrick, born in Rangoon.

CLARE: Was he very much younger than you?

MILLIGAN: About eight or nine years younger than myself.

CLARE: So for all practical purposes you grew up as an only child. What was your schooling in India like?

MILLIGAN: My mother once again tried to keep me away from the realities of the world, which was going to turn me into a neurotic. She sent me to a girls' school, a convent, which was very, very nice. It was a female society all the way round me. I was being matured into a very gentle society and the world wasn't like that. I was reasonably happy. I had some traumatic experiences: I ran away because I had fallen in the mud in the playground once and I could not bear the thought of going back into the classroom with all these girls and myself all covered in mud, so I went back home and the next day this appalling Mother Superior got the whole school out in a line and stood me in front of them and bawled me out left, right and centre and threatened to expel me. I find that appalling in retrospect.

CLARE: And you can still remember that?

MILLIGAN: I can still remember that. It was very painful, yes, and I never got over it.

CLARE: Would you say that you were a sensitive child?

MILLIGAN: Yes, ultra-sensitive. I was very aware of cruelty, I don't know why. One instance was when we were walking at the back of the houses in Poona. They used to shoot the pariah dogs and the dog-shooter saw this pariah dog and he shot it and he blew it in two except for the spine, which was still connected. I noticed that the dog's guts were blown all over the place but the tail was still wagging, and the dog-shooter whistled and it wagged its tail for him! And I said to him, 'Please put it out of its misery,' and he did. He shot it again and the bullet entered its brain and blew its eyes out, they came out like on stalks.

CLARE: What age were you then?

MILLIGAN: About six or seven. As I was growing up I certainly didn't find people pleasant, and I was certainly growing more towards animals than people.

CLARE: Was your brother similar to you in temperament?

MILLIGAN: Yes, we grew up very close together, very like the Brontë sisters. We seemed to turn away from the world; we created our own world called 'The Mania' and we used to make little towns in the garden out of mud and run the country ourselves the way we wanted it run.

CLARE: What became of your brother? Has he had any problems with his sensitivity?

MILLIGAN: None at all. He grew up differently from me. I was psychoneurotic and he wasn't.

CLARE: What is your explanation for that?

MILLIGAN: For my neurosis?

CLARE: For the difference. After all, you were two people growing up in very similar environments.

MILLIGAN: Well, when he was born my mother and father were closer together. My mother was cooling down a bit because, as I say, she was cohabiting, having sexual intercourse, which relieves a lot of stress and strain, I suppose, among adults, and he grew up with me to hang on to as well and my mother had cooled down emotionally a bit. Still a bit of a terror she was, but he didn't have the pressure put on him that I had put on me because my mother was very young and without her man.

CLARE: What sort of pressure? Can you give me an example of the kinds of demands she made on you?

MILLIGAN: Well, 'Eat up all your dinner', and 'If you don't do that God will strike you dead', and I had to go to church, and 'God is watching you and you mustn't play with little black boys, they're Anglo-Indians', and being filled up with a load of gunge, imperial gunge. Deep down I wasn't born to be that type of person. I was meant to be a liberal.

CLARE: Did that make you angry?

MILLIGAN: It did make me angry because the tragedy of childhood is that you have no parliament for the child, all the cards are stacked in favour of the adult. A child can't say I'm going to write to *The Times* about this – he has to accept it.

CLARE: Your mother was a very religious woman?

MILLIGAN: Over religious yes: but it was an automated religion and there was no depth of intellect behind it. I didn't get an education such as I'd like to have got from the Jesuits.

CLARE: Had she been born a Catholic?

MILLIGAN: Yes. Father was a convert who, like most converts, was a stricter Catholic than an ordinary born one and there was church, church all the time. There were confessions: I remember saying when I was very, very young, and I'm horrified now, 'God forgive me for being a sinner', when I was about three or four. I can't believe that they put the word sinner on to an innocent child of four.

CLARE: Did you have nightmares?

MILLIGAN: No, I didn't. I don't think I ever had nightmares. I did suffer a great deal from fevers in India, especially malaria and sandfly, and I used to get nightmares then.

CLARE: Did you have any amateur dramatics at school? Was there any evidence of the talent that was to emerge later?

MILLIGAN: It's remarkable that you should say that. There's a direct answer: yes. When I was at the Convent of Jesus and Mary in Poona they had done the usual Nativity play and they didn't know what to do with me and they said, 'We're going to dress you up as a clown.' So I was dressed up as a clown with a black face. I was six and I remember one thing: they said, 'Now, when all the angels go round the crib you mustn't go on the stage, it wouldn't be right for the clown to be there.' I thought that was wrong and when they were round the crib something intuitive in the child in me made me go out. I stood in front of the crib and I took off my pointed hat and everybody applauded, I remember that to this day.

CLARE: Did they laugh?

MILLIGAN: They laughed at me, without a doubt. In between the scene changes they wanted somebody to go outside, so I used to go outside and pull the curtains and jump up and down and pull funny faces. I heard this laughter and I remember it sounded very good. It's strange that I should start as a clown, and be a clown.

CLARE: You've liked that sound ever since?

MILLIGAN: Yes – I like the sound of being a clown. People say I'm a comic and I'm not, I'm really a clown.

CLARE: From what you've said about it on one or two occasions, coming back to England was quite a change. Your father was a soldier and one of the victims of the Ramsay MacDonald government cuts. They reduced the armed forces and he was out of a job, so you came to

England in the early 1930s. You came to a rather unpromising place, Catford, Lewisham: quite a difference from India.

MILLIGAN: Yes, it was. It was a traumatic change. The English, as I knew them in India, were that much happier and brighter living in the sun out of the gloom. England was infested at that time with the gloom of unemployment. We went to live in an attic, believe it or not, and my brother and I turned right inwards.

CLARE: Did you ever get over that?

MILLIGAN: No, never have. It changed me completely. I got very turned in and, as I say, I think the comedy in me is the only way I can break out and get out to the outside world.

CLARE: You went to a fairly tough school?

MILLIGAN: I went to St Saviour's School in Lewisham. It is a Catholic school, and I had to walk two miles to it every day. They had their quota of bullies there, and I was never a big strong boy.

CLARE: Did you have any contact with girls? Before, say, the army?

MILLIGAN: I was very romantic, when I was very young, about seven or eight. I fell in love with a little Persian girl called Fakrisha and I actually carried her books to school, of all things. Then I fell in love with another girl called Charmaine, and I used to walk around outside her house in Poona whistling an Irving Berlin tune called 'Charmaine'. They thought there was a loony outside! I didn't have much success in my amours until about the age of twenty-one. I was very shy, very shy, terribly shy. I thought sex was evil, kissing was evil – that's the atmosphere that the Catholic Church gave me.

CLARE: Were you anxious in the sense that you bit your nails?

MILLIGAN: I bit my nails a lot, and I was never a very good mixer until I took up music, took up the guitar.

CLARE: You had a passion for jazz?

MILLIGAN: Yes, I did. I liked jazz very much.

CLARE: You still describe yourself as being very tense.

MILLIGAN: Yes, I was very tense, I suppose.

CLARE: And you still are.

MILLIGAN: Yes, I am. It's like a coiled spring, like a cobra waiting to strike. I don't know what it is, that's just how I am – I can't do anything about it.

CLARE: From the story as you have told it, this tension is related to your bomb injury in Italy, but it sounds as if you were always sensitive, always tense, always a rather anxious person.

MILLIGAN: Yes. To prove that I was a neurotic I just had to have that mechanism inside me tripped: this mortar bomb blew me up, and it did it.

CLARE: You use the word 'neurotic'. What does it mean to you?

MILLIGAN: It meant to me a chap who got blown up by a bomb in the war and started to cry and shake and shiver. They said, 'You are a psychoneurotic', and I thought all men who got blown up by bombs were PNs.

CLARE: And now?

MILLIGAN: Now I realise that there's a vast spectrum – a lot of people are uncertain, insecure, frightened, brought up badly or over-cossetted. It also sometimes gives you brilliance, like Van Gogh or El Greco. For all neurotics it's a gift and a curse at the same time. You get the pain much worse than anybody else, but you see a sunrise much more beautiful than anybody else.

CLARE: Would you forgo the one for the other?

MILLIGAN: No, having reached the age of sixty-five I realise that this bath of fire I went through has made me a much more tolerant human being, with a vast spectrum of understanding and tolerance for people. It's like a Toledo blade – you put it into the fire and it comes out much finer.

CLARE: But are you a tolerant man?

MILLIGAN: Not of idiots and fools. If anything is retrograde and pulling the world down and destroying the future for children or imposing suffering on animals, I will combat it. If that's called intolerance then I'm intolerant. I wouldn't say it's intolerance, though.

CLARE: Your secretary, Norma Farnes, once wrote of you: 'He can cause absolute chaos and tension because he can't get someone on the telephone at the precise moment when he wants to talk to them.' Now whatever the rights or wrongs of that, it's not normally something that one would expect of a tolerant person.

MILLIGAN: How would you describe it? You're a psychiatrist: what would you put it down to? Your house is on fire and you can't get through to the Fire Brigade and you're swearing!

CLARE: But that's a very dramatic example!

MILLIGAN: I've just extended the story a little bit!

CLARE: I'd say that there might be some evidence to suggest that you're quite an impatient man.

MILLIGAN: Yes, I think I don't have much patience. And yet at other times I spend hours over one page of script, getting it right. I rewrote *Puckoon* five times. That would be something on the scale of the Bible if you put it all together. I rewrote it five times, such is my desire for perfection. That shows the complete opposite, doesn't it?

CLARE: It illustrates a patience with yourself.

MILLIGAN: Ah very good, *touché*!

CLARE: But with others?

MILLIGAN: I don't know about others, I'm impatient with idiots, yes – to a fault.

CLARE: When you get depressed, as you do from time to time, do you feel guilty about that?

MILLIGAN: No. I realise I'm a victim of a condition, and I go and lock myself in my room and stay away for a couple of days.

CLARE: Do you ever feel you're hard on other people?

MILLIGAN: Please God let me tell the truth: no, I don't think so, Tony. I might demand the truth, but I'm not actually hard on people.

CLARE: When you had your first breakdown, around the time of the bomb, were you invalided out of the army?

MILLIGAN: No, they gave me some tablets. It was the early days of deep narcosis: they gave me some early tranquillisers I think which sent me to sleep, sent me out of the lines for seven days. Then they sent me up to the guns and as soon as I heard them go I started to stammer. I don't know to this day whether I induced the stammer myself, because having failed to get out of the army one way I thought the stammer might do it. I don't know if I'm making this up or not, but I've always been guilty about the fact that I might have run away – and I should hate to think I did, because I didn't want to. I thought it was a just war for a just cause.

CLARE: And what happened then?

MILLIGAN: Then, in the sort of state I was in, they took me out of the line and I went to a psychiatrist. And he said, 'I'm sorry, it would be dangerous for you to go up the line in this condition, it wouldn't be fair to your comrades.' And I said, 'I see that. Will it get better?' He said, 'I don't know. On the whole it doesn't seem that people like you do. We'll put you at a base camp.' So I went to a base camp and had a couple more breakdowns while I was there, and that put paid to me. I did try to get back to the regiment, though. I wrote to the major, but they wouldn't have it, which I understand now. Can't have duff people in the firing line!

CLARE: Did you feel a sense of failure?

MILLIGAN: Yes, and the major stood me up and said, 'You're a coward.' That was an appalling thing to say to a man. No crime in being a coward, mind you, but I didn't think I was a coward in as much as I'd been in action all through the North African campaign and all the way up to Cassino. If I'd been a coward I would have run away the first day, wouldn't I? I think I just ran out of steam, that's all.

CLARE: It is said, and I want to hear your views on it, that the Goons was a turning-point in your life?

MILLIGAN: Yes – it gave me money for a start. I didn't have much money and I didn't really exploit the Goons, but I was very happy letting go with flights of fantasy which were being mouthed by men I thought were superb performers. I've never had the like of them to work for me since – Harry Secombe, Peter Sellers and Michael Bentine.

CLARE: You got married around this time?

MILLIGAN: Yes, I did. I was mad. The girl proposed to me, and said, 'Will you marry me?' and I thought, 'Well, I don't want to disappoint her', so I said 'Yes'. I'd known her about a year. I think it was physical love, though. She had big boobs and I didn't!

CLARE: What age were you then?

MILLIGAN: Seems like the Stone Age from where I'm standing now. I was about thirty-three, I think.

CLARE: But in fact that marriage lasted several years.

MILLIGAN: Well, about five, six years yes. I was impossible. My neurosis was appalling. I was so insecure I was blaming her for everything, and she just couldn't take any more of it. The girl was absolutely right, she was just a nice girl.

CLARE: What do you mean, you were impossible?

MILLIGAN: I was impossible, yes. But I was ill, I wasn't consciously doing it. I was ill and impossible.

CLARE: In what sense?

MILLIGAN: Intolerant. I'd say, 'Don't spend so much money. Don't do this and don't do that. Where have you been and why isn't my dinner ready?' It's appalling. I was screaming at being alive.

CLARE: You were writing scripts for the Goons?

MILLIGAN: Yes, and that was a great pressure, until midnight. It really destroyed me, destroyed my marriage. People would say, 'Did it make you happy?' and I said, 'No, it didn't make me happy.' 'The Goon Show' – no, it was a disaster. I'd lost my children, their mother, it had lost me a wife, who was a very good person, and the scar is unbearably deep, especially with the children.

CLARE: They blamed you?

MILLIGAN: Well, children are wonderful, they don't blame anybody. But I was looking at some photographs I'd kept and I suddenly looked at these faces around that time and I flipped the pages and I suddenly thought, 'My God, how unhappy these children were', and I couldn't believe it. I thought, 'What a terrible thing for adults to do to children.'

CLARE: Why do you use the word 'ill' about that time?

MILLIGAN: I was ill, I was not normal. I was abnormal. I was very strange, I was very strange indeed, almost mentally ill, no two ways about it. I shouldn't have been working, but I had to hang on to this job. It was a very good job, and I went in and out of mental homes about once every six months.

CLARE: Did your colleagues know you were ill?

MILLIGAN: Yes, they did, and they carried on as best as they could and bolstered me up. They wrote up the scripts and did the best they could. They stood by and did as much as they could.

CLARE: But at this time, when you say you were ill, you were turning out classic comedy material!

MILLIGAN: Yes, it was amazing.

CLARE: Could you have done it if you hadn't been ill?

MILLIGAN: It's a strange thing you should ask this, Tony. The best scripts I wrote were when I was ill. I've just recalled these, the ones that I wrote best were when I was ill – a mad desire to be better than anybody else at comedy, and if I couldn't do it in the given time of eight hours a day I used to work twelve, thirteen and fourteen. I did, I was determined. There was a time when I was positively manic. I was four foot above the ground at times, talking twice as fast as normal people. Working on this with great fervour to write this stuff and to hear them do it every Sunday. I couldn't wait for them to do it to hear how it sounded, because it would be acclaimed when it went out. 'I've done it, I've done it' – and then I had to go and start all over again, that was the awful part of it.

CLARE: But there was a sensation of being high?

MILLIGAN: Yes, God it was – and when I look back at it, I think, 'Was that really me, was I ten foot off the ground all the time?' I was – I was terribly manic.

CLARE: Were you ever violent?

MILLIGAN: I wanted to be violent, but somehow I felt inhibited. I thought that would be the last straw if I turned violent, but I did feel violent.

CLARE: You wanted to be violent?

MILLIGAN: I felt like killing people.

CLARE: Wasn't there an episode involving Peter Sellers?

MILLIGAN: He didn't understand mental illness. He kept coming to the flat all the time and his phone had broken down and he wanted to use mine. And I couldn't stand the noise. I said 'Tell him to stop it.' He said, 'Oh tell him not to be silly.' So I got a potato knife from the kitchen. I had been wanting to get into hospital and I felt, 'Why won't they put me in hospital?' I thought, 'If I get a knife and try and kill him they'll put me somewhere', and I did. I went to attack him with a knife. I didn't mean to kill him, but I thought they will hospitalise me. They took me away to a hospital and put me under deep narcosis.

CLARE: What did Sellers make of that?

MILLIGAN: Nothing much! In many ways he was a very cold fish, Peter. He operated at an aesthetic level, but his normal everyday social life didn't operate on a very deep basis.

CLARE: The people immediately around you didn't regard you as ill.

MILLIGAN: They knew I was ill. They were very wary of me. I was very brittle and about to explode at any time. I had terrible tantrums, chucking scripts out of the room. I smashed a room up at Broadcasting House once, all the furniture, because Dennis Main Wilson said something to me. It was the only way to let off steam. I was right, mind you. I started to get an effect right and I knew what the sound should be like and they couldn't get it and I blew my top, I'm afraid.

CLARE: When was the first time you went into a hospital in this country?

MILLIGAN: It was about 1956 – St Luke's Hospital, Woodside, at Highgate.

CLARE: What did that do for you?

MILLIGAN: Thank God, they gave me deep narcosis and I went to sleep for about three weeks, and that seemed to break the tension. But

I was still ill. In fact I think I've only just managed to land again in the last four or five years, I've just started to become myself. It's got better: I think I'm being cured.

CLARE: When was the last time you were in hospital?

MILLIGAN: About seven or eight years ago.

CLARE: And each admission is roughly for about the same sort of thing?

MILLIGAN: Yes, the same thing. Now, of course, I get milder, so I just do it myself. I take a couple of sleeping tablets and you sleep it off. It's short, very brief now, very weakening.

CLARE: And when you're depressed, what is it like?

MILLIGAN: I write poetry. It's the good part of it – I always use my illness to get some kind of productivity, and I write poetry.

CLARE: But sometimes you're so depressed that you can't do anything?

MILLIGAN: Sometimes I just turn out the light, take these tablets and go to sleep, totally blacked out. When I get depressed, I try to get something for this terrible sadness that comes over me and create something in terms of poetry.

CLARE: Do you know when it's coming on, or do you just get depressed overnight?

MILLIGAN: It can be triggered. I was doing a television show on Saturday and I was trying, in all the chaos that goes on in making a show, to get a message across to the actors, and every time I spoke one of them would start telling funny jokes. It drove me stark raving mad and that depressed me so much that I just switched off being me and didn't give a very good performance; but I came out of it by next morning.

CLARE: That's an example of your controlling it to some extent.

MILLIGAN: Yes, I'm getting better at controlling it now.

CLARE: But what about when you're busy and you get depressed and you can't snap out of it. After all, you're like so many people who suffer from this: you must get very irritated with people who say, 'Snap out of it.'

MILLIGAN: That's silly.

CLARE: Yes.

MILLIGAN: Going round with a broken leg – 'Come on, walk, you'll be all right.'

CLARE: It's silly because?

MILLIGAN: Because they don't understand. It's an emotional language.

CLARE: You mean you can't do it, you can't snap out of it?

MILLIGAN: No, you can't. Neurosis, as I say, is an emotional language. You must understand: a person who has suffered it will never say to you, 'Come on, snap out of it.' Immediately he'll reach out emotionally and say, 'What can I do to help, let me sit and talk to you a while.'

CLARE: But most people get depressed.

MILLIGAN: Not to the extent that a neurotic does. You can tell it. It's the mere fact you haven't been this side of the emotional fence. I can tell you've never been this deep down yourself, I can tell it. Difficult to describe.

CLARE: Why is it difficult to describe?

MILLIGAN: It's invisible. There's no written diagrams. It's an abstract, it's a sensation, and if you ask people to paint it most depressives will draw black. Have you noticed that – black paintings all over the place, so we know it has no colour for a start.

CLARE: In the early days, did you get angry with yourself when this happened?

MILLIGAN: No, I never got angry with myself. If I was doing something wrong I'd always try and line myself up to get it right. If I was doing a drawing and did it wrong, my sense of perfection would keep me applying. I wouldn't get angry: I would remove the reason for the mistake, and get it dead right in the end.

CLARE: When you got depressed, you didn't blame yourself?

MILLIGAN: No, I didn't.

CLARE: Or feel that other people would be better off without you?

MILLIGAN: I realised that people would be better off without me. Of course they would have been better off without me. I was just making life hell for everybody. But once again you'd want human compassion to bring you round.

CLARE: Did it ever get so bad that you made an attempt to kill yourself?

MILLIGAN: Yes, I did. I was on a ship and it was taking me back from Australia to England, and while I was there I got a telegram saying my wife was suing me for divorce – and while I didn't mind losing her, I couldn't bear the thought of losing the children. It might have been a token suicide, like lots of them are. I had a bath and got to my cabin and I'd forgotten, or perhaps I hadn't forgotten, that the ship's doctor was coming to have a drink in my cabin with me, and he found me there. Perhaps I arranged it all, Tony. Anyhow the thought of knocking myself off didn't seem all that bad at the time.

CLARE: Can I press you about this? Some people might say, that you describe at times a manipulative ability, that you turn your moods on and off to get things around you changed; so perhaps you have some control over it. But at other times you say that you have no control over it, and that people who suggest that you do just don't know what it's like.

MILLIGAN: In the early days I had no control over it, but it's like getting used to a hump on your back: by the time you're sixty if you're a hunchback you've got pretty used to having a hump on your back.

CLARE: That's getting used to it, but it's not doing anything to reduce it. Can you actually do anything to ease your depression?

MILLIGAN: Well, the circumstances have changed in that I now have a woman in my life who suits me admirably. It's taken a great amount of weight off my shoulders. It's made a great difference to my life, it's given me a great degree of satisfaction, having somebody so loving and understanding with me, which I'd never had before.

CLARE: Is she very tolerant?

MILLIGAN: Very, very tolerant – perhaps it's because she used to work for the BBC!

CLARE: You had a second wife who died, very tragically. Now she, as I understand it, was a very important person in your life.

MILLIGAN: Yes, she was. She was very strong, very powerful and gave my children – who were sort of social orphans at the time – a mother. She gave up her own career, she was a superb singer, to look after my children and I'm eternally grateful to her. She gave me a third daughter who is a sheer delight, the living image of her mother and a talented musician, so that was good.

CLARE: How did she cope with your moods?

MILLIGAN: Very well. She understood: she was a bit of a neurotic herself, but she understood.

CLARE: Do you think you have to be a bit neurotic to understand?

MILLIGAN: Yes, I suppose one murderer will understand another murderer much better than one who isn't!

CLARE: What about the understanding you have of yourself. How would you describe yourself?

MILLIGAN: Well, I'm somebody who developed very late in life.

CLARE: Would you have preferred to stay a child?

MILLIGAN: I think I have stayed a child all my life. That's why I get on much easier with children. As soon as I get a child in my house, I get on with it more than anybody else, marvellous it is, great fun. It's like having a young captive fairy, it's marvellous, all that gurgling laughter that comes out if you do the right things.

CLARE: But there are other characteristics of children – they can be self-centred, demanding, intolerant.

MILLIGAN: Yes, but who isn't? A child is born at the centre of its universe you know, it's born a little savage. It messes in its nappy, but it should be given a chance to extricate itself from the complete abstraction of life. It knows nothing, it has no focal point, no terms of reference, it just sees these things around it, operating on it. Mostly there are people who tell it what to do all the time and you can suppress and iron out a whole personality if you don't give it a chance to present itself. Someone said that 'we are the bow and the child is the arrow and once it's sped on its course nothing can take it from its destiny'.

CLARE: But I'm struck that as you describe the child, you're describing yourself.

MILLIGAN: Is that so? Is that what I've presented to you today? Thanks for the psychiatry.

CLARE: No, not today. But the impatience with the rest of the world and with a lot of the people in it, the feeling that there are much simpler solutions than these highly sophisticated so-called adults have, the desire to cut through it all.

MILLIGAN: Yes, there is a great desire to do that. You know, when I can do it in my own time I find it very pleasing to be able to put my paper in my typewriter and go straight at it and write a book, nothing between me and it, that's a great pleasure. To paint a picture is a great pleasure, but getting into a motor car, getting into the traffic, getting it filled up with petrol, and the shouting and the screaming – it's an appalling world. Nobody's very pleased with it.

CLARE: You're certainly not pleased with it.

MILLIGAN: No, I couldn't be.

CLARE: How do you cope? Are there people in your life who organise it for you?

MILLIGAN: No I'm pretty much the organiser. I have the

cooperation of my wife and my family and my nanna and I handle it like this. I keep up very good standards in my home, we have manners, we're civilised, we do things properly, we have a Sunday tea and friends round, having a boring Sunday English tea with no television or radio, we sit and talk. We go out to dinner occasionally and put on evening dress and I put a rose in my jacket, so we look as if we've got some kind of style. It's not snobbery, it's the fun of dressing up like when you were a child, and my children all love it. I love it, I love putting on the style – it's a yesteryear style though, not the future.

CLARE: In all the episodes involving hospitals, what did you make of psychiatrists?

MILLIGAN: They vary as much as their patients.

CLARE: Was there anyone you were able to talk to about your fears? You said to me earlier that you would quite like somehow to be hypnotised or put to sleep; you would like to have a lot of things unravelled.

MILLIGAN: It would be very interesting. I'd like to hear the recording of what I was like as a child. I only heard the other day that I ran away from home when I came to England because my mother insisted I went to church every Sunday, and I lived for three months with somebody else. There must be things before that – I'd like to know what happened.

CLARE: At that time can you remember intense feelings, like anger with your mother?

MILLIGAN: Yes, I had an exploding temper, on three or four occasions; terrible explosions of temper, savage it was, screaming and yelling. And then I noticed it in my youngest daughter one night. She started to scream and shout and I thought, 'Is this the primeval scream?' Life itself is very very painful for a child. How helpless she must feel, tiny, small, lost, no power, everything being applied to it and they not being applied themselves to anything. She's screaming for the fact that she's alive and it's very painful, and I'm certain I am right on this issue. Sorry I'm banging the table and thumping the mike!

CLARE: Did this lead to arguments with your second wife?

MILLIGAN: None at all.

CLARE: About disciplining children?

MILLIGAN: My second wife was a very prim Victorian lady and wanted them to be very prim and proper and I thought, 'No, I don't want this suppression that's been put on children. I want to see them blossom as much as themselves.' I never hit them. All this beating stuff is out for me. I used to punish them by saying, 'Look that is very wrong, for doing that I'm not going to talk to you for another hour. Don't talk to me.' That would suffice. My children are all civilised now, they're non-violent, and I think I must have done the right thing.

CLARE: Are they like you?

MILLIGAN: They are. Three of them are artistic. I don't know about my son Sean, he's a house painter – I think he's training to be Hitler!

CLARE: I hope not! What do they make of your campaigning, your inveterate letter-writing about the evils of modern suburban life?

MILLIGAN: Well I think they love me, and that's as much as I want. Whether they're proud of me I don't know. You don't have to be proud of anybody. Love is enough. They do come on my campaigns, the CND ones and the Cruelty to Animals, the Seal Hunting. They don't follow me and become vegetarians. They still eat meat, the little devils, and some of them smoke. You don't always win.

CLARE: Do they share your views of children?

MILLIGAN: Yes, I think they do. My youngest daughter said to me, 'Daddy, you're very liberal with me and it's very, very nice.' And I thought, 'Well, if that's a diploma I'll accept it.'

CLARE: In some of your poetry and in the things you say about making people laugh there is a remarkable hearkening back to childhood. For instance, you wrote in 1959 a poem entitled 'Indian Boyhood' which goes

> What happened to the boy I was, why did he run away,
> and leave me old and thinking like there'd been no yesterday?
> What happened then, was I that boy who laughed and swam in the Bund;
> Is there no going back, no recompense, is there nothing, no refund?

Eric Sykes once said about you, 'Spike's the kind of person who should live in a Utopia without rates, parking meters and concrete.' And I thought, 'Well, India was like that.'

MILLIGAN: Yes it was too, wasn't it? But all childhood is free of rates and parking meters, no child ever pays rates. I'm glad you read that poem, it makes me believe that I might have had a happy childhood, because there is a yearning for it there, isn't there?

CLARE: I sense in your view of laughter that you very much associate humour with something childish in the best sense of that word.

MILLIGAN: Well, there's always been a child running through my head, laughing all through my life, all the time. I just don't seem able to get old, not old enough to get away from it. I have a childish charisma inside me, and I love it.

CLARE: Does it get you into trouble?

MILLIGAN: No. It gets raised eyebrows. I'll suddenly talk to somebody in the street, off the cuff. They look surprised but if a child said 'Hullo' they would smile and say 'Hullo'. But if you're a grown-up child like I am they look a bit surprised.

CLARE: Would you say that at times you are bloody difficult to live with?

MILLIGAN: Yes perhaps I might be difficult at times, but I am not known as a difficult person. I'm not an exceptionally difficult person – not really, I don't think so. If they find me difficult they must be an awful pain in the arse themselves.

CLARE: Why are you so frightened of being thought of as bloody difficult?

MILLIGAN: That's a very good question. I suppose because I want to be a decent person. I don't want to make life painful for people because a lot of people made life painful for me and I know how bloody awful it can be to have a painful life and I try to avoid that. For instance, I've never struck my children.

CLARE: It would be very difficult for you to cope with the notion that, despite all your efforts, you've failed?

MILLIGAN: I'm not saying I'm a prophet or an apostle or a disciple or a saint, but I set my sights on some kind of humanity which doesn't exist at this moment, that is on the Utopian scale; so to think that I might actually be just another appalling person, makes me wonder what kind of message I am trying to preach when I myself am committing the very crimes that I'm trying to tell people I don't want committed.

CLARE: I didn't say: Were you a difficult person, I said were you *at times* a difficult person?

MILLIGAN: I did say at times, but as much as you would be difficult and anybody else would be difficult.

CLARE: I don't know whether this is true or not, but you said that before your nervous breakdown you'd been quiet and gentle but afterwards you'd had to become tough to survive.

MILLIGAN: I did, that's so; true, Tony.

CLARE: And some people are at times tough deliberately to survive. In the business world, as you say, you've got to be tough.

MILLIGAN: I want to make an example. I spent an hour three nights ago trying to catch a moth at one in the morning and to put it out the window: I don't know where that puts me.

CLARE: That won't wash, because I'm sure there are many examples you can give of your decency, and at the moment I'm not pursuing your decency.

MILLIGAN: Yes, I suppose I'm all for this cross examination – I find out more about myself, I was just wondering where I was at then. I've admitted to all the things that suggest I am difficult. You asked me a straightforward question – was I a difficult person – and I don't think I am a difficult person at home. You'd have to ask my children.

CLARE: What do you think they'd say?

MILLIGAN: I don't know. I don't know, I wish I could walk on the water.

CLARE: Linked with that is a view you have of life – I seem to be reading all your poetry, but I was struck by another poem. It's much shorter and I'll read it if I may. It goes

> The new rose trembles with early beauty,
> The babe sees the beckoning carmine,
> The tiny hand clutches the cruel stem,
> The babe screams, the rose is silent, life is already telling lies.

In addition to being an interesting insight that is a vision of life as essentially a betrayal – it lets you down.

MILLIGAN: That's very good, Tony, a hundred marks for that! Yes, you're dead right. I'm just trying to agree. You're dead right. Life does let you down, doesn't it? There's no rehearsal for it – there's only one performance, and you never have a rehearsal. So you can never give a good performance.

CLARE: You think most people have that view of life, or is it a particular Milligan perspective?

MILLIGAN: I don't know. I presume that a lot of people in the Third World today are finding life very, very cruel. When little children are beaten to death – you'll get 39,000 cases of beatings of children this year – it's a cruel life. It's a bloody cruel life all the way down the line, and people seek release these days in sex or alcohol, drugs, or discos, because life is very painful.

CLARE: Were you to read something about a really distressing event it would turn the hair on your head.

MILLIGAN: It does unfortunately, alas, but I'm glad it makes me very angry. Then it generates that sort of anger you need to do something about it. I heard about a family just by chance who had let a dog die in a garage a month ago, and they'd been banned by the court from having a dog. I discovered they'd got another dog, so immediately I wrote to the police at Berkhamstead. If I hadn't that anger in me I wouldn't have done it. A lot of people would let it slide – it's a tragedy of life to let something slide, it's appalling.

CLARE: Some people are frightened by cruelty because it attracts.

MILLIGAN: Some people ignore cruelty. I read in the papers yesterday of how a girl of seventeen screamed her head off in a block of flats and in the end she was killed, and the police said they were stunned that nobody came near them. That makes me very, very, very, very angry but the appalling part is that, quite possibly, if that girl was in the house and other people were screaming she wouldn't have interfered either. That puts the human race on the line when it comes to laughingly being called human.

CLARE: And if that girl screamed in the house, what do you think you'd do?

MILLIGAN: I wouldn't hesitate.

CLARE: Without a doubt? You know that about yourself?

MILLIGAN: It'll be the end of me one day, because I will get involved in something that I can't handle. I'll rush across to a punch-up or something to try and save somebody and get killed myself, but that's the way it goes.

CLARE: If you were to pinpoint something about yourself that you dislike most, what would it be?

MILLIGAN: How many hours have we got for this now? God, that's a wonderful leading question: I would like to say I'd plead guilty but insane! It's going to sound as though I'm ego plus, but I can't think of anything particularly at the moment – I wish to God I could. Being, I suppose, ungenerous to the people who can't match me mentally. I suppose I dismiss them too easily, and then I always have terrible resentment about it. That's why I think I try to help people who are handicapped mentally. That's the throw of the dice in life, I think maybe that's what I'm doing. I don't know, Tony, I don't know, truly I don't know.